ERROL WALTON BARROW AND THE POSTWAR TRANSFORMATION OF BARBADOS

ERROL WALTON BARROW AND THE POSTWAR TRANSFORMATION OF BARBADOS

The Late Colonial Period

Hilbourne A. Watson

The University of the West Indies Press
Jamaica • Barbados • Trinidad and Tobago

The University of the West Indies Press
7A Gibraltar Hall Road, Mona
Kingston 7, Jamaica
www.uwipress.com

A catalogue record of this book is available from the
National Library of Jamaica.

ISBN: 978-976-640-711-7 (print)
978-976-640-712-4 (Kindle)
978-976-640-713-1 (ePub)

Cover photograph © Barbados Government Information Service.
Book and cover design by Robert Harris
Set in Scala 11/15 x 24

Printed in the United States of America

CONTENTS

PREFACE AND
ACKNOWLEDGEMENTS

THE STUDY WAS ORIGINALLY CONCEIVED APPROXIMATELY fifteen years ago as a volume on the contributions that Errol Walton Barrow made to the postwar transformation of Barbados, a former British Caribbean colony. Transformation is here understood to be an open-ended, dialectical process of social change, in which social classes, groups and individuals, some with largely contradictory interests, compete and contend to influence or control the state and the exercise of state power, and the political economy. In this sense transformation remains open-ended, consistent with the fact that the process of historical change is inherently non-totalizable. The absence of any full-length study about Errol Barrow's role in postwar change in Barbados made the undertaking more challenging than originally imagined. It became a matter of concern, in the process of conducting the investigation, that it might prove difficult to compress the material into a single volume. When the manuscript was submitted it was recommended (among other options) to prepare it as two volumes. The first volume covers the period from the 1920s to 1966, the year Barbados became a sovereign monarchy within the Commonwealth. The second volume will cover mainly the first two decades of independence from 1966 to 1987, the year Prime Minister Barrow died in office.

The study is not a political biography of the life of Errol Walton Barrow; rather, the emphasis is on Barrow's contributions to the transformation of Barbados, seen through the lens of political economy, which is a social science discipline that studies change from the angle of the social relations of production that humans enter in the process of reproducing themselves in the larger societal and world context.

The postwar transformation of Barbados unfolded within the context of the bourgeois (democratic) revolution, which was designed to canalize the energies of the society, and especially the working-class population, to produce outcomes that would benefit foremost the forces that owned and controlled the means of production and wealth and the political leadership strata, regardless of which groups exercise state power.

The three great crises of the first half of the twentieth century – World War I, the Great Depression and World War II – combined in ways that accelerated the decline of Britain's position in an international environment that was marked by competition from Germany, which tried unsuccessfully to retrace the trajectory of British imperialism (Arrighi 1982), from the United States and from the worldwide, anti-colonial and anti-imperialist struggles for self-determination. The bourgeois (democratic) revolution in the British West Indies (hereafter "West Indies") came to rest on parliamentary democracy (representative government), political party and labour and trade union politics, and juridical freedom or formal equality under the law, all of which are components of the "capitalist social control formation" (Perry 2010, 1).

The struggle for self-determination and the establishment of sovereign states in the West Indies was an integral part of larger world historical struggles that bore the imprint of capitalist modernity, of which liberalism serves as the core philosophical doctrine. The fact that nations and sovereign states are historical institutions rather than naturally evolved entities necessitates parting with the nationalist illusion according to which British imperialism in the Caribbean was a foreign imposition on colonial and postcolonial societies, and the achievement of sovereignty erased imperialism's burdensome imposition as part of the ultimate battle to secure the autonomy of the organic, national body politic. Nationalists imagine the nation as aboriginal – antecedent, immortal and therefore unencumbered by history; hence they tend to read history backward through "retrospective illusions" (Balibar 1991) and imagine that the achievement of sovereignty serves to authenticate the nation-state's place in history. This way sovereignty is made to bear a burden that not even Atlas could shoulder (Agnew 2009; Elden 2009; Gullí 2010; Watson 2015b).

Richard Koenigsberg argues that the "disease of nationalism – of neurosis – grows out of the fantasy of an omnipotent, indestructible part of the self that will never die. A self that can never die cannot mourn;

there is no possibility of intrapsychic change or growth. The object inside the self symbiotically clings or sticks to the self, constituting a burden or encrustation" (2017, 1). The decolonizing elites in Barbados and other West Indian territories were socialized into British cultural norms and institutions and they idealized the British nation-state and fought for change on terms that were fundamentally acceptable to the British. They collaborated with the United Kingdom and the United States to target, isolate and root out the progressive and revolutionary blue- and white-collar working-class forces from leadership in the political parties and the labour movement, to deny them any role in shaping the process and outcome of the decolonization and independence struggles.

Grantley Adams viewed British colonialism and the British Empire as preferable to other variants of European imperialism, and he boasted about the superior standing of Barbados among all British colonies. Alexander Bustamante (Jamaica) declared in London in 1952 that democracy could not be guaranteed in the postwar world without the survival of the British Empire. Eric Williams (Trinidad and Tobago) and Norman Manley (Jamaica) reminded West Indian critics of the "Westminster model" of representative government that it represented the authentic form of democracy they considered fitting for the West Indies. Errol Barrow plumbed the depth of England's pre-modern, absolutist institutions in search of what he saw as the original sources of Barbados's autochthonous constitution. Barrow traced Barbados's political stability, representative government, the rule of law and respect of the rights of colonial citizens to institutions of the ancien régime that undergirded English tyranny during the time of the Stuart dynasty, largely ignoring the role of the resistance and struggles the toiling masses waged, from slavery to decolonization, for political relief and freedom.

In his discussion of the "decolonization that might have been", Gary Wilder (2015, xii, xiii) focused on those "transformative possibilities that may have been sedimented within existing arrangements . . . through decolonization, to remake the world so that humanity could more fully realize itself on a planetary scale". Wilder notes that we are still without a robust critical language with which to speak about "postnational democracy, translocal solidarity, and cosmopolitan politics in ways that have not already been instrumentalized by human rights, humanitarianism, and liberal internationalism" (xiii).

In fact, cosmopolitan politics is part of the dominant state-centrist discourse and practice that treat liberal internationalism as the definitive universality, which subsumes struggles for self-determination and freedom under the right to exploit that complicates the struggle for our full humanity.

The proponents and defenders of the liberal, nationalist project of self-determination under capitalism tend to naturalize and thereby privilege the domination that comes with class rule, and subordinate justice under the state's security (Gullí 2010). Liberal discourse also separates economics (capital and the market) from politics (state), the economy from the state and civil society, the individual from society and the nation from world humanity (the international). This approach, which privileges individualism and alienation, intentionally fragments and externalizes the social, makes it difficult to appreciate that all forms of freedom, justice, human rights, equality and democracy under capitalism presuppose the right of private capital to exploit labour for the ends of private capital accumulation and thereby makes inequality seem natural.

The late colonial and postcolonial nationalist project in Barbados has been portrayed as an "empowering" response, with advocates in the state and civil society deflecting appropriate attention away from the way the exercise of state power shelters private economic power and wealth and domination from necessary scrutiny and critique in an ostensibly social democratic polity. Nationalists make what they imagine and desire to be the realization of the national unity of the body politic the high point of the achievement of state sovereignty. The experience of Barbados and the West Indies with decolonization and independence confirms that the nationalist elites embraced the bourgeois (democratic) revolution on terms the British largely framed and ordered (Mawby 2012) for them to manage.

The US strategy for boosting its hegemony included a demand for its European allies to free their colonial possessions in a responsible manner. Britain proceeded with attention to American expectations and even oversight. The reality that Gerald Horne (2007) aptly refers to as a "cold war in a hot zone" found Britain playing a subordinate role under American hegemony with reference to shaping the outcome of the contradictory process of decolonization in the Caribbean. Britain was forced to rely on the United States to protect the far-flung economic, commercial, military and financial interests of the UK state and its ruling class in the world. The real motive of the United States in demanding decolonization was to deepen the integration of the region into the postwar international capitalist order it was crafting. Washington refused to accept competing geopolitical centres of military power within the Atlantic Alliance, a development that reflected the weakness of the European powers and helped to shape the outcome of decolonization and independence in Barbados and the West Indies. The United States succeeded in seeing to it that working-class interests did not prevail in shaping the outcome of the decolonization struggles. It does not mean, however, that the working class did not play any role in shaping the outcomes, as such an assertion would be tantamount to denying agency to the oppressed and exploited in the freedom struggles.

In the course of conducting research and preparing the manuscript I incurred debts to a number of organizations and individuals. Bucknell University provided important support in the form of travel and research grants over several years to conduct the investigation in the United Kingdom and in Barbados and deliver presentations at several conferences. The British National Archives (Kew, London), Barbados National Archives, University of the West Indies Federal Archives (Cave Hill, University of the West Indies), and the West Indies Collection (University of the West Indies Library, Cave Hill) were the main sites where I did the research. Professor Sir Hilary Beckles listened attentively and keenly, offered suggestions and provided office space in the CARICOM Research Building during my 2008–9 sabbatical year. Several colleagues and friends – Linden Lewis, Dave Ramsaran, Alex Dupuy, Don Marshall, Andrew Downes, Harold Codrington, DeLisle Worrell, George Belle and Nigel Bolland – offered suggestions at different points. Several individuals granted me interviews for which I am truly thankful: Sir Courtney Blackman, Sir Shridath Ramphal, Sir Erskine Sandiford, George Lamming, Dr Peter Laurie, the Hon David Thompson, Maurice King, QC, Freundel

Stuart, George Belle, David Commissiong, Peter Morgan, Carlisle Carter, Horace King, Michael King, Maizie Barker-Welch, John Connell, Mitchell Codrington, Woodville Marshall, Astor B. Watts, Tennyson Beckles, Yvonne Walkes, Marjorie Lashley, Antoinette Thompson, Norma Jackman, Carlton Brathwaite and Gwen Hurst, among others. Conversations with Cedric Licorish, Jeb Sprague and others proved valuable especially during the writing phase. Thanks to the two anonymous reviewers and to the editorial and production team from the University of the West Indies Press.

ABBREVIATIONS

BGWILC	British Guiana and West Indies Labour Congress
BLP	Barbados Labour Party
BPL	Barbados Progressive League
BWU	Barbados Workers' Union
CADORIT	Caribbean Area Division of the Inter-American Regional Organization of Workers
CARICOM	Caribbean Community and Common Market
CC	Caribbean Commission
CCSP	Caribbean Christian Socialist Party
CLC	Caribbean Labour Congress
CO	Colonial Office
CPA	Caribbean People's Alliance
DL	Democratic League
DLP	Democratic Labour Party
HMSO	Her [or His] Majesty's Stationery Office
ICFTU	International Confederation of Free Trade Unions
JLP	Jamaica Labour Party
NAACP	National Association for the Advancement of Colored People
PNP	People's National Party
PPP	People's Progressive Party
UN	United Nations
UNIA	Universal Negro Improvement Association
WA	Workingmen's Association
WFTU	World Federation of Trade Unions
WINCP	West Indian National Congress Party

1.

MAPPING THE STUDY, FRAMING THE ARGUMENT

THE ISSUES THIS STUDY ADDRESSES ARE examined within the context of the bourgeois (liberal democratic) revolution that the anti-colonial struggles which unfolded as part of the much larger anti-imperialist movements forced Great Britain to extend to the West Indies.

The weakening of Britain's domestic and international position was hastened by the international capitalist crisis of the 1930s and by the negative impact and consequences of World War II, which extended to the loss of its empire. The introduction of liberal democratic reforms in the West Indian colonies was a very uneven process that did not occur on terms and conditions that were set and determined by the local anti-colonial forces on their own initiative. Extreme economic, political and social backwardness and unevenness characterized the societies and condition of most of the populations inhabiting the West Indian colonies. Britain's international position had begun to weaken from late in the nineteenth century and deteriorated with the Great Depression and World War II and its aftermath. Britain, however, managed to reform the colonial system without sacrificing the benefits to dominant interests in Britain and the colonies. Colonial reform and practice in the West Indies are best understood as features and expressions of the bourgeois democratic revolution that was exported to the colonies in modified form, in line with British interests, in the context of liberal internationalism.

There was nothing inherently democratic about the bourgeois democratic revolution. From the perspective of the working class, the

1

"democratic" content in the bourgeois democratic revolution had to do with the means to greater ends that are associated with the acquisition and exercise of popular power, in contrast with ruling-class forces, whose interests rest on denying popular control and determination of economic and political priorities. Any assertion that colonial reform in the West Indies was subject to the demands of the broad mass of the oppressed and exploited population has the effect of masking the motives and interests of both the dominant agro-commercial interests and those of the decolonizing elite who inherited the postcolonial state and sheltered the same dominant interests from necessary exposure and critique, bearing in mind that those struggles occurred within an international context.

The bourgeois democratic revolution in the West Indies operated as a top-down process that reflected the intentional supervisory role the British colonial authorities played, with input from the local capitalists and the decolonizing elites, in ways that constrained the anti-colonial assertiveness and resistance that working-class majorities mounted, beginning during the 1930s. In the process the colonized populations would be compelled to reproduce themselves during the transition from colonialism to independence with the economic, political and ideological "handcuffs" (Perelman 2011) of liberalism and capitalism firmly in place, a strategy that is based on the "theoretical detachment of ideology and politics from any social determinations" (Wood 1998, 25). The anti-colonial struggles were harnessed and towed through the canals of the bourgeois democratic revolution, which simply could not create an equitable environment for the spread of its most repeated and vaunted principles of parliamentary democracy, representative government, freedom, equality and justice, precisely because of the class basis and exploitative foundations of capitalist societies. Liberalism, which is modernity's "philosophical doctrine" (Goldberg 2002), capitalist private property, the modern bourgeois (national) state and the cultural institution of the nation-state are founded on substantive inequality, which has nothing to do with forces of nature that supposedly direct human affairs. On the contrary, certain reactionary class-based characteristics from the pre-capitalist moment that Ellen Wood calls the ancien régime, notably patriarchy, economic exploitation, class inequality, gender oppression and other antipathies, survive under the fantastic guise of naturalness (1998). Among modernity's most enduring contributions to history is the claim by liberal Enlightenment luminaries that race, rather than the exploitative, capitalist organization of society, is the source of inequality in society (Malik 1996). This liberal tactic has featured in the racialization of everything from modern world history to human nature, culture, politics and economic and social life: it remains a defining marker of modernity and it anchored colonial policy and practice over the centuries. Contextually, rather than combat British colonialism and imperialism based on a clear understanding that it is the economic (capitalist) organization of society that leads to the racial classification of humanity, the West Indian decolonizing elite negotiated decolonization and independence on the basis of the model of the sovereign monarchy, with the queen as head of state, and asserted that the colonized were equal as humans to their oppressors: for equality to matter substantively, it must transcend the terms on which oppressors are prepared to concede it to victims. The point here is that the law of the state does not and simply cannot bring equality into existence; rather, the law registers and normalizes the fact of the recognition of humanity as the most concrete form of social existence under conditions of domination. In other words, to embrace the notion of deontological equality under a system that is structurally unequal is opportunistic and politically defeatist, as it also rests on the dangerous myth of race as an objective, scientific category (Montagu [1942] 1997).

Largely, the forms of liberal freedom, justice, equality, individual rights and democracy that developed unevenly in European societies during the bourgeois revolutions rest on the right to exploit on which capitalism is based. The culture of negative freedom is associated with deontological rights, freedom, justice, equality and the alienation of power, with human nature assumed to be fixed and flawed. This pseudo-religious, ideological perspective is common where the means of production assume the form of capital with production organized for private capital accumulation. The bourgeois democratic revolution in the West Indies developed in keeping with the strategy of the Colonial Office, which assumed that the colonized had to be slowly guided toward self-government and independence, a position that Grantley Adams embraced unapologetically. The introduction of universal adult suffrage and of internal self-government was subsumed under the right to exploit, which was mediated by the racialization of class exploitation and social relations, including gender and other ideological expressions of social life.

Rather than view British imperialism as a foreign imposition on Caribbean colonies, it would be more accurate to treat imperialism as the central structuring force in the making of colonial societies, which is to say that the colonial experience and capitalist imperialism that conditioned it were mutually constitutive dimensions of bourgeois modernity. Terms like "black Anglo-Saxons" and "Anglophiles" that were applied by nationalist critics to the nationalist leaders in the West Indies spoke to the eagerness with which those leaders embraced the bourgeois democratic revolution and equated it with the upper limits of substantive freedom.

Grantley Adams and other Barbadian leaders and their West Indian counterparts embraced the "moral epistemology" of British imperialism, as was reflected in their conviction about the superior virtues of the British Empire, in comparison with, say, French and Dutch imperialism. There was no special way in which the "moral epistemology" of British imperialism and the Anglophilia it engendered were internalized in Barbadian society: the indoctrination process was a necessary part of the colonizing project. The internalization of the ideology gathered momentum after emancipation with the introduction of public education, an island-wide constabulary, the village constable, a neo-Victorian sense of propriety, the inculcation of the mother-country syndrome and the strengthening of the Christian ethic, all of which served as necessary components of the hegemonic project of the "social control formation" of colonialism and imperialism. The fact that Barbadian society at large rallied around the decision the established leaders agreed upon to advance Barbados to sovereign statehood under a monarchy speaks to the effectiveness of the "moral epistemology" of British imperialism in shaping the contours of Barbadian national consciousness and self-image.

The decolonizing elite in the West Indies exemplified what Victor G. Kiernan (1969) had in mind when he observed that the European imperialists congratulated themselves on their success in producing non-European leaders in the colonies who were racially different but culturally British in their values and commitments. Kiernan argues that from the perspective of the imperialists, with the period from enslavement to emancipation and beyond in mind, the "discontented native in the colonies [and the] labour agitator in the mills were the same serpent in alternate guises. Much of the talk of barbarism or darkness of the outer world which it was Europe's mission to rout was a transmuted fear of the masses at home" (1969, 316). Culturally and politically, the discourse of nationalist, anti-imperialist ideology in the West Indies did not represent a break with the philosophical doctrine of modernity. Largely, the anti-imperialists have been nationalists rather than anti-capitalists, in relation to the struggles the working-class forces mounted for human rights and civil rights, with a view to living as full human beings.

The tendencies within nationalism in the region range from progressive to conservative, consistent with the forms of social consciousness that inspired the motives and goals of its leading advocates. Gary Wilder (2015, xiii) says insightfully, "For twentieth-century African and Antillean populations there did not exist a simple 'outside' from which to contest empire or pursue different futures, an outside that was not already mediated by relations of colonial domination." Wilder does not deny that any "transformative possibilities" existed. Rather, he argues that in writing *Freedom Time, Negritude, Decolonization and the Future of the World*, he moved "away from a critique of impossibility and toward a reflection on utopian potentiality".

To make decolonization and self-determination appealing to the exploited and oppressed people, nationalists equated the struggle for freedom and sovereignty with the fight against imperialist oppression, while tracing exploitation to the workings of the laws of racism and the operation of the laws of nature in human affairs. This ahistorical tendency renders plausible the separation of the moment of coercion (state-based political domination) over the colonial society from the moment of compulsion (exercise of capitalist economic power via the market) in civil society (Wood 1995).

It does not mean, however, that Grantley Adams, Errol Barrow and other West Indian leaders did not take any realistic action to limit the crippling and stifling impact of British imperialist power in the West

Indian colonies and post-colonies. It is necessary to understand the nature of the changing relationship between the post-colonies and the exercise of British state power, bearing in mind what Richard Drayton calls the "Secondary Decolonization" in the British Caribbean, which he views as an "ongoing" process (2014, 132). In fact, "Secondary Decolonization" signals that the decolonization experience was substantively compromised and therefore mirrors the fact that national sovereignty – which is not the outcome of history for any national state or society – and capitalism combine in ways that make substantive self-determination extremely difficult to secure on any definitive or sustainable footing.

The nationalist leaders and their organic intellectuals pursued decolonization and independence on terms that the British self-consciously and deliberately ordered in line with their security interests (Mawby 2012). The British understood the full range of their postwar liabilities, which included a qualitative decline in their international power (Conway 2015, 354). In the early 1940s the British government acknowledged that Britain would have to grant independence to West Indian colonies, partly on the insistence of the United States, and because it would be better positioned to benefit from the postwar hegemonic (international) order the United States was constructing by pursuing decolonization in a responsible manner. The United States did not insist on decolonization and independence for the colonies out of altruistic motives: Washington was bent on deepening the integration of the colonial regions around the world into its capitalist and geopolitical orbit as part of the restructuring of the postwar international system.

The outbreak of the Cold War forced Britain to adapt to a new set of conditions in which it would play a subordinate role under American hegemony, as Britain was no longer in a position to protect the far-flung economic, commercial and financial interests of the British ruling class. From the outset of the Cold War, the creation of the Atlantic Alliance was intended to create a single centre of geopolitical power organized under American hegemony (Panitch and Gindin 2012). The United States called on its European allies with colonies to supervise decolonization responsibly to avoid unpredictable and unmanageable outcomes. During the first decade after World War II, the progressive and radical sentiments and plans the West Indian decolonizing elite harboured toward federation, internal self-government and independence, with working-class needs and interests as their priority, were dutifully sacrificed at the altar of the Anglo-American Cold War project. In the discussion that will follow throughout the book, I will attempt to substantiate the claims that I make about the contradictions that formed part of the bourgeois democratic revolution, aspects of which Britain extended to Barbados and other West Indian territories under conditions that Whitehall found ways to control.

AIMS OF THE BOOK

The study is being organized in two volumes. Broadly, the aims of the work include (1) bringing to the attention of an audience of generalists and specialists (academics, students, public officials and technocrats) certain information and knowledge about the political and other contributions that Errol Walton Barrow made to the postwar transformation of Barbados from the early 1950s, when he began his career in party politics, to the end of the first two decades of independence; (2) accounting for the cultural (economic, political and social) environment in which Barrow had to operate, bearing in mind the domestic and international contradictions and constraints that flowed from a crisis-ridden and disintegrating British Empire and the US-led Cold War project; (3) contributing to the body of limited scholarly material about Barrow's contributions, partly by examining available primary and secondary sources and his actions as a leader; (4) humanizing Barrow by liberating him and his contributions from the highly subjective accounts that superimpose on him an iconic status as "national hero" and "Father of the Nation", which have had the effect of putting him and his accomplishments above appropriate critique; (5) accounting for the role that the racialization of Barbadian cultural life and social processes – its history, politics, economics, class relations and gender and ethnic issues – plays and how political parties and labour unions framed the "agreed-upon" discourse of the body politic; (6) contributing to our understanding of the role that the Barbadian working class played in the making of the contradictory process of change that Errol Walton Barrow helped to direct; (7) making sense of the claim that the creation of the Democratic Labour Party (DLP) worked against the development of the working class into an independent political force in Barbados; (8) keeping in focus the role that those who exercised state power played in managing the transformation process, by attempting to subsume the priorities of private capital under those of the late colonial and postcolonial state; (9) drawing attention to the patriarchal ordering of gender relations, with attention to the DLP's approach to gender issues via its handling of matters that affect women, households and families; and (10) locating the postwar transformation process in Barbados within a regional and globalizing context.

The work represents the first full-length study of Barbados that seeks specifically to locate Barrow as an architect of an important period within Barbados's postwar transformation. The idea for a study of the role Errol Walton Barrow played in Barbados's transformation originated when I did research for a chapter – "Errol Barrow (1920–1987): The Social Construction of Colonial and Post-colonial Charismatic Leadership in Barbados" – that was published in *Caribbean Charisma: Reflections on Leadership, Legitimacy and Populist Politics*, edited by Anton Allahar (2001).

The study begins with an overview of developments during the 1920s and 1930s, when the personalities and conditions that would influence the formation of Errol Barrow's social and political outlook, values, commitments and ideological consciousness began to develop, with special attention to the foundational work that his maternal uncle Dr Charles Duncan O'Neal (1879–1936) and several others did that contributed immensely to the making of modern Barbados.

As social agents we are compelled to act on the stage of history under conditions that we cannot individually control and determine. The pursuit of our ambitions is always tested and constrained by the limits of the possible. The fact that the outlines of the future are inevitably constructed in the present means that we are never necessarily the victims of fate or circumstances, considering that the world we make is the world we change, bearing in mind that actual history is inevitably open-ended and non-totalizable.

THE LOGIC OF THE INDIVIDUAL IN HISTORY
VERSUS THE PEOPLE IN HISTORY

Chinua Achebe says, "There is that great proverb – that until the lions have their own historians, the history of the hunt will always glorify the hunter. . . . It's not one man's job. . . . But it is something we have to do, so that the story of the hunt will also reflect the agony, the travail – the bravery, even, of the lions" (quoted in Smith and Smith 2015, dedication page). Achebe's metaphor of the lion as the prey conveys a subtle message of the strength and power of the hunted, as the lion, king of the beasts and of the jungle, is typically represented as the hunter. Achebe's metaphor can be applied to the potential of the unorganized working-class mass, who have typically been treated as objects rather than agents of history. History is not kind to those who concede the right to write their story to exploiters, oppressors and their organic intellectuals. Ideas, knowledge and theory are always produced for someone, some purpose or end, and can be transformed into a material force for purposive action, where and when those ideas take hold of ordinary people, who then consciously employ them to make sense of their potential to change history, rather than allow themselves to be reduced to the objects of history by others.

It is therefore necessary to interrogate the tendency to interpret historical change in ways that overdetermine the actions of particular individuals or "great men". Viewing historical change from the angle of individual actors is not a waste of time or energy; under liberalism, philosophical individualism and methodological nationalism treat the individual in history as the irreducible unit of analysis, and locate the individual above the actual historical process, reducing thereby those very social forces that act as the purposive actors and agents and products of change to epiphenomena. The irreducible individual is a figment of the liberal imagination. It is necessary to locate the individual within the larger sociohistorical context. Errol Barrow's strategy of working through organized political parties, party politics and in close association with labour unions and capitalist interests to exercise state power and bring about social change in Barbados required mobilizing and politicizing the broad mass of the working-class population and appealing to them along populist rather than class lines, under the banner of the DLP. His approach to expanding the scope of the bourgeois democratic revolution combined nominal politicization with strategic demobilization, to complete the decolonization process and lead the people into independence under the sovereign monarchy, waving the banner of the bourgeois democratic revolution.

It is important to consider the roles that the various social classes and their strata and groups play in the production of social relations around the interplay of antagonistic interests. When we reduce working-class people and others to passive bystanders who are assumed to be in search of a political messiah who can deliver rewards in exchange for joining political parties and labour unions and voting for the chosen leaders, we often devalue the role of the "people" as historical agents acting on the world stage, and we miss the significance of the larger struggle to control the state and exercise state power and transform society. The separation of the direct producers from their means of production left them disorganized, vulnerable and insecure, given the anarchy of production under capitalism and the fragmentation of social life that is an integral part of that contradictory process.

The major institutions and organizations that operate within the state and civil society form embedded components of the "social control formation of capitalism" (Perry 2010, 1), a reality that reflects the alienation of power (Wood 1995). Those institutions and several others form part of the protective apparatuses through which so-called great men operate to control the working class and the broader society, to reproduce and exercise "disciplinary power" (Gill 2003) along what are accepted as legitimate, constitutional lines. The leaders do not operate in isolation from the interests they represent, which is to say that neither the leaders nor the interests they represent can be understood by disaggregating the social forces and the processes in which they participate and focusing on individual consumers or firms or other micro-entities at the expense of the contradictory, open-ended, heterogeneous totality. The fact that actual history defies totalization and absolutes should remind us that social forces and the processes they engineer are best understood as operating within the limits of the possible and are therefore subject to its logic and process.

During the 1930s, in Barbados and across the West Indies, working-class forces erupted in rebellious action to demand the reform of the bankrupt British colonial order. In 1924, Charles Duncan O'Neal and a group of collaborators formed the Democratic League (DL) to respond to the challenges the working class faced: they disseminated progressive (social democratic) ideas for improving the lot of the heavily racialized, oppressed and battered working-class mass. Among the DL forces was Clennell Wickham, who used the *Herald* newspaper to raise the awareness of the general public of the legitimate grievances of the working class against the great political repression and economic exploitation it suffered at the hands of the agro-commercial capitalist strata that also exercised state power. The political environment for working-class struggle in Barbados became increasingly favourable, given the lingering material effects from World War I, extremely low wages, crushing and demoralizing poverty, abysmally poor housing and overcrowding, a highly restrictive franchise, and social and political agitation by demobilized soldiers returning from war service. Returning migrants from Panama and Cuba added to the ranks of the unemployed and restless. Black nationalist ideas from the local branch of Marcus Garvey's Universal Negro Improvement Association (UNIA) also percolated and resonated with many among the yet-to-be-organized working-class mass.

The demands that were made by the decolonizing elite, largely in their own interests, under which the needs of the working class would be subsumed, were hardly anti-British, considering that the "anti-colonial consciousness" (Drayton 2014, 121) of the elite and the masses in the West Indies did not inspire the exploited and oppressed to make disloyalty to the British Empire a tenet of their struggle.

A number of reforms were introduced in Barbados in the aftermath of the 1937 working-class rebellion, in keeping with the recommendations of the West India Royal Commission (Moyne Commission), which the British government appointed to investigate and report on the causes of the "disturbances" and recommend reforms. The colonial state in Barbados enacted the Trade Union Act (1939), which led to the formation of the Barbados Workers' Union (BWU) in 1941; the Workmen's Compensation Act (1943); Shops Act (1945); adopted the Bushe Experiment (1946); the

Factories Act (1947); the 1949 Amendment to the Trade Union Act of 1939, which instituted the right to peaceful picketing; the Representation of the People Act (1950), which provided for universal adult suffrage, which took effect in 1951; and the introduction of ministerial government (1954).

The Barbados Labour Party (BLP), which was formed in 1946, replaced the Barbados Progressive League (BPL), which grew out of the DL; the DLP was created in 1955 (Smith and Smith 2015, 77–79). In 1945, Oliver Stanley, secretary of state for the colonies, dispatched a document to all British governors in the West Indian colonies that set forth British policy for constitutional reform in the British Caribbean and declared Britain's commitment to the promotion of full self-government within a federation in the speediest possible fashion. In 1948 the Colonial Office issued the Colonial Empire 1947–48 (Cmnd. 7433) report, according to which the "central purpose of British colonial policy is . . . to guide the colonial territories to responsible self-government within the Commonwealth in conditions that assure to the people . . . a fair standard of living and freedom from oppression from any quarter". The Colonial Office issued the 1949–50 report *The Colonial Territories 1949–50*.[1] The term "colony", which appeared in the Colonial Empire 1947–48 report, was replaced by "territory" in the 1949–50 document, which identified economic self-sufficiency, energy and enterprise, honesty and a capacity for skilful administration as core elements of the self-government the UK government was prepared to grant to the West Indian territories. The two reports mentioned above coincided with the outbreak of the Cold War and made it unambiguously clear that Britain was not about to allow the West Indian territories to chart their path to self-government and independence on their own terms at the expense of British, American and broader Western interests.

The bourgeois democratic revolution that came to the West Indian territories would be introduced under the auspices of the Colonial Office. The colonial state introduced the Bushe Experiment in Barbados in 1946 to create a framework for an orderly transition to decolonization through internal self-government, in anticipation of the mandate that was sent down by the secretary of state for the colonies. Sir Frederick Smith and

Alan Smith summarize the political provisions of the Bushe Experiment as follows:

> Governor Grattan Bushe (1941–46) announced in 1946 (1) that the 4 Assembly members of the Executive Committee (the governor's policy advising committee) would now be chosen on the advice of that member of the Assembly best able to command a majority, i.e. the leader of the majority party; (2) the four members would henceforth be responsible in the Assembly for the different departments of the government, though the actual administration of the departments would remain under the Colonial Secretary; and the majority leader of the Assembly, and not the Attorney-General, would be the government spokesman in the Assembly. This was the major first step towards making the democratically elected members of the Assembly responsible for government. (Smith and Smith 2015, 78)

Sir Frederick Smith and Alan Smith stress that the provisions of the Bushe Experiment were "used wisely by the labour movement to enact lots of reforms that benefited the working class". The authors emphasize that the labour movement strategy "was resisted strongly by the planters and merchants" (2015, 78). The Bushe Experiment became an integral part of the social contract within the unfolding bourgeois democratic revolution that subsumed decolonization, based on black majority rule, under the prevailing racialized (white) capitalist economic hegemony. Sir Frederick Smith hints at this fact, when he notes that Grantley Adams

> never moved on economic matters unless he conferred with Sir Archibald Cuke and K.R Hunte, two captains of Barbados industry. With such titans of the Barbados corporate world being Sir Grantley's consiglieri, in a Barbados still under the watchful eye of a post-war Britain, in a world where the Cold War was heating up by the day, you always knew on which side of an issue Sir Grantley would come down if asked to choose between what he viewed as fiscal prudence as against investing in social programmes. (Smith and Smith 2015, 85)

Sir Frederick Smith also confirms that the decolonization initiative was ordered and supervised from Whitehall with the full cooperation of

the decolonizing elite, which is in contrast with the ideologically motivated nationalist assertion that decolonization and independence were
demanded and achieved according to conditions that were set by the
decolonizing elites and the colonial populations. Whitehall put the recalcitrant capitalist class forces in Barbados on notice that it was in their
interest to accept the provisions of the Bushe Experiment (Belle 1988).
In their reluctance to embrace the Bushe Experiment, the dominant
economic and political forces acted deliberately and decisively to ensure
that the unequal power relationship between the decolonizing state and
capital on the one hand and the working-class mass and their leaders on
the other was maintained as fully as possible. The ministerial government provisions of the Bushe Experiment became an integral part of the
sociopolitical control mechanism for ensuring that black majority rule
under universal adult suffrage would not be exploited by black political
state managers to undermine white supremacy and capitalist economic
hegemony in Barbados. British imperialism had put structural obstacles
in the way of economic modernization, as W. Arthur Lewis noted in 1949,
when he criticized British colonial policy and practice for retarding the
development of the colonies and their populations (1949, 37–41; 1978).

The British Guiana Labour Union was formed in 1919. The Guianese
and West Indian Federation of Trade Unions and Labour Parties was created in 1926 and convened four meetings in British Guiana and Trinidad
by 1938. It gave way to the British Guiana and West Indies Labour Congress (BGWILC), also in 1938, which morphed into the Caribbean Labour
Congress (CLC) at its founding meeting in Barbados in 1945. The 1945
meeting brought together (for the first time) labour and working-class
delegates from throughout the West Indies to strategize about the future
of the colonies, with the interests of the working class in clear perspective.
In the communiqué that the CLC issued in Barbados, Grantley Herbert
Adams declared that the only hope for any viable future of the Caribbean
would depend on the creation of a socialist Caribbean Commonwealth
(Phillips 1998, 15; Bolland 2001; Watson 2004).

As World War II was winding down, Britain was forced to acknowledge the impossibility of maintaining the British Empire. The United
States increased pressure on Britain, France and the Netherlands to free

their colonies in a guided manner. The US strategy proved decisive in framing the discourse of decolonization along US-mediated Cold War lines. The United States began by testing its Cold War strategy in British Guiana (1953) against Cheddi Jagan and the People's Progressive Party (PPP), against Jacobo Árbenz Guzmán in Guatemala (1954), and against the Cuban Revolution beginning in 1959. Britain became a signatory to the US-led (Anglo-American) Cold War project, which yielded important benefits to the increasingly powerless European imperialists via the Marshall Plan and the Atlantic Alliance.

The United States resolutely opposed the adoption of any working-class-controlled decolonization and independence strategies in the West Indies, whether through a federation or via territorially based internal self-government. This study will show that the decolonizing elite in the West Indies faced major geopolitical, economic and other challenges and hurdles that arose from the making of the postwar international order under US hegemony. Whatever Errol Barrow had to say regarding his socialist birthright and credentials, when it came to matters of Cold War geopolitics, he acted in the most pragmatic and transactional manner, simultaneously embracing and criticizing American hegemony and the "megalithic corporations", while self-consciously never advancing any semblance of a critique of hegemony.

LOCATING ERROL WALTON BARROW

Errol Barrow spent most of the first six years of his life (1920–26) living with his parents in St Croix, US Virgin Islands, where his father, the Reverend Reginald Barrow, was assigned to the Episcopal diocese of Puerto Rico. In St Croix, the Reverend Barrow delivered sermons that addressed the racist and oppressive basis of US colonial policy and practice, class (economic) exploitation, and other issues that did not endear him to the American authorities. He openly participated in trade union organizing activities in St Croix and was instrumental in helping to organize a branch of the African Methodist Episcopal Church there. He was dismissed from the diocese and forced to leave St Croix, whence he travelled to New York, where he joined the African Methodist Episcopal

Church and spent many years participating in activities that supported decolonization in the Caribbean, before he retired to Barbados during the early 1960s (Blackman 1995, 113–14).

Theodore Sealy notes that Errol Barrow informed him that his father's involvement in the "trade union movement" with Hamilton Jackson in St Croix led to him having been invited "on board an American warship and taken away surreptitiously. That was the last we saw of him for years. Eventually he found his way to the United States to put his case, but he stayed on there and . . . he joined the Garvey Movement and the African Methodist Episcopal Church in the United States" (1991, 24).

In 1926 Barrow's mother returned to Barbados with her children. Errol attended the Wesley Hall Boys' School and completed his secondary education at Harrison College. In 1939, the same year he was scheduled to enter Codrington College to study classics, Barrow joined the Royal Air Force to fight for Britain as a loyal colonial subject, having asserted that Britain needed him more than Codrington College did. After he completed his military service, Barrow was decommissioned in 1945–46, and studied economics at the London School of Economics and law at the Inns of Court. He returned to Barbados in 1950 and joined the BLP under Grantley Adams; he won his first election to the House of Assembly on the BLP ticket in 1951.

Beginning in 1954–55, Barrow and certain other BLP dissident back-benchers began to object publicly to the slow pace of the decolonization process, which Grantley Adams's BLP government was implementing less enthusiastically than Britain was prepared to tolerate (Belle 1988). Sir Frederick Smith says the "growing set of dissidents within the BLP were led by Barrow, and included Cammie Tudor, myself, T.T. Lewis, and Theodore Brancker. The left of the party . . . was entirely excluded from ministerial posts in 1954" (2015, 83). Barrow delivered a speech in the House of Assembly on 14 April 1955 in which he asserted that his standing as a "socialist from birth" made his association with "certain members of the Government . . . one of bitter disappointment from beginning to end". He said, "The charges which I would like to lay at their heads are a lack of political and personal morality, also a lack of sincerity in their insisting always to use public funds of this island for vote-catching purposes and other personal reasons." He declared that he was "severing all connections with the BLP" (Smith and Smith 2015, 84).

Sir Frederick Smith mentions that a catalyst in the decision to form the DLP was that Cameron Tudor "ran as an independent in a by-election in St. Lucy in 1954 and trounced the BLP candidate" (2015, 88). The early signs of the weakening of the position of the BLP in the House of Assembly and in the society came when the BLP failed to win the St Lucy seat, which L.A. Williams had vacated to assume an appointment in Grenada. Tudor contested the vacant seat as an Independent Labour candidate, having left the BLP in 1952, and campaigned on social programmes such as improved housing, free secondary education, social security and programmes to benefit fishermen. During the bitterly contested election campaign, Tudor accused Adams of alienating intelligent and independent-thinking individuals from the BLP. In response, Adams accused Tudor of being part of a subversive and disruptive tendency that was willing to sacrifice party unity for selfish ends. Adams understood party unity as submissiveness to his autocratic ways – a characteristic feature of the authoritarian colonial social and political tradition. Tudor polled 1,518 votes, exceeding the "combined strengths of his two opponents" (1,312): Garner of the BLP received 761 votes and Greaves, from the Electors' Association, got 551 votes (Cheltenham 1970, 117, 118).

Tudor won the seat without the backing of any political party, having crushed the BLP and the Conservatives in a constituency that solidly supported the BLP in 1951. Richard Cheltenham argues that the BLP government's front bench was the only core support Garner received from within the BLP, while Tudor earned greater support from within the broad ranks of the BLP. During the campaign Adams visited London on official business about the deep-water-harbour project that was being considered for Barbados. The governor's speech from the throne did not inspire confidence among the bulk of the electorate, and the official Opposition – the Electors' Association – seemed out of touch with the pressing issues of the day (Cheltenham 1970, 117, 118).

The BLP began to experience turmoil in its ranks before the middle of the 1950s. Various monthly reports from the governor of Barbados to the secretary of state for the colonies drew attention to a range of problems such as the poor performance of BLP ministers in Parliament, the activities of the rebel faction within the BLP (Barrow, Smith, T.T. Lewis, and others), the systematic attacks on the BLP administration by Frank Walcott, the head of the BWU (even though Walcott voted more or less consistently with the government party), Walcott's deep personal and political rift with Adams, and the consistent voting against the BLP government by Wynter Crawford and Owen Allder. The larger issue was the impact of the Cold War on domestic politics and ideology in Barbados and the West Indies.

Drawing on Peter Laurie's doctoral dissertation, Smith and Smith point out that Adams's opposition to Sleepy Smith's becoming president of the BWU "was part of an intense Cold War campaign being waged against the left wing of the labour movement in Barbados, who were all branded as communists and traitors". Adams announced at a public meeting on 22 June 1954 that there existed "a wilful, wicked, atrocious and diabolical plot by certain persons to capture power in the union and then the Labour Party and then destroy the Labour movement as it now exists" (quoted in Smith and Smith 2015, 81; originally in the *Beacon*, 26 June 1954). Adams's anti-working-class and anti-communist defence of British imperialism at the United Nations Special Session held in Paris in 1948, the purging of the "left" from the People's National Party (PNP) in Jamaica by Norman Manley, the undermining of the Trade Union Council in Jamaica by 1952, the Anglo-American strategy for removing Cheddi Jagan and the PPP from power in British Guiana beginning in 1953 (Smith and Smith 2015, 91–93; Rabe 2005) and the strategic role that Adams and Frank Walcott played in destroying the CLC by the early 1950s formed part of the operation of the Cold War project in the West Indies (Watson 2004; Horne 2007).

The formation of the DLP in 1955 was part of the evolving local, regional and international political context in which the Cold War played a pivotal geopolitical and ideological role. Sir Frederick Smith asserted that he "was definitely not a communist" and elaborated that colonialism had an enduring psychological effect by "acting as a drag and a weight". He asserted that by "setting up the DLP, we were fighting for a real removal of the chains once and for all. I had no intention, having done that, to then be re-shackled by communism" (Smith and Smith 2015, 97). Sir Frederick's notion of removing "chains" rings hollow, given that there was absolutely no break with the institutional framework that anchored British imperialism and its strategy for controlling political moderniza- tion in Barbados. Sir Frederick misread decolonization for a substantive break with the British system, and he introduced a false inside-outside dichotomy between colonialism and imperialism on the one hand and decolonization on the other, when in fact the two have been mutually constitutive. Whitehall was forced to follow orders from Downing Street, which joined the United States in directing the anti-communist crusade that appealed to Sir Frederick and other social democrats. Their invest- ment in the bourgeois democratic revolution extended to British-style party politics and British political institutions like capitalism and parlia- mentary government, which to their thinking epitomized the realization of human freedom, justice and equality.

The Barrow-led "young Turks" broke with the BLP and formed the DLP on 1 May 1955, with Frederick "Sleepy" Smith becoming the party's first president (Smith and Smith 2015, 24, 77–98). The DLP defeated Adams's BLP in the general election of 1961: Barrow served as Barba- dos's second premier (1961–66) and led Barbados into independence as a monarchy (that is, with the Queen remaining its head of state) within the Commonwealth in November 1966, consistent with the decoloniza- tion provisions that Whitehall announced. He served as prime minister of Barbados for two terms (1966–71 and 1971–76) before the DLP was defeated by the BLP under Jon Michael Geoffrey Manningham "Tom" Adams, Grantley Adams's son, in the two successive general elections of 1976 and 1981, in which Barrow retained his seat. The DLP won the general election of 1986 under Barrow, who died in office in June 1987 in his sixty-seventh year, having been reelected to the DLP stronghold constituency of St John in every election since 1958 (Smith and Smith 2015, 90).

By 1965 Barrow had become visibly frustrated over the slow prog- ress toward the creation of a replacement for the Federation of the West Indies, which was dissolved in 1962. Barrow acted decisively to promote independence for Barbados alone, a move that generated opposition from within the DLP and intense public criticism from the BLP and certain others in Barbados. A year after Barbados became independent in 1966, Barrow joined the leaders of Guyana, Jamaica, and Trinidad and Tobago and the non-independent territories that made up the federation to create the Caribbean Free Trade Area in 1967 and later the Caribbean Community and Common Market (CARICOM) in 1973. Barrow, however, did not view independence for Barbados as grounds for looking inward at the expense of the West Indies and the wider world: his international perspective helped to inform his view that sovereignty should help to equip newly independent states to build toward closer world understanding and cooperation in the interest of human progress. His criticism of the workings of the international system did not rise to the level of a critique, a way of acting that was consistent with his populist perspective, which was not intended to politicize and mobilize Barbadians for any radical action. He embraced American hegemony, criticized the workings of the international economy and felt strongly that the United Nations should be permitted to direct the development process to benefit the less developed countries. He did not seem to understand that the UN model of sovereign autonomy was not designed to allow the newly independent states to exercise their sovereignty to frame their own development trajectory under the liberal international order.

METHODOLOGY: CONCEPTUAL, PHILOSOPHICAL CONSIDERATIONS AND LITERATURE CONCERNS

Goran Therborn argues that historical materialism provides "a critique of the indeterminate abstractions of the economists, in which historically specific forms of production and property are volatized into concepts of production . . . and property in general" (1976, 43). The methodology the "economists" and other mainstream social scientists routinely employ relies on a technique that reduces social relations between humans (classes, social strata, groups and individuals) to technical relations between individuals and things (commodities).

In *The Grundrisse*, Karl Marx takes exception to volatization, which mirrors fetishization and alienation. Marx argues that when we study the social relations of production in actual societies we must be prepared to offer concrete analyses of concrete situations by paying attention to the "real and concrete . . . with e.g. the population, which is the foundation and the subject of the entire social act of production". Marx stresses that the "population" as a concrete form should not be taken at face value, however. He says,

> The population is an abstraction if I leave out, for example, the classes of which it is composed. These classes . . . are an empty phrase if I am not familiar with the elements on which they rest, e.g. wage labour, capital, etc. These latter in turn presuppose exchange, division of labour, prices. . . . For example, capital is nothing without wage labour, without value, money, prices, etc. Thus, if we were to begin with the population, this would be a chaotic conception . . . of the whole, and I would then by means of further determination, move analytically towards ever more simple concepts . . . from the imagined concrete towards ever thinner abstractions until I had arrived at the simplest determinations. ([1939] 1973, 100–101)

Marx understood that the social (whole) appears to the naked eye as random, chaotic and disorderly and requires closer examination to appreciate the underlying complexity by arriving at the "simplest determinations".

Following Marx, Goran Therborn rejects the liberal (positivist) habit of objectifying social reality by reducing it to a product of "our own self-alienated subjectivity". He is mindful that historical materialism steers clear of neo-Weberian (liberal) philosophical individualism and methodological nationalism (idealism), which discount the fact that the knowing human agent (subject) is internal to the movement of nature, society and knowledge. It is not possible for humans to acquire scientific knowledge of a detached and alienated world that is propelled by supposedly objective and autonomous laws of nature, history and society that purportedly operate independently of human (social) agency and determination. As a product of human activity, all knowledge is created intersubjectively, such that human subjectivity and the production of knowledge are social expressions of human action and determination. By extension, the class struggle in society is not reducible to an instrumental phenomenon.

With Errol Barrow's role in the postwar transformation of Barbados in mind, I treat economic change as part of the larger social process, which I understand as complex, open-ended and contradictory, with potential and possibilities that depend on combinations of social and political forces and the constraints that are imposed by the operation of capitalist power in the economy, state and civil society and by the operation of the international system. The fact that capital accumulation is a global process means that those constraints are historically conditioned and rooted in the global political economy. In fact, national states never seem as sovereign as when they act to defend and protect capitalist property rights and rightful property income, domestically and internationally (Agnew 2009).

The fundamental aim of development under capitalism is to secure conditions that broaden opportunities for private capital accumulation. Capitalist development depends on the transformation of the essential means of production into capital, a contradictory process that involves the separation of direct producers from their means of production and their transformation into wage-dependent workers. Where and when capitalists own and control the bulk of the means of production, they never make the economic development of any country, region or any other part of the world their priority, which means that capitalist commodity production is not organized to meet socially determined human needs. The production and accumulation priorities of capitalists are fundamentally antisocial.

Benjamin Selwyn argues that mainstream thinking on development as well as certain Marxist tendencies rests on a paradox that claims to help the poor and promote democracy, while employing authoritarian methods that work against the real interests of the poor. Selwyn proposes an alternative he labels as development that is led by labour, a process in which the world's labouring classes define and shape their own development priorities, based on putting an end to exploitation (Selwyn 2016). It is the class struggle that conditions the reproduction of social classes and the options that are available to the working class to improve the conditions of its existence in everyday life, with attention to the policies the state implements that are constrained by the imperatives of capital accumulation and the politics associated therewith.

The pursuit of private capital accumulation compels capitalists to search for ways to overcome constraints from state-mandated policies that limit the movement of capital within and across national borders. Their priority is to increase the rate of profit: capitalist investors treat the international economy as their real economic space, in contrast with each sovereign state and nation, which view national (sovereign) space as the effective unit of analysis for making sense of the pursuit of economic and political ends.

During the postwar decades, which witnessed the deepening of the internationalization of capital (in the direction of globalization), key areas of national economic decision-making authority were slowly transferred to the world level (Holloway 1995) under the gaze of the dominant states, international capital, and the multilateral institutions like the World Bank, International Monetary Fund and others. This process paved the way for the emergence of the neoliberal transition, beginning in the 1970s–1980s, when the conditions and provisions that anchored the postwar accumulation strategy became exhausted (Robinson 2004).

Sir Arthur Lewis advanced certain arguments that are worth examining, as he was the leading economic adviser to West Indian and Commonwealth Caribbean governments on the economic development strategy he deemed appropriate and necessary to attract international capital to achieve economic development and international competitiveness. A review of two of Lewis's main economic claims will suffice: the first is his assertion that imperialism retarded the development of the colonies between 1875 and 1945, a situation which he claims was responsible for the rise of political radicalism among the colonial intelligentsia and the spread of anti-imperialist struggles that wasted precious time which he claims would have been better spent promoting economic development (1978). Lewis's (1954) second claim pertains to his two-sector model of economic development with unlimited supplies of labour. Lewis's subjective (social democratic) view of imperialism resonated with J.A. Hobson's idea that imperialism approximated an irrational policy of capitalist states (1902), that the imperialists could use laws or other means to achieve alternative development outcomes, without attention to the imperatives of the capitalist production and accumulation. Lewis assumed idealistically that transforming the economic and social conditions in the colonies and thereby forestalling the costly anti-imperialist class struggles would pre-empt certain contradictions that arise from exploitation and oppression under imperialism.

Lewis discounted the fact that imperialism signalled the expansion and deepening of capitalist production on an international scale within a specific world historical conjuncture. He understood commodities as products (things) that connect countries via the international division of labour, rather than as expressions of capitalist social relations of production that transcend territorial borders (Roberts 2016, 31, 38–44). Contradictory (capitalist) social class relations are not part of Lewis's conceptual schema. His positivist outlook rests on a false inside-outside dichotomy between Europe and the rest of the world, and he sees Europe as the developed geographical region, with the non-European world trapped in a condition of original (natural) backwardness with "unlimited supplies of labour" and lacking an internal capacity for self-movement. In this sense Lewis was a proponent of postwar modernization theory and deology. In his thinking the non-West had to wait for the rational, capitalist West to introduce the trappings of modernity to transform these "unlimited supplies of labour" into productive (value-creating, commodity-producing) labour. This notion ignores centuries of European domination and incorporation of the non-West into sites for commodity production for the world market, and the fact that uneven and combined development are inherent to the capitalist process.

Beate Jahn points out that European thinkers produced a "redefinition of authentic and legitimate political community" that produced the artifice of a "political community built on natural law". Jahn notes that such an ahistorical Eurocentric outlook "inevitably led to the universalist conception of the state of nature" which informed an unrealistic "worldview based on a hierarchy of cultures which serves as the basis for a theory of unequal relations between political communities" (2000, 95, 96; see also Noble 1998, 256–59).

The state of nature simply is not the appropriate starting point for thinking about the origins of social life (Levins and Lewontin 1985). The mutability of human nature means that change is nature's abiding constant. Biology and biological differences cannot account for the conflicts and enmities that occur among different groups of humans; rather, it is exploitation and oppression which inform and condition the racialization of history and social life that condition cultural conflict and other contradictions (Montagu [1942] 1997, 261–63).

Lewis's notion of "unlimited supplies of labour" as the original condition of certain parts of the world is at variance with the history of actually existing societies. His methodology, influenced by state-centric "epistemological territorialism", made it difficult to appreciate that the open-ended, non-totalizable process of capitalist economic and social transformation on an international scale is marked by combined and uneven development, which characterizes commodity production and capital accumulation based on the operation of the law of value (Pradella 2015). When we understand that combined and uneven development lies at the heart of the capitalist production and accumulation processes, we lay the basis for parting with geographical determinism, which informs dichotomous representations of developed and developing countries that informed the "colonizer's view of the world" (Blaut 1976).

Giovanni Arrighi and John Saul (1973) subjected Lewis's "unlimited supplies of labour" thesis to appropriate critique in their study of European colonial expansion into Southern Africa, with special reference to Southern Rhodesia, an area that Britain transformed into a site of "unlimited supplies of labour".

Unlimited supplies of labour were created in Southern Rhodesia only after African lands were expropriated and cattle, agricultural production and basic exchange processes and other aspects of social reproduction systematically uprooted, a deliberate move that transformed largely self-sufficient farmers into landless masses who were then compelled to exchange their labour power for wages on terms that were set by the expropriators (Arrighi and Saul 1973; Watson 2008b, 2008c). The development of capitalism in Southern Rhodesia under the British followed the traditional path of forcibly separating the direct producers from their means of production and converting those means of production into capital via direct coercion and physical compulsion that resulted in two types of commodity owners – new European capitalist owners of the means of production (capital) and African owners of labour power that had to be exchanged for the means of subsistence.

Anievas and Nişancioğlu (2015) argue for "an internationalist historiography" that understands capitalism as transcending Europe and capital accumulation as a global process, to situate Europe's contribution to world history within a scientific framework that locates combined and uneven development at the heart of the fundamental capitalist process (Warren 1980; Kay 1975). The discussion of contradictions associated with combined and uneven development under capitalism is relevant for a few reasons. First, my discussion of the Lewis model of economic development shows that Lewis embraced the positivist logic of development and underdevelopment as two separate processes, and he made development in the "underdeveloped" regions dependent on capital and technology inflows from "developed" areas.

Second, the managers of West Indian and Commonwealth Caribbean states like Barbados that embraced his model did not seem to appreciate that there is no definitive, long-term national solution to the contradictions of development for the ends of private capital accumulation, even as they acknowledged their dependence on access to international capital. The state managers subjectively declare their intention to take their countries out of their condition of underdevelopment and transform them into developed countries by some imaginary date. They labour under the misguided notion that the real challenge they face is to discover and adopt the proper mix of public policies to attract the requisite amount of productive capital from abroad, while preserving national economic and political sovereignty and interpreting economic development as a national process in a global economy. The ideology of epistemological territorialism, which they embrace, rests on the myth that there are discrete national economies with corresponding national (sovereign) states that possess irreducible sovereignty. However, they adopt development strategies that give concessions to global capital and increase the insecurity of the labouring majority.

Third, they believe that they and their technocrats can harness private capital and bring capital accumulation priorities under effective national (state) control via indicative planning, even though their actions as state managers make their priority the protection of private capital's right to exploit labour for private capital accumulation. Much like Lewis, the Caribbean leaders failed to appreciate that what passes for development and underdevelopment is symptomatic of the uneven and combined development that is characteristic of the fundamental capitalist process of production for private accumulation ends.

The absence of biographical work about Errol Barrow and of an extensive corpus of scholarship on his contributions to change in postwar Barbados made researching and preparing this study challenging. The whereabouts of Barrow's papers, three decades after he died, remains a mystery.

The larger problem is that, as Alan Smith notes in the foreword to *Dreaming a Nation*, as far as chronicling the civic memory of Barbados is concerned, "there is no tradition of statesmen or key citizens leaving accounts of their lives" (Smith and Smith 2015, 11), a sentiment shared by Harold Hoyte (2012, vii). Much like Grantley Adams, Tom Adams and other "key citizens" of Barbados, Errol Barrow did not publish any material, scholarly or otherwise, on his role as an elected politician and leader that is available for public scrutiny. His life and political contributions remain the least studied when compared with his contemporaries from Guyana, Jamaica, and Trinidad and Tobago.[2]

My earliest attempt to research Errol Walton Barrow's charismatic political leadership began with *Speeches by Errol Barrow* (Haniff 1987) and a scholarly article by Hilary McD. Beckles (1989); Beckles's *A History of Barbados: From Amerindian Settlement to Nation-State*; Peter Morgan's *The Life and Times of Errol Barrow*; and Francis Blackman's *Dame Nita: Caribbean Woman, World Citizen*, a biography of the life of Barrow's sister in which the author devotes limited space to Errol Barrow's political career. On Barrow's death in 1987, the *Nation* newspaper (Barbados) published an extensive keepsake edition (10 June 1987) that was devoted to Barrow's career as seen through the eyes of relatives, a representative number of key political figures, associates, intellectuals, journalists and certain other members of the intelligentsia.

Beckles's *Chattel House Blues: Making of a Democratic Society in Barbados, from Clement Payne to Owen Arthur* (2004b) adds to the relevant literature and is useful for studying Errol Barrow's contributions to the transformation of Barbados; however, Beckles says very little in *Chattel House Blues* about Barrow's contributions, which is unfortunate and regrettable, given the historical scope of the book. The late Peter Morgan's *The Life and Times of Errol Barrow* (1994) is a biography that chronicles Barrow's rise and the development of his political career. Morgan, an Englishman of long residence in Barbados, served in Barrow's cabinets, held an appointment as high commissioner to Canada and wrote very sympathetically about Barrow.

Morgan's brief study is intended for a general audience. He comments also on political contributions by other major figures in the DLP, among them Douglas Lynch, a white Barbadian who served in World War II, later became an attorney, and unsuccessfully contested a seat on the DLP ticket. Sir Frederick Smith remarks that Lynch became "a captain of industry as chairman of the Barbados Shipping and Trading Group, the island's largest conglomerate for several years. Errol always continued to consult with him on finance and commercial matters over the years" (Smith and Smith 2015, 87). Douglas Lynch was to Barrow what K.R. Hunte and others were to Adams, as noted by Smith. Whatever might have been the basis of Lynch's close political relationship with Barrow and the DLP, it is indisputable, considering insightful arguments that Richard Cheltenham (1970) makes with reference to the Bushe Experiment that informed the "historic compromise", that Lynch had his own motives for joining the DLP and becoming a close adviser and confidant of Barrow. Lynch's strategic move allowed him to monitor the decision-making process and protect the interests of the white-dominated capitalist order from any undesirable regulation by black majority governments in a society where white monopoly power permeated all areas of economic and social life.

F.A. Hoyos wrote two biographies, one of Grantley Adams and the other of Tom Adams (1974, 1988), both of which paid limited attention to Barrow's role in Barbadian politics. Theodore Sealy drew heavily on conversations with Barrow for a chapter on Barrow's political development, his social democratic (socialist) worldview, his participation in Barbadian politics, his difficult personal and political relationship with Grantley

Adams and the BLP and his outlook on and involvement in regional political cooperation (1991). Woodville Marshall edited Wynter Crawford's autobiography (Marshall 2003), which covers a period that began before and overlapped with Barrow's rise and participation as a politician, a member of Parliament, the second premier and first prime minister of Barbados. Crawford joined the BLP when the West Indian National Congress Party (WINCP) folded, as the electorate stopped supporting its candidates at the polls. He later broke with the BLP and supported Barrow and other dissidents to create the DLP; he served in the cabinet under Barrow, with whom he had a number of public disagreements over federation and the appropriate path to political independence for Barbados. Crawford was an unambiguous supporter of regional cooperation. He believed that he, rather than Barrow, should have become the leader of the DLP, and unsuccessfully challenged Barrow for leadership. His autobiography throws light on tensions and contradictions in the late decolonization period as well as the early independence movement under Barrow and the DLP.

Gary Lewis published a study of his uncle T.T. Lewis's social and political life and career and his role as one of the BLP dissenters who broke with Adams and helped form the DLP in 1955. T.T. Lewis was broadly viewed as a "white rebel" and maverick for breaking with the white establishment and passionately and unambiguously defending black working-class interests, for which he was rejected and isolated by the white-dominated establishment in Barbados (1999). Barrow sincerely, honestly and openly embraced Lewis as a member of the DLP. Sir Frederick Smith said of T.T. Lewis,

> I remember T.T. I can see him now: a man of absolute integrity. If there was one man who has suffered for politics and for championing the cause of the poor downtrodden, that man was T.T. Lewis. Truly he paid the price for his commitments. He was a dedicated socialist and cared for the common man even though he himself was not a man of affluence. He could have easily gone over to the other side and as a white could have made it easy on himself. (Smith and Smith 2015, 86)

Sir Frederick Smith's autobiography, jointly published with Alan Smith

(Smith and Smith 2015), makes a timely contribution to the very limited body of literature for the period from the 1950s to Barrow's death in 1987 and beyond that locates Barrow at the centre of important arguments and processes within the bourgeois democratic revolution. The book adds to our knowledge of Barrow's contributions as a political leader in Barbados, while highlighting political tensions and disagreements between Sir Frederick and Barrow and the DLP.

NEGATIVE FREEDOM: DIALECTIC OF BOURGEOIS DEMOCRATIC REVOLUTION IN BARBADOS

Sir Frederick Smith acknowledges that Barrow exhibited an authoritarian streak, a tendency that has been characteristic of the political behaviour of the decolonizing elite and postcolonial leaders throughout the British Caribbean. Tom Adams appropriately traces authoritarianism to the repressive and antidemocratic nature of colonialism and imperialism.[3] Authoritarianism has been a characteristic of the top-down, highly centralized leadership of the political parties, labour unions, business interests and others that manage and regulate the conditions under which the working class reproduces itself.

Patrick Emmanuel (1988) and Richard Cheltenham (1970) argue that the BLP and DLP remained committed to the "historic compromise" that formed an integral part of the political settlement on which Barbados's postwar decolonization and independence strategies came to rest. Both authors argue convincingly that the two labour parties pursued policies that strengthened white capitalist (economic) hegemony in the political economy of Barbados.

The dominant capitalist forces created organizations and exploited every opportunity to protect their strategic interests to make it easier to influence public policy under black majority governments.

All revolutions are expressions of contradictory interests and processes. The bourgeois democratic revolution was a "passive revolution" for cementing class and other forms of domination from above. In that sense, hardly any aspect of the social relations of production was beyond the reach of the bourgeois democratic revolution, notably the organization of state power, parliamentary government, liberal democracy, property relations and rightful property income, individual rights, workers' rights, labour organizations, political freedom and ideological issues of religion, patriarchy, race and gender. The edifice of private (capitalist) property rights, through which a handful exercise dominant economic power over the majority, is customarily interpreted by liberals and social democrats as compatible with the achievement of democratic freedom.

Contrastingly, Michael Hardt and Antonio Negri discuss the expansion of the exploitative basis of capitalist private property and production in colonial societies in the following terms: "The primacy of property is revealed in all modern colonial histories. Each time a European power brings new practices of government to its colonies in the name of reason, efficiency, and the rule of law, the primary 'republican virtue' they establish is the rule of property" (2008, 14). According to Lucia Pradella, "Marx's notebooks of the 1840s provide evidence that the 'international' had a central place in the elaboration of the materialistic conception of history, which proceeded hand in hand with that of the labour theory of value and of the revolutionary socialist programme." Pradella notes that Marx "conceived of the economic systems of the European powers as colonial systems. He also analysed processes of deindustrialization and impoverishment in colonized and dependent countries, delving into the concrete situation of an impressive range of countries" (2015, 169).

Thomas Holt reminds us that the "global configurations" wrought by capitalism have "continued to frame ideologies of work and citizenship, systems of labor mobilization and exploitation and diverse claims for participation in the modern world" (2000, 31, 32). Capitalism is not the end of history: contrary to what liberals might claim, capitalism and liberal democracy are best understood as representing a moment in the development of world historical time. Liberal democracy is one form of class democracy. If we were to accept that capitalism is the ultimate democratic way to organize economic life, we would logically have to accept that the separation of direct producers from their means of production is natural – antecedent to and unencumbered by history – and that the separation of economics from politics, the alienation this practice engenders in society, the obscene concentration of wealth in the world and the abysmal poverty associated therewith are also inevitable. There is no empirical basis for the claim that the institutions and structures which certain groups devise and back up with state coercive power and violence, which they cover over in the tracks of the market in order to rule over society, are natural. The open-endedness of history reminds us that we make our world and have the wherewithal to change it.

Juridical equality, which is a tenet of liberal democracy, is a mask for class inequality that is rooted in private ownership of the means of production. The Barbadian labourer evolved into the proletariat on whose labour the reproduction of the capitalist class order and the entire political economy depends. The institutionalization of racialized domination based on whiteness in the Caribbean began with genocide against the native population and the enslavement of Africans, processes that engendered and normalized the segregation and regulation of social and political life. The idea that all "men" are created equal had no place in the practices of the saintly religious institution of the Anglican Church in the colonies that rationalized the oppressive, exploitative, dehumanizing system. Domination and oppression extended to all areas of social and sexual intercourse and sexual and gender relations, via forms of racially mediated force and violence in the hegemonic ordering of the economy and society. The exploitative basis of production for profit and private capital accumulation remains the bedrock of the political culture of Barbados. It would have been unusual, if not impossible, for the situation to have been much improved in the colonies, bearing in mind that the working class in Britain was forced to accommodate itself to bourgeois class power and rule and the terms and provisions of political gradualism that the Reform Acts of 1832, 1867, 1911 and 1948 helped to normalize in the name of the democratization of social and political life.

The culture of negative freedom is a defining characteristic of the bourgeois democratic revolution, of which liberal democracy is a principle that was built into the independence project in Barbados. Independence under black majority governments in Barbados has worked to normalize and regulate market-mediated economic compulsion and state-mediated political coercion to reproduce the capitalist order. This is largely how liberal democracy operates in Barbados: no amount of nationalist tweaking can abolish the alienation of power and the extremely limited social content which is a characteristic feature of liberal and social democracy. Sir Frederick Smith nonetheless views Barbados as an exemplary democratic country, even as he deeply lamented the survival of the high concentration of the wealth and economic power in the hands of a small number of whites in the country, after fifty years of independence under black majority rule. Smith understands rights in deontological (abstract) terms, which implies that he is uncomfortable with making those rights demandable by the "democratic" polity, in which popular power presumably resides. His lamentation speaks to what Ellen Meiksins Wood calls "democracy without social content": democracy that is organized on the basis of the alienation of power from popular control and determination in class society (see Wood 1995).

Substantively, those changes that were wrought under Barrow and the DLP and to which Her Majesty's Loyal Opposition contributed in substantive ways were of a social democratic reformist type; both political parties have employed state power to modify the framework without abandoning its bourgeois democratic character and content. There have never been any substantive content or provisions in the economic and political programmes of either political party in Barbados that were intended to produce any socialist transformation in Barbados, a fact that has not been seriously addressed in the available scholarly literature.

ORGANIZATION AND OVERVIEW OF THE BOOK

The following overview of the chapters offers a sense of the scope and relevance of the volume. Chapter 2 begins with the 1920s, when Dr O'Neal founded the DL and the Workingmen's Association (WA) – two organizations that were pivotal in anchoring popular struggles for economic, political and social reform then and during the 1930s, and helped to elect a number of progressive individuals to the Barbados House of Assembly. The chapter locates the personalities and social forces that helped to shape Errol Barrow's development and his political awareness and interests within the context of struggles for economic and political reform. Barrow said he stumbled into politics after he returned from the

United Kingdom in 1950, after studying economics and law in Britain. He also credits his maternal uncle Dr Charles Duncan O'Neal with exposing him to socialist ideas in his teenage years (see Sealy 1991).

The chapter also pays attention to Barrow's socioeconomic background within the propertied black middle strata on his mother's side. His mother's family formed an integral part of a small and prosperous, educated and cosmopolitan-oriented black petite bourgeoisie: the family owned a respectable amount of landed property and commercial real estate. In contrast, Barrow's paternal grandfather was a man of much lower social origins: he was a blacksmith. Overall, the O'Neal family had relatively broad West Indian representation that spanned Barbados, St Vincent, Tobago and Jamaica. Both sides of Barrow's family embraced progressive political activism that proved effective in shaping the political struggles to uplift the downtrodden rural and urban working-class population in Barbados. Barrow's father, the Reverend Reginald Barrow, was treated very shabbily and unprofessionally by the Anglican Church establishment in Barbados: he was forced to abandon his position as a tutor at Codrington College at the instigation of a white South African, A.H. Anstey. The racist Anglican establishment strongly opposed the progressive ideas the Reverend Barrow communicated through his sermons when he served as a curate at the St George and St Lucy parish churches. He was hounded out of the Anglican Church, which was a bastion of white supremacy and a staunch defender of British imperialism in the colonies. The Reverend Barrow took a job as headmaster of the Alleyne School in St Andrew; he successfully transformed the school by expanding the enrolment of black students and admitted black girls to the student body for the first time in the school's history, an accomplishment that impressed neither the Anglican Church nor the colonial education system.

The chapter ends with Barrow and the DLP coming to power in 1961 and with an overview of the period through 1976, and pays limited attention to the return of the DLP to power in 1986, the year before Barrow's untimely death. The world and Barbados had changed considerably, and Barrow's passing made it impossible to be definitive about how he might have responded to the changing situation then and later on.

Chapter 3 focuses on the two paths to self-government that unfolded in the West Indies and pays close attention to the antinomies of decolonization and sovereignty in the British Caribbean. It concentrates on developments in the West Indies roughly between 1947 and 1962, which constituted the formative period of the origin, political life and dissolution of the Federation of the West Indies, and the ensuing debate that unfolded in Barbados around the appropriate path to independence, which was achieved in 1966. Errol Barrow claimed that Barbados had an "autochthonous" political constitution, an assertion that influenced the discourse of the politics of decolonization and sovereignty and conditioned the self-image that Barbadian leaders and the population acquired and projected onto the West Indies and beyond. The notion of an "autochthonous" constitution contributed to the strongly held belief that Barbados was exceptional among British colonial possessions throughout the world, a claim that was originally made by Grantley Adams as early as 1952, when he was knighted by the Queen.

Errol Barrow was more subtle and diplomatic in making his case for Barbadian exceptionalism, which he traced to the original "independent" constitution that England granted to the early settlers in Barbados in the seventeenth century. The chapter considers the unacknowledged influence of the white supremacist ideology of "racial Anglo-Saxonism", which the English invented and invoked to place England and Great Britain above Europe and the world. I argue that this racist ideology resonates subtly in the crevices of the nationalist ideology that permeates the Barbadian political imagination. Barbadian exceptionalism was at work in Barrow's approach to federation and in the closer association efforts that were launched to create the "Little Eight" and the "Little Seven", after the dissolution of the federation in 1962.[4]

The chapter also addresses issues from Western secular modernity – for example, global white supremacy, nationhood, national identity, sovereignty and citizenship – that are imbued with prejudices that limit the possibility of achieving our universal humanity. I will explain how those themes that cradle state-centric nationalist ideology influenced the behaviour of Barbadian and other West Indian leaders as they grappled with decolonization within the spatial (geopolitical) context of the

Anglo-American Cold War project. The chapter explores how issues like territorial primacy in relation to internal self-government, which are best understood as problems within an open-ended process of world change, were treated as definitive solutions to political problems by Barbadian and other West Indian leaders.

The chapter also sets the stage for advancing a critique of the commonsense notion that Jamaica was uniquely responsible for the breakup of the Federation of the West Indies. A number of factors contributed to the demise of the federation, not necessarily in the order here presented. First, there was US opposition to any form of working-class control or determination of the priorities of internal self-government and federation, before sovereign autonomy became the alternative. Second, Britain's early decision during the debate on closer association to assign equal, if not greater, weight to internal self-government over the federation helped to tilt the scales against the formation of a federation with strong central powers. Third, Britain's failure or inability to underwrite the financial requirements of the West Indies Federation weighed heavily on the West Indian leaders, who were aware that the territories largely lacked the financial resources to make the federation viable and sustainable. Fourth, Britain's nod to Jamaica's Norman Manley that Jamaica would not suffer any penalty for withdrawing from the federation and seeking independence alone reinforced scepticism and strengthened the commitment to territorial self-government. Lastly, the ultimate decision-making power in the colonies of the Crown in the West Indies did not rest with the colonial elite, but rather with the United Kingdom (Lewis 1968). It follows therefore that Barrow's preoccupation with the romantic notion of Barbados's original constitutional autochthony remains substantively difficult to defend on juridical, empirical and intellectual grounds.

In chapter 4 I deal with the working-class political trajectory with special reference to the scope and influence of the Cold War project in the Caribbean and I examine the role the Cold War played in shaping decolonization in the West Indies, with attention to the framing of the domestic and international geopolitical environment in which Barrow developed into a political leader. The chapter seeks to answer questions about the implications of the crisis of British imperialism and the decline of the British Empire for decolonization struggles in Barbados and the West Indies. More broadly, the chapter addresses the problem of how the integration of the United Kingdom into the postwar hegemonic international order, which the United States led the way in constructing, affected the ability of the United Kingdom to manage decolonization in the West Indies.

Several important questions will be addressed in the chapter. How did the United Kingdom's acceptance of the primacy of US security interests in the Caribbean condition its approach to self-determination for its West Indian territories? What role, if any, did the Cold War project play in determining how the UN model for self-determination and independence for the colonies influenced thinking on approaches to self-government in the West Indies? Did the West Indian decolonizing elite embrace Cold War designs around the restructuring of the economic, geopolitical and labour (labour unions and working-class) arrangements for managing the international capitalist order? What role did Barbados play in aiding and abetting the trajectory of Cold War geopolitics in the British Caribbean? How did the Cold War–mediated labour politics strategy affect the political development of the working class in Barbados?

The chapter treats the state as a set of institutions rooted in power relations that form an integral part of the social relations of production. The state, sovereignty and power are not things that are technically connected or remain tethered to territory in any predetermined geographical sense, given that they exhibit certain "migratory propensities" (Agnew 2009). The state is a site of intense, contradictory struggle and contestation that the different classes and their factions seek to exploit in order to advance their antagonistic interests. It was this fact, more than any other concern, that influenced the Anglo-American strategy to prevent the working class from gaining control of state power, while asserting the liberal democratic basis of the decolonization and independence processes. Liberal democracy serves as a controlling force rather than a liberating institution on behalf of the working class in capitalist societies.

Chapter 5 focuses on the role of labour unions, political parties and the formation of political consensus for governing Barbados. A major claim the chapter will investigate is the contention that the creation of the DLP by Barrow and other dissident BLP parliamentarians in 1955 led to the fragmentation of and political divisions within the working class, and compromised and undermined its development into an independent force in the society. The chapter argues that the development of the working class involves a fraught and contradictory process, with fragmentation and division as integral parts of the economic and political conditions that help to keep it disorganized under the best of circumstances. I argue therefore that no single political party can be held responsible for the contradictions that plague the working class in its rise, development and reproduction under capitalism and liberalism in Barbados, bearing in mind that those organizations were never innocent bystanders to that process. Labour organizations and political parties do not address working-class needs and interests from a politically neutral vantage point, and the interests of the working class are never neutral in any class society.

When the DLP was created in 1955, the working class in Barbados was a predominantly rural mass that was heavily concentrated in low-wage, unskilled agricultural work, and there was a relatively small urban component of the class that was heavily concentrated in services. The productive forces in Barbados were largely pre-industrial, with traces of semi-industrial activities that were heavily concentrated around primary production. Barbados lacked a modern productive base in research and development; there was hardly any manufacturing industry that was organized around modern science and technology and research and development with the capacity to create and absorb any appreciable sup-plies of professional and technical labour that could compete on a world scale. It was not the mission of imperialism to create such conditions in the colonies.

By the time the DLP was formed in 1955, the BLP and the BWU had already gone over to the side of the Cold War project and they partic-ipated actively in the destruction of the CLC under Anglo-American direction, a development that subordinated the working classes in the West Indies to Cold War–oriented labour party and trade union politics, under the banner of representative government and formal trade union democracy (Watson 2004). The formation of the DLP therefore expanded and intensified a process that had already been set in motion, bearing in mind the trajectory from the DL to the BPL and the BLP. Cold War geopolitical priorities and intrigue contributed to the deepening of the fragmentation of the working class in Barbados and limited the options for exercising sovereignty, when it was achieved. The DLP and the BLP worked out an understanding for governing Barbados, based on their willing embrace of the "historic compromise", which means that the DLP did not become the solution to the problem it encountered when it was created. The conceptual and methodological framework provided in the preceding discussion sets the stage for the analysis that follows in chapter 2 and in subsequent chapters.

2.

FAMILY MATTERS

FROM CHARLES DUNCAN O'NEAL
TO ERROL BARROW

ROBERT BARROW, ERROL WALTON BARROW'S PATERNAL grandfather, served in the British West Indies Regiment in Jamaica during the 1870s and saw military service in the Ashanti Wars in West Africa and in the Boer War in South Africa. Robert Barrow was twice married: his first wife was a Jamaican and his second wife, Frances, was a Vincentian of Carib descent. Robert and his Jamaican wife had two children, and he and Frances had four children – Reginald, Florence, Jonathan and Bellingham.

Thomas Whitford O'Neal, Ruth Alberta O'Neal's grandfather, acquired Friendship plantation in the parish of St Lucy (Barbados) during the 1840s. Joseph O'Neal of Nesfield, St Lucy, married Catherine Sarah and they had six children – Charles Duncan, Ruth Alberta, Ebenezer Walton, Thomas Prescod, Inez Malvina, and Joseph Edwin O'Neal (Blackman 1995).

Charles Duncan O'Neal was born on 30 November 1879 and died on 20 November 1936, in his fifty-seventh year. Ruth Alberta O'Neal, daughter of Joseph J.C. O'Neal and Catherine Sarah O'Neal née Prescod, who was born in Tobago, married Reginald Barrow: they had four children – Graham, Sybil, Nita and Errol (Blackman 1995). The Barrow and O'Neal families thus included representation from four West Indian colonies – Barbados, Jamaica, St Vincent and Tobago.[1] The O'Neal family became part of a "growing black community of small, but stable, business people" (Blackman 1995, 5), beginning in the early post-emancipation period.

Errol Barrow's maternal grandfather, Joseph J.C. O'Neal, bought two small plantations – Nesfield and the Garden – in the parish of St Lucy, and became a shareholder in the Barbados Building and Loan Society, which was registered in 1889. Joseph O'Neal purchased four additional properties in Bridgetown, in addition to Mount Pleasant estate, in 1895, which consisted of "39 acres and with sugar works". By 1920, the year O'Neal sold Mount Pleasant estate for some £3,700, he had accumulated a sizeable amount of real property. He earned sufficient rental income from his Bridgetown properties to support his widow, their children and grandchildren. His family members were among the most "privileged blacks of Barbados" at the time (Blackman 1995, 6; see also Stafford 2005, 193).

CHARLES DUNCAN O'NEAL: SOCIAL DEMOCRACY AS SOCIALISM IN BARBADOS

Charles Duncan's father was a Barbadian of working-class origin – a blacksmith turned shopkeeper, who later became an owner of plantation property he acquired from his wife's inheritance. Charles Duncan began his secondary education at the Parry School in the parish of St Peter, from which he transferred to Harrison College, where he excelled in mathematics, placing second in the competition for the single Barbados Scholarship in 1899. His father sent him to Edinburgh University, Scotland, from which he graduated with a medical degree in 1904, in his twenty-fifth year; Edinburgh University appropriately recognized him for his outstanding achievement in surgery (Simpson 1973, 35, 36; Hoyos 1972, 109). He returned to Barbados in 1910, then moved to Dominica and practised medicine there for a short time before going to Trinidad, where he set up a thriving practice. There he met the trade unionist Captain Cipriani, collaborated with him in labour and political matters and became an active participant in the activities of the local branch of the International Workingmen's Association.

Duncan returned to Barbados in 1924 and became involved in political activities that benefited immensely from the invaluable experience he had acquired in Scotland and in Trinidad (Hunte 1988, 23). F.A. Hoyos describes Charles Duncan O'Neal as an individual who "from his student days . . . became a thorough-going socialist. From that time to the end of his days, he remained convinced that socialism was not just a plaything for politicians but a grand philosophy for the regeneration of the human race" (1972, 110). Theodore Sealy credits Dr O'Neal as "not only an outstanding medical practitioner but one who had great political insight . . . a forward-looking Socialist, the first person in . . . Barbados to lift the banner of Democratic Socialism. It was Dr. O'Neal who founded the old Democratic League, which was an attempt to galvanize the . . . black working people into some conception of what their life could be if society were changed in their direction." According to Sealy, "Errol Barrow inherited that same sense of mission, which was his guiding light in politics" (1991, 23).

O'Neal eschewed and repudiated racism and race-baiting; he insisted that an ethically informed, holistic view of society was necessary to give equal weight to the "interests of the field-labourer, mason, carpenter, blacksmith, and governor", a view that was consistent with his socialist sense of "mission to awaken the social conscience of the local decision-makers", and which resonated with his way of amalgamating Christian socialist and Fabian socialist beliefs and action (Hunte 1988, 28). He understood that the racialization of society and social relations by the British and their surrogate Barbadian (white) ruling class was decisive in framing the formation of class power and rule, and he organized on the basis of class interests to change the oppressive, racialized, exploitative economic and political order to transform all of society for the better.

In O'Neal's time the political economy of Barbados operated on a division of labour that was organized predominantly around primary agriculture. Sugar cane and sugar production dominated social life for the owners, the toilers and those who fell in between. The bulk of the labouring population and their offspring remained bound to the soil, forced to endure the harsh whip of a small and predominantly white capitalist class of mainly planters and merchants that owned and controlled most of the landed property, the export-import trade and other important commercial businesses. The remainder of the society consisted largely of a "small and impoverished middle class . . . and . . . a large number of manual workers". The ruling agro-commercial capitalists "monopolized the seats in the House of Assembly and provided the bulk of the Legislative Council, nominated by the governor. It also controlled the vestries, the Church, the law courts, the press and the academic institutions" (Blackman 1995, 6).

Keith Hunte argues that when O'Neal returned from Trinidad in 1924, Barbados was "securely in the economic and political grip of a planter-merchant ruling class. The commitment of that class to the preservation of the 'old representative system' of government was total and without qualification. The virtue of defending the constitution of the colony was espoused by generation after generation of local legislators" (1988, 28). Under the old representative system, the "Barbadian ruling class shared political power with the imperial government and effectively excluded from participation in the political process the vast majority of the population". Hunte notes that O'Neal and others, notably Clennell Wickham, Chrissie Brathwaite,[2] Erskine Ward, Grantley Adams and H.A. Vaughan, also believed it was possible for the system to be "made responsive to the interests of all classes in the society" (1988, 20, 21). By their convictions and political action, they and many others demonstrated that class-based racial oppression was part of the ruling-class strategy for maintaining domination and inequality in the society. Racial oppression served as part of a political strategy for separating certain groups from others and mediated the process through which a minority defined its own freedom negatively as the denial of freedom to and for others.

THE DIALECTIC OF REGINALD BARROW'S SOCIAL AND POLITICAL TRAJECTORY

Reginald Barrow[3] received his early education in St Vincent and Barbados, where he completed his secondary education at the Combermere School and studied at Codrington College, earning a licentiate in theology from Durham University (England), with which Codrington College became affiliated in 1875 (Jemmott and Carter 1994–95, 96). Reginald Barrow was forced to withdraw from the staff at Codrington College (see Pilgrim 1988a, 29) and was hired as the lay assistant to the rector at

St George Parish Church. After his ordination he was "appointed to curate in the St. Vincent diocese, which included the islands of Bequia, Union Island, Mustique, Carriacou and Canouan". After serving in St Vincent, the Reverend Barrow returned with his wife, Ruth, to Barbados in 1916 and went to live with his wife's parents. He was appointed curate of the St Lucy Parish Church at a meagre salary (Blackman 1995, 8; Pilgrim 1988b, 29), which was in marked contrast with the high-level status and significant material benefits the Anglican clergy in Barbados typically enjoyed. They routinely received good salaries, vicarages and rectories such that an "appointment to an official position in the state church in Barbados was an enviable post not only for local and West Indian Caucasians – but even for Englishmen!" The Reverend Barrow became the "second non-white clergyman in the island and the first to serve in the Parish of St. Lucy" (Pilgrim 1988a, 30).[4]

According to Francis Blackman, the

> sermons of Rev. Reginald Barrow often pointed to the inequalities of Barbadian society. Such preaching was disturbing to the privileged class and therefore the rulers of the church and of Barbados. He was an oddity at the time in that he was a black priest. Among all the British institutions, the Anglican Church had remained the most staunchly sexist, the most overtly racist and the most rigidly conservative and class-ridden institution in Barbados. On many counts its history was so tied to privilege and rank, viewing the black population as a mass of largely inferior labourers and toilers much the way the core of the racialized agro-commercial strata that dominated the political economy of the colony saw things. (Blackman 1995, 9; see Chamberlain 2010, 111)

It was made known to Barrow that "his unorthodox, if not radical (and not yet identified as socialist) views were disturbing. Consequently, when the post of headmaster of the Alleyne School, a grammar school ... situated in St. Andrew, a north-eastern parish ... became vacant, Rev. Reginald applied for the post and was appointed". The Alleyne School was established in 1785 under a financial bequeathal from Sir John Gay Alleyne (1724–1801),[5] a wealthy planter-aristocrat from St Andrew, for the "education of whites" – white boys – which means that the school "catered mainly to the plantocracy" (Pilgrim 1988b, 31). Sir John Gay Alleyne also served as speaker of the House of Assembly (Watson 1998, 21). In addition to his job as headmaster of the Alleyne School, the Reverend Barrow also "performed duties as an assistant priest in the parish of St. Andrew" (Blackman 1995, 9). He served as headmaster of the Alleyne School from 1917 to 1919 and managed to achieve highly commendable results at the institution and for its students during the two years he served as headmaster.

The Reverend Barrow described it as

> the period in the island's history when, with the progressive development of the sugar industry, small plantations and peasant holdings had been taken over and merged into large plantations. So there were few families with ownership and managerial backgrounds to make use of the Alleyne School. In fact, when I took the offer as Headmaster there were fewer than ten pupils – all boys! When I left the school in 1919, there was a roll call of some 40 boys and 20 girls.

He worked steadfastly with the head teachers of the elementary schools in his parish to identify and select children "who could pass the improvised entrance examination, to be enrolled as students of the Alleyne School. In this way the school could be said to be the first quasi-co-educational secondary school in the island" (Pilgrim 1988b, 31).

The Reverend Barrow modified the racialized class and gender composition of the student body, secured financial subsidies for the qualifying working-class pupils, and resisted attempts to close the school. His accomplishments as headmaster owed much to the unstinting support, dedication, effectiveness, commitment and contributions of his wife to his work and to the local community (Pilgrim 1988b, 31). His wife tutored black girls in their home to prepare them to take advantage of the openings they both created for them to exploit opportunities in secondary education in St Andrew. Torrey Pilgrim quotes the Reverend Barrow as saying, "In addition to participating in the conduct of church services and pastoral work, I helped in an embryonic adult education programme that had been provided for those in the community who were not in a position to obtain high school education" (1988a, 29). The actions of

Barrow and his wife "made it possible for the children of artisans, carpenters, masons, blacksmiths, shopkeepers, and store hands to obtain an academic education – which included such subjects as Latin, Greek, Spanish and math" (Pilgrim 1988b, 31).

The Reverend Barrow came under strong pressure and resistance from the influential and powerful Anglican-based planter establishment in St Andrew, and he was forced to resign from the Alleyne School in 1919. He viewed his departure as an advantageous move in his career; however, he was not aware at the time that he had been a "victim of a scheme evolved by the Bishop and his close associates". He soon thereafter took up a position in St Croix, US Virgin Islands, which formed part of the Episcopalian diocese of Puerto Rico. He said, "I had been got out of the island by being kicked upstairs." He added, "With a family of four children – Graham who was born in St. Vincent, Nita, Ena [Sybil] and Errol, who had been born in Barbados, a salary twice as much as I was getting on the island and a residence thrown in for good measure, such a post did offer prospects too inviting for me to refuse – an ideal 1919 Christmas present indeed" (quoted in Pilgrim 1988b, 31).

The material advantage the Reverend Barrow gained did not dampen his eagerness to contribute to the progressive struggle in St Croix, where he took up the cause of the black majority population and drew attention to the dehumanizing conditions under which they were forced to live. He was soon pressured to vacate his position within the Episcopalian diocese in St Croix, after which he worked with a number of local groups to organize a "local branch of the African Methodist Episcopal (AME) Church", which became an independent vehicle through which he exposed the social, economic and political contradictions that existed in the US Virgin Islands. He approached the "liberalizing" mission as an international project and took to heart the cause of the working-class population wherever assignments in the Anglican Church took him (Blackman 1995, 113–14).

In St Croix the Reverend Barrow also served as acting editor of the *Herald* newspaper, a position he used to draw attention to the incompetence of the local administration. Francis Blackman notes that the "role played by the *Herald* was immensurable" in exposing the "dehumanizing influences, inequalities and cruelties associated with the plantation system" (1995, 11). From his new base within the newly founded branch of the African Methodist Episcopal Church, Barrow "formed the St. Croix Benevolent Society" which helped to "provide benefits which were not ordinarily available" to members. He was deported from St Croix in December 1922 "on the order of the Governor Henry Hough", on the grounds that his criticism of the local administration and his support for labour union activities made him an "undesirable" (Blackman 1995, 11, 13). The Reverend Barrow moved to New York, which became his base for several decades. According to Theodore Sealy, Errol Barrow informed him that because of his father's involvement in the trade union movement with Hamilton Jackson in St Croix, he was invited "on board an American warship and taken away surreptitiously. That was the last we saw of him for years. Eventually he found his way to the United States to put his case, but he stayed on there and . . . joined the Garvey Movement and the African Methodist Episcopal Church in the United States'" (1991, 24).

The Reverend Barrow's wife and children returned to Barbados in 1926 and supplemented the family's resources with a portion of the rental income from property "inherited by Catherine from her late husband Joseph". Blackman notes that "Ruth's sense of independence and concern for her children's future eventually led her to leave the five young Barrow children with their grandmother and seek employment in the USA", where she joined her husband (1995, 15). Errol Barrow spent an important part of his early life, which lasted through his completion of high school in Barbados, under the guardianship of his mother's relatives.

ECONOMIC AND SOCIAL CONTRADICTIONS AND THE RISE OF THE DEMOCRATIC LEAGUE

It is important to focus on Charles Duncan O'Neal's contribution to the origin and development of modern party politics in Barbados, out of which evolved the institutional base and structure on which Errol Barrow would make his political debut as a social democrat, within fifteen years of the untimely death of his uncle in 1936 (Blackman 1995, 16), having spent seven of those years in military service in World War II.

According to Blackman,

> Duncan O'Neal set up practice in Newcastle, England, where he saw pov-
> erty such as he had never seen before: poverty which deprived its victims
> of all self-respect, poverty which resulted in hungry children attending
> school in the depths of winter and where prostitution was not a social
> inconvenience but a livelihood. His sensitivity and commitment to assist-
> ing the less fortunate in retaining dignity led him to become a represen-
> tative on the Sunderland County Council.[6] Duncan . . . soon heard the
> call of home where there was equally important and similar work to be
> done among his own people. He . . . returned to the Caribbean . . . finally
> settling down in Barbados in 1924. (1995, 16–17)

O'Neal spent fourteen years (1910–24) working as a doctor in Dominica and in Trinidad, where, according to Hoyos, he "distinguished
himself as a doctor, as a politician and as a lover of horse-racing"
(1972, 110).

Sir John Mordecai argues that the British Caribbean territories were
caught in the throes of a protracted economic depression that lasted from
the 1870s to the 1930s (see also Roberts 2016, 36), and stresses that the
period between the 1920s and 1934 saw a dramatic fall in the export price
of sugar. In 1923 the price was "£23 10s per ton, c.i.f. London. By 1929
it was . . . down to £11.5s per ton, c.i.f and by 1934 it stood at £5 per ton.
Wages were slashed, and unemployment mounted. By the middle of the
1930s discontent was endemic. A series of riots and disturbances swept
through the islands, starting in St. Kitts in 1935, out of which an organized
trade union movement was born" (1968, 21; see Marshall 1988, 2, 12).

The dominance of agriculture and sugar in the political economy of
Barbados and over the lives of the labouring population was part of the
much larger problem of a lack of a modern industrial manufacturing base
or other appreciable production diversification; tourism was in its infancy
and made a very marginal contribution to revenue and employment.
The imperialist division of labour militated against industrial diversification in the West Indies, as it was cheaper to produce primary export
goods like sugar with a large pool of unskilled, low-wage labour than to
invest in modern science, technology and skilled labour to stimulate the

development of manufacturing industry and the general advancement of the colony.

W. Arthur Lewis argues that imperialism retarded the economic and industrial transformation of the colonies between 1875 and 1945 (1978; Roberts 2016, 36–38). Nigel Bolland notes that the entire Caribbean region was experiencing major economic and related difficulties between the eruption of the Great Depression and the rebellions that took place in the West Indies during 1935–38 (2012). Robert Morris notes that the Great Depression unfolded "against a background of increasing structural fragilities in the economic and social life of the . . . economies of the British Caribbean and can be seen as a significant precipitant of the disturbances which erupted in the region after 1934" (1988, 39).

The largely pre-industrial character of the Barbados economy was reflected in the preponderance of employment in domestic service – mainly housemaids, gardeners, butlers, cooks, chauffeurs and nursemaids – and a heavy dependence on imported goods that added to the high cost of local production. Banking was limited in scale and scope, catering mainly to agro-commercial interests; the working class was forced to depend on friendly societies as the "financial intermediaries through which they got access to loans" (Morris 1988, 39). The colonial state depended on direct and indirect taxes for revenue to maintain government services and subsidize capitalist production, and there was little room for stimulus spending in the face of a tradition of balancing the budget.

Population growth continued apace, while the production and capital accumulation processes remained largely static, in conjunction with low productivity and weak employment and exports. A number of sugar plantations ceased production in the face of relentless international competition. The great mass of rural and urban toilers and dwellers endured extreme material deprivation, poverty and poor health, which were compounded by a high birthrate and a high level of net return migration. Estimates of the net return migration figures over emigration numbers ranged from fourteen thousand during 1925–37 to forty-three thousand for 1921–38, according to Colonial Office reports (Morris 1988).

The Great Depression had a profoundly negative impact on the volume and content of remittances. According to Morris, there was a "decrease in the number of registered articles received in Barbados from the USA, the Canal Zone and the United States Virgin Islands from 245,037 in 1930 to 14,226 in 1937" (1988, 50, 51; see Richardson 1985; Newton 1984; Senior 2014). Employers routinely took advantage of the prevailing economic depression to reduce even further the meagre wages they paid and widen the wage gap between male and female workers, at the expense of females and many households. It was also reported that the prison population was better fed than "the lowest grade of agricultural labourer" (Morris 1988, 40–46, 47).

Robert Morris draws on the 1937 study by the Dean Commission, according to which there was "no justification short of the bankruptcy of trade and industry for the maintenance of so low a standard of wages. . . . We have been impressed by the high dividends earned by many trading concerns in the island and the comfortable salaries and bonuses paid to the higher grades of employees in business and agriculture" (quoted in Morris 1988, 48). Working-class consumers were at the mercy of merchants across the island. According to evidence presented to the Olivier Commission in 1929, at least "32.7% of the population or some 50,000 persons . . . were on poor relief costing the government over $192,000.00" (Morris 1988, 52). The state was thereby subsidizing the agro-commercial capitalists to keep the mass of the labouring population in the state of destitution to which they were reduced.

The devastating impact of the Great Depression on the local population also helped to keep the number of eligible voters low: rapidly falling incomes among the better-off segment of the working class meant that certain individuals among them no longer met the minimum income qualification of $240 required for exercising the franchise. The incarcerated population increased from 831 prisoners in 1927 to 1,124 in 1935 for mainly "larceny and crimes against . . . persons, all indicators of the darkening mood within the country". The "pauperisation, immiserisation, and marginalisation of the workers . . . played a significant role in the accumulation of resentment which exploded in the disturbances of July 1937" (Morris 1988, 52, 54–55; see Belle 1988; Lewis 1938).

The foregoing overview captures important aspects of the material conditions in the social environment in which the DL emerged and developed into a political party that managed to obtain limited representation in the Barbados House of Assembly. When Dr O'Neal founded the DL in 1924, he drew on the experience he gained in Scotland from working professionally and politically among the working class through his involvement with Keir Hardie's Miners' Union and the Independent Labour Party socialist programme. He also benefited from his exposure to the ideas of the Fabian Society, which was established in London in 1884 with a vision of promoting socialist ideals based on the nationalization of landed property, government participation in industrial and commercial enterprises and the abolition of discrimination based on sex and gender. One of the planks of the platform of the Fabian Society was educational reform to achieve social change in society along gradualist lines that advocates expected to lead to socialism – an outlook and approach that resonated with the delayed subversiveness that was part of the outlook of the Second International (Pelling [1953] 1965, 76; see Drayton 2014, 120).

O'Neal was very mindful of the political significance of education, which can be harnessed to promote an awareness of the need to change prevailing power relations as part of the process of creating an informed and engaged population. Clennell Wilsden Wickham shared O'Neal's view of education, mindful that struggles for democratic change in society have historically arisen from below, among the exploited and oppressed. Wickham, who had served in World War I in the British West Indies Regiment, returned to Barbados and joined Clement Inniss at the *Weekly Herald* newspaper, which Inniss used as a vehicle to "arouse the political consciousness of the people" (Blackman 1995, 16). F.A. Hoyos acknowledges that

> without exaggeration . . . one of the most important events in Barbados after the First World War was the foundation of the *Weekly Herald* newspaper. . . . From 1919 until it was forced to close its doors in 1930, the *Herald* was engaged in a strenuous but exhilarating battle in the cause of democracy and its record entitles it to a place as the greatest radical newspaper in the Island's history since the Liberal of Samuel Jackman Prescod. (1972, 117; see also Jemmott and Carter 1994–95, 93)

The military experience that Clennell Wickham got in World War I gave him first-hand exposure to European barbarity on the battlefields of the inter-imperialist conflict. His keen sense of the economic, political and other excesses of the racialized capitalist order in Barbadian society was instrumental in framing his approach to journalism, which he correctly identified as an integral part of the prevailing social relations. Blackman says, "when necessary he would use his pen as a weapon, and with devastating effect; or he would apply it as a scalpel to the seat of incipient social gangrene" (1995, 16). Hoyos notes that Wickham "gave the *Herald* the stamp of his own individuality and established himself as the greatest interpreter of the aspirations of the common people that Barbados has ever known.... Wickham ... was that rare combination – the soldier who was not afraid to die in battle and the journalist who was not afraid to tell the truth in politics." As a "socialist of the advanced type", Wickham was also "moved to protest against the rigid lines he saw drawn everywhere in Barbados, to demolish the barriers that protected the privileges of a narrow and selfish minority" (1972, 121–22; see James 2007).

The DL benefited immensely from the work that individuals like Clennell Wickham were doing among the intelligentsia and the rank and file.[7] Wickham used the *Herald* as a vehicle to bring to the Barbadian public the message and programme of the DL, which emphasized universal adult suffrage, old age pensions, employment insurance, workmen's compensation, compulsory education, industrial modernization, cooperatives and trade unions, and other measures to improve the lot of the masses in the society (Seekings 2006). The Workingmen's Association was created in 1926 as a unit within the DL to agitate for improved working conditions. The system of public education in Barbados at the time did not produce the much-touted high literacy across the population, considering that compulsory education did not exist, elementary school attendance rates were in the range of 70–76 per cent, and there was "material deprivation within the lower class and other cultural deficiencies that constitute the social barriers to educability such as poor parental motivation, aspiration, and indifference" that conspired to keep some children out of school (Jemmott and Carter 1994–95, 94).

The WA was a precursor of sorts of the coming of the labour and trade union movement to Barbados and much more. In 1929, the WA presented the case of the workers before the Olivier Commission, which was set up to study the causes of the crisis in the West Indian sugar industry. The workers mobilized under the banner of the WA[8] and the UNIA and responded enthusiastically to Clement Payne's efforts to articulate their sentiments and highlight their frustrations and aspirations. It was out of this seemingly amorphous mass that the forces that would lead the embryonic working-class movement emerged and provided some measure of direction for the 1937 rebellion (Morris 1988, 54). Largely, the black middle-strata liberal intellectuals did not rush to populate the DL and the WA: mainly the labouring poor, tailors, shopkeepers and tradesman were regulars at the meetings and finance was a common concern and problem for the organization. The black middle strata depended for employment and livelihood on the ruling class that also dominated local politics (Hoyos 1972, 112–13; Farley 1987, 34–42).

Blackman suggests that there was some degree of influence from Marcus Garvey and the UNIA on the ideas of the DL (1995, 17; James 1998; Hoyos 1972, 108; Hunte 1988, 21–22; Morris 1988, 54; Beckles 2004b, 187–89; Stafford 2005, 188–92). When the DL was founded in 1924, the population of Barbados approximated 156,000; however, a mere 3,385 individuals, or 2.2 per cent, were registered voters, the majority of whom were concentrated in the Bridgetown and St Michael areas, where much of the assessed commercial property was concentrated (Deerr 1949; Beckles 2004b).

O'Neal was elected to the House of Assembly in 1932 and held his seat for four years, until his death in 1936 (Hunte 1988, 32). His political programme and campaign emphasized proposals to abolish child labour, reduce high unemployment, lower the franchise qualification to increase the number of eligible voters to bring the franchise to the working class, compulsory free education, workmen's compensation, higher wages and improved working conditions (Farley 1987, 44–50 passim). Certain demographic shifts in the composition of the population and residential patterns in several electoral constituencies improved the chances of DL candidates being elected, especially in parts of St Michael. Hunte notes that between 1921 and 1937, "the electorate grew out of all proportion to the overall population increase. While the total population increased by

22.15% in 1921–1937, the electorate grew by 186.52%. The phenomenal growth in the size of the electorate in all constituencies . . . was substantially a reflection of the increase in the number of property owners coincident with the spread of villages." This demographic shift, however, did not mean that the new black property owners did not continue to face "bread and butter considerations" or the fear of recrimination that imposed certain "constraints on their ability to exercise the franchise" (Hunte 1988, 25, 27).

An important factor which contributed to the increase in the number of black property owners was the return of twenty thousand or so black Barbadians from Panama around World War I: among them were people with enough money to become independent artisans, shopkeepers and small landowners. Ralph Jemmott and Dan Carter argue that the catalyst for change in Barbados during the 1930s was not education as "subversive activity" but rather the "strains of the material culture", bearing in mind that the travails of the working class were "unemployment, underemployment, low wages, political under-representation, poor health conditions, and substandard housing" (1994–95, 92). O'Neal's maiden speech to the House of Assembly was part of a reply by House members to the inauguration speech by the governor. O'Neal said,

> This House regrets the absence of any proposals in your Excellency's address for alleviating the distress among those who are suffering most severely from the effects of enforced unemployment and desires to affirm that in their opinion steps should be taken to provide a legislative grant to supplement the funds available for poor relief through the Board of Guardians of the various parishes of the island and that a committee of the House be appointed to consider and report on other phases of the employment question.[9]

O'Neal and other DL members did not leave a record of significant parliamentary achievements, which was not for a lack of effort, as the proposals they introduced faced relentless opposition either in the House or in the Legislative Council (Hunte 1988, 36). They were viewed as a radical anti-establishment minority in the House of Assembly, and they could not rely on the black middle strata for popular support on behalf of

the blue-collar working class they worked tirelessly to represent in Parliament. The black middle strata endured economic and social insecurity
and feared political reprisals and retribution, which helps to explain why
they adopted a gradualist view of social change, and why most of them
avoided any participation in political activity. By their actions they helped
to reinforce the racialized, anti-working-class order.

Nonetheless, the contributions of the DL extended far beyond O'Neal's
personal involvement in parliamentary politics and extra-parliamentary
activities. It seemed in many ways a thankless task, as the low level of
social and political awareness and consciousness and the deeply rooted
repression, material insecurity, alienation and cynicism among the masses
made many of them afraid to respond favourably to his political entreat-
ies. Their great dependence on the capitalist planters and merchants for
employment, and in many instances access to marginal tenantry land and
dilapidated chattel housing, took a severe emotional and psychological
toll on their resolve. Practically every aspect of the agricultural workers'
daily lives was subject to impositions by the agro-commercial capitalists
and the colonial state they dominated.

The DL adopted a creative approach to electoral politics via political
meetings, canvassing, campaigning, pamphleteering and other means to
reach the working class, raise their political awareness and bolster their
self-confidence. By those and other means O'Neal and the DL introduced
popular education to the political process, thereby laying the foundation
for universal adult suffrage that would be granted almost three decades
later. He argued that the predicament in which the working class found
itself was strictly the result of historical circumstances rather than natural
forces, and could therefore be transcended by direct human action. He also
contributed to the rise of trade union consciousness via the work of the
WA in a political environment in which trade unions were not yet legal.

O'Neal helped to forge a basic sense of political party identification
within the context of an embryonic form of party politics in Barbados
(Hunte 1988, 24, 29) that worked in contradictory ways – mobilizing
people to fight for their interests along populist lines, while simultaneously canalizing their interests under the rubric of political parties whose
motives and interests do not necessarily converge with the real needs of

the working class. Populists operate via political parties to gain control of the state to exercise state power; however, they opportunistically claim to unite the people, with the real beneficiaries of their strategy being the reproduction of the bourgeois democratic order, which is designed to benefit foremost the capitalists and the populist political leaders. Among the main contradictions that arise from capitalism and bourgeois party politics is the fragmentation of the working class, with political parties competing for the votes and allegiance of workers. This liberal strategy, which also reflects the fragmentation of the division of labour and everyday life within the capitalist reproduction process, is deployed to canalize the energies of the working class by tethering workers to political parties, electoral politics and trade union democracy, with contradictory consequences across the political spectrum. Populists convey the impression that their real objective is to achieve national unity and consensus rather than promote political polarization, by treating objective differences subjectively.

Alienation, which is a characteristic feature of production for private capital accumulation, feeds into the ways liberal-democratic class politics operates and influences the class struggle in ways that portray social class differences as technical problems between equal individuals in society. Fragmentation and alienation are readily exploited by the state managers, as they claim to speak for the "people", casting exploiters and exploited in the same mould as equals. Their real aim is to control the majority by enlisting it into a brand of politics that makes it easier for a minority class to control the vast majority via representative (parliamentary) government, party politics and so forth. The DL emerged at a time when the material and political advancement of the working class was hampered by the pervasive backwardness of the productive forces, limited forms of politicization and the lack of machinery for self-organizing political activities by the working class. It was extremely difficult for the largely pre-industrial working class, which was confined to village life, to process the idea of becoming a class in itself, where problems of everyday life posed seemingly insurmountable challenges and abiding hardships.

O'Neal imagined that if the programmes the DL was fighting for were implemented by the state, the benefits would have helped the entire society. On O'Neal's death in 1936, Chrissie Brathwaite said that the label of "Father of Democracy" belonged to him, and C. Mahon, a white member of the House of Assembly for St Thomas, acknowledged O'Neal's pioneering contribution to the struggle for democracy in Barbados, saying: "I do not know if the future will produce a man capable to fill the place of Dr. O'Neal and carry things further than he has done."[10]

O'Neal was committed to the idea that the struggle for democratic change consistently emerges from below. It is this undeniable fact that exposes the limits of liberalism when it comes to standing for the qualitative transformation of the conditions of the working class, bearing in mind that liberalism is a bourgeois philosophy and there has hardly been any sustainable "radical liberalism" (see Mills 2010, 247; 2016) that suffices to bring the working class to power. The class-based unequal economic, political and social institutions are promoted and defended by those who live by the right to exploit and their organic intellectuals. It is in their interest to anchor structures of oppression and the racialization of social relations to maintain durable inequality, while extolling deontological forms of equality, freedom, democracy and justice based on the primacy of the irreducible individual, all of which reflect the alienation of power.

The backwardness of the productive forces and other constraints imposed by the colonial order, and the backward capitalism it protected, limited the options that were open to the small black middle strata of educated, professional and small business people that rose through education, the professions and the vestry (local government) system. The DL helped to bring to the fore a number of the black middle-strata leaders who shared an interest in alleviating the plight of the highly marginalized and insecure mass of working-class people. Those middle-strata leaders understood that their own professional, material and political advancement could be enhanced by taking the initiative to address the needs of the working class. A number of black businessmen also participated in the struggle for political and social reform during the early 1920s, notably James A. Tudor (father of Cameron Tudor), the Reverend Reginald Barrow, "John Beresford Beckles, Nathaniel Bullen, Christopher Brathwaite, Aurelius Washington Harper, Beresford Branford and his brother William, Nathaniel Clairmonte, and . . . Thomas P. O'Neal"

(Blackman 1995, 17). Those individuals were also members of the Barbados branch of the UNIA.

O'Neal, Clennell Wickham and other DL stalwarts were mindful that a political and often professional price is always exacted for becoming involved in popular struggles to improve the lot of the working class (see James 2007). Blackman says, "Duncan O'Neal appeared to be in no doubt about the price which he would be required to pay for his involvement with the poor and depressed people of Barbados. In material terms, his private medical practice would be reduced. Socially, he would be ostracized, regarded as a virtual outcast for associating closely with the poor" (1995, 17). Dame Nita Barrow said:

> I remember one of our matriarchs who "held court" every afternoon, even after she had a stroke, saying, "He is a traitor to his class." . . . I remember him much earlier being quite affluent. He lived in a large house . . . with a beautiful rose garden which he looked after himself. He lost all that when he began to champion the poor. He came to live at "Park House" where he had his surgery. On Christmas he would cook enough to feed all who came, which to me seemed to be never less than 500. (Quoted in Blackman 1995, 18)

The Barrow family "matriarch" was appalled that Dr O'Neal unselfishly took up the cause of Barbados's oppressed, exploited and marginalized population.

F.A. Hoyos says, "O'Neal was really a phenomenon. It was the first time in the Island's history that a man of his class, with a university education and an independent profession, had identified himself so completely with the masses of the people" (1972, 114).[11] Blackman adds that O'Neal's

> anger and aggressive approach found favour neither with the white oligarchy nor with the coloured conservative professionals, including F.W. Holder, W.W. Reece, D. Lee Sargeant and E.R.L. Ward, all of whom were elected to the House of Assembly partly through the help of the DL. They, however, did not join those who attached such damning labels to Duncan as communist, Bolshevist, and activist. In spite of the difficulties that his style caused him, he would not change it in order to gain votes, and he

repeatedly failed to gain a seat in the House of Assembly until 1932. (Blackman 1995, 18; see Hoyos 1972, 114–15)

Hoyos (1972, 113) notes that O'Neal's style did not prevent C.A. Brathwaite from being elected to the House of Assembly in 1924 on the DL ticket, "to be followed by D. Lee Sargeant, Charlie Elder, Henry Wallace Reece and E.R.L. Ward".

The initiative that the Reverend Barrow and his wife took to make it possible for black girls to obtain secondary education during his tenure at the Alleyne School paid larger dividends when Nathaniel Bullen, who was elected churchwarden in the St Michael vestry in 1923, introduced a motion in the vestry for the creation of a secondary school for girls in Bridgetown. Colleagues in the vestry and supporters in the House of Assembly garnered "overwhelming support for Bullen's motion, the result of which was the creation of the St Michael's Girls' School on 7 May 1928" (Blackman 1995, 18). The quality of life improves for society at large when the educational, social and material advancement of the female population becomes a priority and a reality. Errol Barrow was conscientiously committed to the advancement of women and girls, which he pursued, albeit along patriarchal lines, always conscious of the fact that the electorate and society at large were often sceptical about taking big steps to address any problems.

ERROL BARROW'S ANTI-IMPERIALIST AND SOCIAL DEMOCRATIC PHILOSOPHY

Errol Walton Barrow was born on 21 January 1920 at Nesfield estate, his maternal family's property in St Lucy. He was born at a time when the franchise was limited to those with property with an annual value of at least £5 or who had an annual income of £50 or a university education. Certain members of the Barrow family met the qualification to exercise the franchise, at a time when the number of eligible voters "was less than 2,000 in a . . . population of more than 182,000". The 1891 census reported a population of "15,600 whites, 44,000 coloureds and 123,000 blacks in Barbados" in which most blacks lacked the property and other requirements to exercise the franchise (Blackman 1995, 6).

Errol Barrow's earliest childhood recollections were of St Croix rather than Barbados: he was merely three months old when his family migrated from Barbados to the US Virgin Islands, and he returned to Barbados for the first time in 1926, in his sixth year. He lived in Barbados until 1939–40, when he enlisted in the Royal Air Force, where he served until 1944.[12] Important social and political influences on Barrow's life, beyond his exposure to his uncle's political work, came during the time he studied at the London School of Economics under Harold Laski, who espoused a "left of centre" social democratic politics (Holder 2015, 58). When the Barrow family returned to Barbados from the US Virgin Islands, Charles Duncan O'Neal was actively building the DL and the WA. Errol attended the Wesley Hall Boys' (Primary) School, which was modelled broadly on the Tuskegee Institute in Alabama, which headmaster Rawle Parkinson had visited in 1912: the Tuskegee Institute model was based on Booker T. Washington's philosophy, which stressed the acquisition by blacks of a combination of basic, marketable, hands-on skills and pragmatic accommodation with "Southern" white supremacy (Blackman 1995, 15; Watson 2015a). Barrow told Theodore Sealy that he lived in the house with his uncle and became aware of the existence of "a Socialist organization called the Democratic League and there were only three black men in the House of Assembly out of 24". According to Sealy, Barrow said, "I was growing up in a home with my uncle completely absorbed in these matters and I went around with him to his political meetings . . . and I was very involved in his elections and that kind of thing in my early teens" (quoted in Sealy 1991, 25).

J.C. Tudor provides a plausible description of the O'Neal family:

> The whole O'Neal family were gifted. All of them without exception made a contribution to the public life of Barbados. But more than that, they were a sort of leading light in their community; in education, in the arts and matters of the mind as well as in practical affairs. His mother, Ruth, was one of the best educated women of her generation, and an outstanding musician. She . . . had a very beneficent influence on young women of the generation that came after her. And . . . all of her children . . . were brilliant. . . . I think his mother played an exceptional part in the mould-

ing of his character and in shaping the outlines of his career. . . . And, of course, his mother's mother, Kathleen O'Neal, she was a matriarch and it was largely . . . her influence along with her daughter's that shaped Errol's destiny. (Quoted in Sealy 1991, 29)

The fact that Errol's parents lived in New York during his formative years means that they were not directly involved in the development of his political consciousness. His military service in Britain, however, was significant in shaping his political awareness and his understanding of Britain and its relationship with the West Indies and with Europe and the wider world. It was in World War II that he saw firsthand the brutality that European ruling classes executed in waging warfare.

Barrow was as comfortable discussing the harsh nature of British imperialism as he was in celebrating his notion of the "cultural heritage" which, he insisted, Barbados inherited from England and Great Britain. In the following remarks, which he uttered in criticizing British imperialism, he was not intentionally anti-British:

> When you talk about political immorality, you have to understand that there is a country which has ruthlessly taken hold of the economy of other countries, people who are more benighted than ourselves and less advanced in what they choose to call a civilization; they have murdered, detribalized and suppressed their religious activities . . . forbidding them to use their own language. You cannot be surprised that the residual effects of that kind of harsh treatment must still be manifested in the behaviour of some politicians of the colonial territories today. (Quoted in Holder 2015, 59)

Errol Barrow's embrace of British "cultural heritage" with special reference to "jurisprudence and constitutional and parliamentary institutions" was captured in what he called the "autochthonous" foundation of the constitutional heritage and development of Barbados, which he traced to seventeenth-century English institutions, with hardly any attention to the institutions that developed in Barbados during the modern colonial period. He emphasized the primacy of the English cultural connections during the talks on constitutional independence for Barbados that were held at Lancaster House in 1966 (Holder 2007, 65). Barrow spoke of

Barbados's "autochthonous" constitution, silent about the fact that "laws made by these legislatures were secondary to English law" (Drayton 2016, 7; see Lewis 1968, 97).

In rejecting the "nebulous affinity" he associated with the black cultural (Africa-centred) nationalism that informed the ideological perspective of the Black Power movement in Barbados, Barrow insisted that Barbadians were "bound together by historical and physical accidents, because we looked to one metropolitan country for control and leadership and because the pattern of jurisprudence, the pattern of constitutional institutions and parliamentary institutions which we have followed all along has been the pattern which has been given to us by the government of the United Kingdom" (quoted in Holder 2015, 45). Barrow intentionally muffles the authoritarianism his government exercised in dealing with Black Power by subtly acknowledging that the British had largely succeeded in what they had set out to accomplish via colonialism and imperialism. They created non-European colonial subjects who fully internalized and embraced the core values, cultural norms and institutions of British imperialism, which made it remarkably easy to deal with them when they assumed state power in the late colonial and postcolonial moments (Kiernan 1969).

Substantively, imperialism understood as a particular moment in the historical development of capitalism, rather than an external imposition on colonies, could not therefore be negated by decolonization and independence. Realistically, imperialism was preserved as concrete cultural (economic, political and ideological) markers of British ruling class and state power in the construction of both the colonial and postcolonial order. The inheritors of the postcolonial state embraced British values and institutions with hardly any restraint, a phenomenon which the Black Power movement in Barbados attempted to expose, often incoherently (Drayton 2016).

FRAMING THE TRAJECTORY OF BARROW'S
SOCIALIST IMAGINATION

Jean Holder notes that Errol Barrow was not a doctrinaire or "extreme" socialist. Here Holder follows the well-worn ideological path of viewing socialism in the rhetorical manner in which Barbadian political leaders and their political parties and organic intellectuals described it and the public accepted at face value. Holder does not interrogate the philosophical doctrine of Fabian socialism or the limits and limitations of its social democratic principles in capitalist societies like the United Kingdom and Barbados, where the bulk of the essential means of production is owned and controlled by a few. Holder acknowledges, however, that the Fabian political tradition was essentially reformist, with leadership for the working class coming from outside to control and channel its political energies. British Fabian socialists like Sidney and Beatrice Webb and Harold Laski wrote or spoke in the name of the British working class with every liberal inclination to uplift them; however, they never imagined the possibility or appropriateness of the working class rising to a position to exercise state power under any circumstances (see Malik 1996).

Hilary Beckles demystifies the problem that Holder leaves unresolved when he says,

> Barrow was not a socialist in the Marxist use of the term; neither was he advocating the re-structuring of the Barbadian socioeconomic landscape. He was within the O'Neal tradition of Fabian socialism, that sentimental and moral expression of concern for the poor, and the belief that organized governments should place at the centre of their agendas policies directed to their material and social upliftment. Placing the reins of power directly in their hands was another issue altogether. Barrow was also in the Prescod tradition of advocating "responsible and conscientious middle-class government". (Quoted in Holder 2015, 60–61; see Beckles 1989)

J.C. Tudor waxed populist when he argued that Barrow had "a single well-oriented personality and his outlook and his ways of dealing with people are the same whether it is in connection with public life or his private life. He is forthright, straightforward, (and) intensely compassionate, though he will go to any lengths to disguise his compassion and gentleness", which, in Tudor's opinion, masked the fact that he was "more private a person than . . . a public person". Tudor suggests that it was possible to get a glimpse of the real Errol Barrow by interacting with him "away from public life". Tudor says, "What gives him the strength of purpose and character in public life is that . . . he is an intensely serious and efficient person . . . The second thing is that he has a sense of mission" that came "from the O'Neal lineage" (quoted in Sealy 1991, 28, 29).

Tudor is silent on the authoritarian tendencies that were characteristic of the entire colonial elite that led Barbados and the West Indian territories into independence. In fact, authoritarianism is a characteristic feature of political rule in societies where the means of production are organized for the ends of private capital accumulation, an arrangement that is impossible to maintain without the subordination of the majority, the subsumption of labour under capital and the use of the coercive power of the state to mediate and uphold the system. Such top-down modes of governance and regulation, which typify the postcolonial state, are part of the legacy of modernity.

Jean Holder also draws attention to the eclectic basis of the liberal-democratic tendencies in Barrow's political philosophy, when he mentions that in a speech Barrow delivered to the DLP Academy of Politics in 1980, he "identified with President Franklin D. Roosevelt, who said that the first basic [sic] that people expected of their political and economic system was 'Equality of opportunity for youth and others'". Holder mentions that Barrow also drew on Sir Arthur Lewis's observation on socialism to express his socialist perspective. According to Lewis,

> Socialism is about equality. A socialist believes that the purpose of human history is to achieve a society dominated by the concept of equality. Equality involves a society where the exploitation implicit in the class system has ceased. A society where there is . . . truly equal opportunity for all to share in a rich and varied life and to develop the many and varied solid talents of the human individual. That is development. (Quoted in Holder 2015, 61)

Lewis here does not only express the classic liberal perspective, but also a subjective notion of socialism. He did not rise above the ideology of social democracy that informed the British Fabian tradition. He also emphasized equal opportunity for unequally situated social classes (Watson 2008c). A society dominated by what Lewis called the "concept of equality" is not a society where a non-negotiable "ground of tradition" or freedom (Žižek 2012) exists as the foundation of material, economic, political and social rights. Liberal capitalist societies necessarily privilege abstract (deontological) rights over substantive (demandable) social and material rights because it is not possible to achieve substantive social equality in any society where production is for the ends of private capital accumulation, with a small group owning and controlling the means of production and thereby dictating the priorities around production, distribution and accumulation.

US president Franklin D. Roosevelt was a patrician, who never imagined a world without capitalism. Roosevelt was compelled to adopt the New Deal in the wake of the Great Depression of 1929–33 as the most realistic way to mediate capitalism's structural contradictions. His real intention was to find ways to neutralize the great labour and working-class militancy of the time. Roosevelt's notion of "Equality of Opportunity", which Barrow accepted, is part of the liberal populist tactic that emphasizes income distribution to help the working class, while leaving undisturbed private ownership of capital and the concentration of wealth in the hands of a few. The notion of equal opportunity for the owners of wealth and the dispossessed working class represents an ideological tactic that is designed to justify the subordination of the working class to the power of private capital in the state and civil society.

Richard Hofstadter argues compellingly that "the New Deal was designed for a capitalist economy that . . . Roosevelt took as much for granted as he did his family. For success in attaining his stated goals of prosperity and distributive justice he was fundamentally dependent upon restoring the health of capitalism" (1973, 455). The New Deal helped to set the conditions for workers' wages to rise in line with productivity, and "ongoing additions to government programs and aggressive black activism" contributed to making the 1930s to the 1970s a "remarkable period when Americans enjoyed the highest standard of living they had ever experienced and capital experienced its greatest defeats" (Nasser 2014, 5).

However, in the space of a decade the working class fought for and won battles at the workplace and beyond. Following the implementation of the New Deal, the American bourgeoisie launched a massive counteroffensive to roll back those gains (Finamore 2014). The anti-working-class strategy had broad congressional backing with the passage of the Taft-Hartley

Act, the Landrum-Griffin Act and the National Security Act, all between 1947 and 1959. The gains from the capitalist counteroffensive exist in the form of the adoption of anti-working-class "neoliberal policies since the early 1970s" (Watson 2015a, 391–92 passim).

The "equal opportunity" tactic appealed to social democrats like Errol Barrow and other "progressive" liberals who accepted a "mixed economy" in which capitalists own and control the bulk of the means of production and wealth, with private ownership of wealth largely undisturbed, the working class removed from any direct participation in economic decision-making and the state tinkering selectively and narrowly with income redistribution. Where capitalists own the means of production, workers are compelled to reproduce capital as the necessary precondition for reproducing themselves. Equal opportunity, which is layered onto exploitation and inequality, cannot abolish economic exploitation in class societies. Liberal capitalist democracy lacks social content, given that the concentration of wealth in a few hands goes with the alienation of power, considering that all manner of rights, freedom, justice, equality and democracy presuppose capital's right to exploit labour, a reality that is socially constructed and has no basis in natural law. When Barrow and the DLP won power, he set about to modernize the economy rather than to socialize it (see Holder 2007, 33).

THE POLITICAL ENVIRONMENT OF ERROL BARROW'S SOCIAL DEMOCRATIC POLITICAL PHILOSOPHY

Certain challenges that Dr O'Neal faced would return in altered forms and circumstances to haunt Errol Barrow. Grantley Adams (born 28 April 1898) did not join the DL and refused to support the proposals its elected leaders presented to the House of Assembly. Barrow would contend with Grantley Adams, who, for Cold War–inspired ideological and political reasons and because of his liberal inclinations, accused him and other BLP dissidents of creating a "Communist cell" in Barbados, a claim that resonated with McCarthyism in the United States (Smith and Smith 2015, 16). Barrow and other colleagues who formed the DLP also had to contend with opposition from certain black middle-strata elements which included small businesspeople, professionals, politicians and certain others.

Barrow did not believe that one's ideology should necessarily predetermine political outlook and strategy, and there is hardly any evidence that he changed his political style to win the admiration of his friends, critics or opponents. He sought to improve the lot of the working class along social democratic lines that were not necessarily at odds with ruling-class expectations: as a social democrat, Barrow did not promote or embrace a strategy for putting the working class in charge of state power. Much like his late uncle, he moved freely and comfortably among the working class; however, he never failed to remind middle-strata individuals and politicians, many of whom he viewed as shallow, insincere and reactionary, that he was born "in a plantation Great House, not a tenantry"; he also noted that he "as a schoolboy was entrusted with a rifle in the suppression of the 1937 riots and was dispatched to guard the white suburb of Worthing" (Drayton 2014, 120). One might reasonably ask what Drayton's comment that Barrow "had always been identified socially with order and respectability" (2014, 120) might reveal about the ambivalence that was demonstrated by his habit of reminding especially certain other leaders about his class pedigree. It certainly raises questions about his self-confidence in the fuller context of the oppressive, racialized social relations that anchored Barbadian society.

On the "Communist cell" to which Adams accused Barrow and other BLP "young Turks" of belonging, J.C. Tudor would subsequently accuse Adams of exhibiting authoritarian and dictatorial tendencies, given the way he treated the party dissidents during the early 1950s. Tudor said:

> I have been a member of this House since 1954, Sir Grantley Adams used to occupy the seat where I am now, and I can remember standing over where the junior member for St. Andrew is now sitting and hearing him deny our request for the use of radio time. All this the Barbados Labour Party has done. All those protagonists for freedom now have gone down in black and white on record of denying opportunities for freedom and the expression of members of the Opposition when they had the Government. This is the dictatorship now that they want to make the outside world believe is the Government of Barbados.[13]

Under the racialized class order in Barbados, the black population was largely viewed as socially inferior, regardless of the class position of some of them. Blackman attributed the racist behaviour to the white-supremacist perspective of "the white Barbadian and English staff that any black person performing a service for a wage was in effect rendering servitude, a remnant of the slave and master relationship of a period less than one hundred years past" (1995, 22). The point here is that at its core, liberalism, which is modernity's "philosophical doctrine", harbours intense antipathy toward blackness. Hilary Beckles remarked that especially after World War II, the "first generation of black women were knocking on doors of a profession reserved for white women since the slavery period. Creole white women perceived that they had the most to lose and were not willing to retreat on the issue. Trained nurses imported from England, who held positions of authority, tended to see black probationers as labourers rather than colleagues and successors" (2001, 28–29).

The racialization of social life proved instrumental in anchoring the misconception that the descendants of former enslaved Africans could be trained to labour, but not to govern or rule. The devastating impact of World War II on Britain's domestic and international position forced the British state to implement decolonization without sacrificing white supremacy and hegemony.

Barrow returned to Barbados in 1950, the year the Representation of the People Act was passed, with provisions for universal adult suffrage. Based on comments Barrow made to Theodore Sealy in a 1976 conversation, it did not appear that he intended to become involved in politics. He said,

Well, in 1950 I came back home and in 1951, largely through the persuasion of Dr. Cummings – I was reluctant, but they were short of candidates – I stood for election and won my seat. I had wanted to do research and planning instead. Cameron Tudor, who had just come down from Oxford, joined with me, and the two of us . . . wrote the 1951 *Manifesto* and a chap called "T.T" Lewis, a white Barbadian, but a very strong character and very much a Socialist, was with us. Grantley Adams assigned to us the job of writing the *Manifesto* and for the first time the Barbados Labour Party got a clear majority in the House. Before that the Barbados Labour Party had . . . 12 members but one had to be Speaker, which meant . . . they had a minority on the Floor. In this 1951 election we got 16 [*sic*] seats then. Frank Walcott was with the Labour Party, but by that time Hugh Springer had gone to the University of the West Indies since 1948 and Frank Walcott had taken over as General Secretary.[14] (Quoted in Sealy 1991, 27)

According to Sealy, Barrow informed him that while they were happy they had a majority in the House,

> it was like a colonial administration. Because on the Executive Council of the Barbados Government, the Financial Secretary was an Englishman and the Attorney General was another Englishman and four members of the House of Assembly – and that included Grantley Adams. It amounted to representative government; although we had Universal Adult Suffrage we did not have full responsibility in government. That was not a situation that we liked; so a lot of friction began to develop. In 1952 Cameron Tudor was the first person to quit; he did not win a seat in 1951 but he had run in 1953 as an independent. In 1955 we formed the Democratic Labour Party. It had its ups and downs but eventually came into office and held office for 15 years. (Quoted in Sealy 1991, 27)

Barrow appreciated that having a majority in the House in "a colonial administration" that was dominated by certain British expatriates in strategic positions on the Executive Council of the Barbados government intentionally limited the effectiveness of universal adult suffrage. He linked Grantley Adams to the state of affairs the Bushe Experiment was designed to produce. The friction that developed between Barrow and Adams had much to do with the slow pace of change the BLP was implementing via the governmental process.

The DLP defeated the BLP in the 1961 general election and retained control of the government in 1966 and 1971, the first decade of independence. It was defeated in 1976 by Tom Adams and the BLP, which held power for two consecutive terms (1976–1986). With the defeat of the DLP in mind, Sealy suggests that the more pressing issues that Barrow and the DLP faced revolved around his relationship with the religious community, bearing in mind that Barrow had taken up the question of disestablishing the Anglican Church in Barbados. Barrow had a strained relationship with the Anglican Church: he was mindful of the humiliation to which his father had been systematically subjected by the church establishment, dating back to the time when he was dismissed from his position as a tutor at Codrington College. The Reverend Barrow was also subjected to humiliating treatment at two Anglican parish churches in St George and St Lucy (Pilgrim 1988a, 1988b).

Theodore Sealy mentions that his conversation with Barrow in the summer of 1976 did not focus on any of the achievements of his governments from 1961 to 1976; rather, the issues they discussed revolved around a raging "dispute between Prime Minister Barrow and the Ministers of the Gospel" about his proposals for constitutional amendments, which the dean of the Cathedral of St Michael and All Angels intentionally politicized. Barrow found it problematic that the "Dean of the Anglican Church would have his stern reply to his proposals published in the *Barbados Advocate* before the Prime Minister even got it". Barrow found the dean's behaviour "so ill-mannered" that he refused to reply, considering also that the "churches had apparently been organized by the Opposition and by the conservative elements" (quoted in Sealy 1991, 30).

Barrow reportedly reminded Sealy that it was the norm for the governor general to appoint the chief justice on the advice of the prime minister. In the matter of the appointment of puisne judges, Barrow told Sealy that the governor general had

> made the proposal . . . that the Puisne Judges should also be appointed by the Governor General on the advice of the Prime Minister. This would mean that when a Chief Justice came to be named from among them it could not arise that they were Puisne Judges approved by the Judicial Services Committee only (independent of the Prime Minister) who might not be acceptable later on for appointment as Chief Justice. The government's proposal that the Puisne Judges, like the Chief Justice, be appointed on the advice of the Prime Minister, created hostile criticism. The critics claimed that it was a tendency to interfere with justice, beginning with dictatorship and the like. The Dean had published virulent statements like that. (Quoted in Sealy 1991, 30)

The notion of dictatorship had little to do with Barrow as an individual leader, considering that despotism and dictatorial characteristics are institutional features of all forms of organized state power. The real issue remains the embedded authoritarian tradition that was bequeathed by British imperialism via colonialism and which remains entrenched in the political culture of British Caribbean societies (Bolland 2001). Richard Drayton argues appropriately that "the parliaments of the Caribbean were always able to repeal old laws or introduce new ones, but the savings clauses wrapped an externally-imposed legal order formed by centuries of despotism and structural inequality in a knot which naturally became encrusted with political and public inertia until it became our own". Drayton argues pointedly that much like "victims of a long period of confinement, we thus carry the manners of the prison even after our liberation". He notes compellingly that the "worm in the mango of our constitution is an idea of law as domination and subordination. . . . That British constitutional tradition to which we remain a satellite has at its centre a theory of the law as a system of irresistible sovereignty, for which the rights of subjects and citizens were secondary" (2016, 16).

Barrow argued correctly that the criticisms that were directed at his proposals for revising judicial appointments were politically motivated. He was bent on implementing changes to weaken the staying power of the saving clauses on which he had compromised during the London (Lancaster House) 1966 conference on the Independence Constitution, now that his party had the necessary two-thirds majority to implement changes (quoted in Sealy 1991, 30). The official Opposition intentionally and opportunistically sided with the British government, which it knew had deliberately inserted the savings clauses in the Independence Constitution of the sovereign monarchy of Barbados. Barrow felt the time had come to remove the weight of the compromise his government had made at Lancaster House that harped back to the pernicious and injurious savings clauses.

Hoyos notes that Tom Adams accused Barrow of attacking

> the Lord Bishop of Barbados, the Rt. Rev. Drexel Gomez, Mr. Clyde Brome, the Roman Catholic Bishop of Bridgetown and Kingstown, Anthony Dixon, Dean Harold Crichlow, the Moderator of the Methodist Church, the Rev. Philip Saunders, the lawyers of Barbados . . . Mr. Justice Deighton

Ward, later to become Governor-General of Barbados, the Chief Justice, Sir William Douglas . . . the Chamber of Commerce, the Barbados Youth Council, the Anglican Young People's Association, various Barbadian manufacturing and employers' organizations and the Jaycees. (1988, 67)

The opportunist and politically motivated accusations that Tom Adams and other critics levelled against Prime Minister Barrow produced the intended effect in an election year. The assertion that Barrow and the DLP had declared war against the heart of civil society in Barbados with dictatorial intent took its toll in 1976. Barrow and the DLP were forced to wait for ten years before returning to power in the 1986 general election; however, Barrow would die in office on 1 June 1987, in his sixty-seventh year.

Drayton notes that "Barbados's 1974 constitution made no amendment to the savings and ouster clauses, but instead added to the powers of the Prime Minister, who already nominated the majority of members to the Senate, the right to nominate the judiciary" (2016, 17). More broadly, the "Order in Council, Letters Patent, Royal Instructions, laws passed in Westminster: these autocratic instruments of law were the legal foundations for colonial constitutions, and indeed for political independence". The point of Drayton's argument is that Commonwealth Caribbean leaders do not necessarily have to invent ways to be authoritarian, dictatorial or despotic, as those characteristics form a durable dimension of the constitutional core and political character of liberal "Westminster undemocracy" (2016, 9). The notion of "Westminster undemocracy" is best interpreted as democracy without social content that is founded on the double alienation of power, first in preserving authoritarian features from the colonial order in the Independence Constitution and second in the body politic. Liberal representative government is based on power as *potestas* – alienated power as domination – in contrast with disalienated, enabling popular power – *potentia* (Holloway 2002). Through a process of tactical and ideological dissembling and displacement, the UK government expressed concerns about Barrow's alleged dictatorial tendencies (Holder 2007, 58).

A close reading of Simeon McIntosh (2002) and Drayton (2016) shows that Barrow's action was in line with the power of the sovereign state of Barbados, and the notion of dictatorship and despotism should have been redirected at the colonial institutional foundation that was preserved in the postcolonial Barbadian state. The larger issue, however, was the impact of the international economic crisis of the early 1970s and the associated economic and financial insecurity and fallout that threatened to undermine the consumerist-driven fragile "middle class life style" of people who fetishized the notion of "middle class", which is a rather unstable and elusive social category under capitalism, with its built-in crisis propensities (Robinson 2004; Watson 2015a). Delisle Worrell argues that the impact of the 1973 international oil crisis, inflation and declining performance in sugar and tourism, as well as other challenges, combined in ways that marred the record of the DLP (Worrell 1994–95).

Barrow's perspective on economic and social development planning in Barbados was based on the plausible notion that state managers and their technocrats could effectively plan and manage the capitalist economy by realigning and bringing the capital-accumulation priorities of the dominant business strata under effective state regulation. He seemed therefore to believe that bringing capitalists directly into the decision-making process with membership on various statutory boards and government corporations and seating them directly at the table of political power would get them to synchronize their accumulation priorities with the state's development goals and with popular needs. The reality, however, is that where production is for private ends rather than to meet social needs, there was and is no incentive for capitalists to realign their priorities with those of the state. The postwar settlement on which decolonization and independence came to rest in Barbados was built on a strategy that subsumed black majority rule under white (capitalist) economic hegemony that was built into the "historic compromise".

After independence, Barbados joined the Commonwealth of Nations, the United Nations, multilateral institutions – the International Monetary Fund and World Bank, the General Agreement on Tariffs and Trade, the Inter-American Development Bank and the Organization of American States – forged close economic, financial and geopolitical ties with the United States, United Kingdom and Canada, and promoted regional cooperation with Commonwealth Caribbean states via the Caribbean

Free Trade Area in 1967 and CARICOM in 1973. Barrow declared at the United Nations that Barbados would avoid becoming involved in East-West geopolitical entanglements, by being pragmatic and becoming a friend of all and refusing to become a satellite of any. He argued, however, that the nature of global geopolitics and the constraints of size, limited resources and the lack of the means to exercise "effective sovereignty" in world affairs forced Barbados to embrace the West under US hegemony.

Barrow criticized the foreign-investment strategies of what he labelled "megalithic corporations" and the aid and development assistance programmes of the dominant states, on the grounds that their actions often produced negative consequences for the developing countries. He was persuaded by Jamaica, Guyana, and Trinidad and Tobago to establish diplomatic relations with Cuba, and he permitted Cuban aircraft ferrying troops and military material to the liberation forces in Southern Africa (Angola and Mozambique) to refuel at Barbados, until the United States objected. He supported attempts at the Organization of American States to restore Cuba to official membership in the inter-American system.

As leader of the Opposition in Barbados (1976–86) Barrow openly criticized the US invasion of Grenada in 1983, and did not support the decision of the BLP government to allow Barbados to be used as a staging ground for the invasion. He opposed the creation of the Barbados Defence Force and the formation of the Regional Security System, claiming that the latter would entangle Barbados in the deepening of the militarization of the Caribbean by the United States. He understood that it was not the economic development of the Caribbean that underscored US foreign policy under Ronald Reagan, but rather a Cold War project for deepening the military integration of the region into the US security strategy.

A period of "fierce social and class struggles . . . and national liberation struggles . . . 'forced' capital into a class compromise" that expressed itself variously as "redistributive capitalism" or "social democracy", otherwise called "Third World developmentalism". What was occurring in Barbados during the early 1970s was part of the broader process of the transition to neoliberal capitalist globalization that was being propelled by an emergent transnational capitalist class "and its political representatives to reconstitute its class power by breaking free of nation-state constraints on accumulation". It would take a few decades into the late twentieth century for the transnational capitalist class to "take advantage of newfound mobility and new forms of globalized spatial organization of social processes to break the power of territorially bound organized labor, to develop new capital-labor relations based on the fragmentation and flexibilization of labor and to shift the worldwide correlation of class and social forces in its favor" (Robinson 2014, 54). The contradictions of neoliberal capitalist globalization would overwhelm the DLP in the early 1990s and keep the BLP off balance until it was defeated by the DLP in 2008. The DLP would once again be forced to confront a protracted economic and financial malaise that continues to take a severe toll on blue-collar and white-collar working-class people in Barbados. At the global level, increasing numbers of highly trained and technically proficient middle-strata professional workers (such as lawyers, engineers, scientists, doctors, academics, and others) are facing unprecedented challenges in areas such as employment, income and personal and professional advancement in fields where robots and other smart tools are replacing human workers (Brynjolfsson and McAfee 2014; Edsall 2018).

CONCLUSION

Paying close attention to Errol Walton Barrow's social background offers a useful way to highlight his social origins in a petit bourgeois, property-owning family and to show that ownership of property in the means of production did not suffice to protect his uncle or father from discrimination and rejection by the dominant forces at different historical junctures. The social democratic values Errol Barrow learned from his uncle and from his academic study at the London School of Economics did not come to naught: he made a conscientious effort and succeeded, within the constraints he faced, in helping to modernize and transform the colony (Morgan 1994), with men like Wynter Crawford carrying much of the load through the commitments they made, the policy proposals they advanced and the battles they waged.

Social democracy is not a qualitative alternative to liberal capitalism. Social democracy became in Barbados the face of the bourgeois democratic revolution, indicating that the balance of social forces within the capitalist order did not favour the achievement of working-class power and hegemony in the state or society at large. Barrow built a close working relationship with key elements among the dominant capitalist strata, which used their access to the state to enhance their strategy for controlling the economic process under the late colonial and postcolonial state. Those capitalist forces became intimately involved in shaping the public policies of the DLP and BLP administrations via the business organizations through which they promoted and secured their interests, consistent with the "historic compromise" from 1946[15] that was designed to preserve capitalist hegemony into the postcolonial period.

Barrow's break with Adams and the BLP was not based on major disagreements on philosophy or economic strategy. Under capitalism, the role and impact of the electorate are secondary to the power of private capital, a fact that highlights what it means to speak of democracy as representative government without social content that ostensibly anchors the idea of government of, by and for the people. The limits and limitations of social democracy can be seen in the contradiction between formal juridical rights and substantive economic and material inequality. Barrow did not undertake initiatives that were designed to undermine the hegemony of private capital in the political economy of Barbados. Jean Holder states confidently that Barrow rejected policies that were sympathetic to the "expropriation of private property and personal liberty" (2015, 60). Liberals and social democrats routinely subsume individual or "personal liberty" under the primacy of private property in the means of production and the right to exploit,[16] which is consistent with the state's defence and protection of private property in the means of production over social (collective) rights. Tom Adams insightfully observed that people who were saddled with the burden of colonialism accept a lower standard of liberty[17] for themselves than those who have not endured the whip of colonialism and imperialism.

Barrow's public defence of the inheritance and durability of British jurisprudence and constitutional and parliamentary institutions in Barbados confirmed that certain characteristic features of the class-based order were preserved in the postwar transformation process. Drayton says,

"In Barbados . . . in strict constitutional terms political independence is premised on the Barbados Independence Act 1966 c. 37, passed by the House of Commons on 17 November, 1966, which in theory the British parliament could repeal tomorrow" (2016, 9–10).

Barrow spoke unambiguously about the importance of continuity as a defining characteristic of the postcolonial order in Barbados, when he said: "May our people draw deeply on our cultural heritage. May we use independence not as an end in itself but as a turning point in time when we discover new energies for a massive and successful assault on the problems facing a small community" (quoted in Holder 2015, 46). He pointed with considerable satisfaction to what he understood to matter most to the population, suffused with populist symbols – Barbadian nationalism as exceptionalism, a monarchical form of state sovereignty, a sovereign nation-state as the seat of formal popular democratic power and electoral and political stability – themes about which the polity was neither encouraged to think seriously nor to take the initiative to debate or contest at any time.

3.

THE SELF-GOVERNMENT
TRAJECTORY IN THE BRITISH
CARIBBEAN
THE POLITICS OF DECOLONIZATION
AND SOVEREIGNTY

THE CHAPTER FOCUSES ON POLITICAL CHANGE in Barbados and the West Indies, mainly from the 1940s to the period of the dissolution of the Federation of the West Indies in 1962, and the ensuing political debate in Barbados on the question of the appropriate path to independence. I will argue that Errol Barrow's assertions about Barbados's "autochthonous" political constitution, which he claimed made the colony exceptional among the West Indian territories, influenced the discourse of the politics of decolonization and sovereignty. Contextually, the chapter will address the subtle influence of the white-supremacist ideology of British racial Anglo-Saxonism (see Horsman 1981) that influences Barbadian nationalist consciousness.

I will also discuss the role played by Barbadian exceptionalism with reference to how the Barbadian decolonizing elite approached federation (1958–62) and the post-federation initiatives for the "Little Eight" and "Little Seven", from which sprang the Eastern Caribbean Federation after the Marlborough House Conference, which set the terms and conditions for the dissolution of the Federation of the West Indies in 1962. I will argue that largely unexplored themes from Western secular modernity,

for example, global white supremacy, nationhood, national identity, ethnic exceptionalism and sovereignty, helped to condition the behaviour
of Barbadian and other West Indian leaders as they grappled with decolonization. With the question of modernity in mind, I will argue that
self-determination and sovereignty, rather than representing definitive
outcomes and solutions to struggles waged by West Indian leaders and
their societies for freedom and political autonomy, are best understood
as particular historical problems of world order, which I understand to
be an open-ended, contradictory process. The point here is that national
sovereignty and capitalism render substantive national self-determination elusive, if not impossible, to secure and maintain as an end in
itself, considering that capital accumulation is a global process and the
main priorities of national states are customarily defined as territorially
delimited. In other words, what capitalists see as means to other ends,
nation states treat as ends in themselves.

Historically, all attempts at building self-determining societies and
sovereign states in the Caribbean have faced challenges associated with
Western secular modernity, which rests on particularistic (Eurocentric) –
exclusionary and contradictory – notions of universality (Wood 1991).
Several important historical developments come to mind: the Haitian
Revolution, the Cuban "Wars of Independence" in the nineteenth century,
the US annexation of Puerto Rico and the granting of citizenship to Puerto
Ricans under the Jones Act (1917) without the right to elect the US president, the adjustment of Puerto Rico's colonial status to commonwealth
in 1950, the deepening of the integration of the French Antilles into the
French Republic after 1848 and their transition to overseas departments
in 1946, the adoption by the Dutch of strategies to modify the political
status of their Caribbean territories in 1954, the Cuban Revolution (1959),
and the British handling of decolonization struggles in the West Indies.

The West disavowed sovereign Haiti's relationship with modernity and
Haiti was forced to indemnify the French state and French capitalists for
abolishing chattel slavery. France granted citizenship without sovereignty
to the inhabitants of its Caribbean colonies in 1848 and reclassified those
colonies as overseas departments in 1946, in a move that was designed
to limit American influence and UN control of decolonization in the

French Antilles, fully aware that the outcome of World War II would not augur well for the future of European imperialism. In the War of 1898 the United States invaded and occupied Cuba and rejected the terms and conditions for sovereign autonomy that the Cuban revolutionary forces proposed for ending Spanish colonialism. The US occupation of Cuba set the conditions under which a sovereign Cuba could expect to exercise sovereignty. Since 1959 the Republic of Cuba has been forced to endure the burden of an illegal US economic embargo and other international challenges directed from Washington that draw attention to the historically contingent nature of sovereign autonomy.

In 1953 the United States presented to the UN General Assembly the case for "associated statehood" with reference to Puerto Rico, with the intention of limiting the purview of the United Nations in the "internal affairs of the territory". The measures that were adopted by France, the United States, the Netherlands and the United Kingdom for dealing with their Caribbean possessions were part of a larger Cold War geopolitical initiative to control and shape the process leading up to self-determination and independence for colonized societies.

In 1947 the British secretary of state for the colonies, Arthur Creech Jones, convened a conference with delegates from West Indian territories at Montego Bay, Jamaica, to discuss British proposals for closer association. The United Kingdom was determined to control decolonization in the West Indies, with US security interests looming large. The West Indian delegates arrived at Montego Bay hopeful of the creation of a sovereign West Indies Federation based on dominion status within a disintegrating British Empire. Their thinking reflected a hodgepodge of anti-colonial and anti-imperialist sentiments that were not the least anti-British: as creatures of Western modernity the delegates hardly imagined any future outside a British framework. Among the West Indian delegates were pro-labour individuals who had attended the meeting of the CLC in Barbados in 1945. They were hopeful about creating a federation that could build on nominal working-class politics and labour rights; however, the framers of the Anglo-American Cold War project had other plans for the region that necessitated derailing and destroying the CLC vision expressed in 1945.

By 1953 most West Indian labour and political leaders were ready to support the Anglo-American plan to destroy the attempt by Cheddi Jagan and the PPP to build a social democratic ("socialist") state and society in British Guiana (Hart 2004; Rabe 2005; Horne 2007). Jagan insisted that his vision for a socialist British Guiana was based on concepts he adopted from the Puerto Rican model and from ideas and proposals that Henry Wallace put forth; his argument did not appeal to Washington, which intentionally lumped progressives, anti-imperialist nationalists, socialists and communists together and viewed all of them as threats to US security interests.

During the parliamentary debate on independence for Barbados, Premier Barrow strengthened the case for Barbadian exceptionalism that Grantley Adams made in 1952, when he was awarded a knighthood by Queen Elizabeth II. Barrow argued before the secretary of state for the colonies at Lancaster House in 1966 that Barbados occupied a unique position among West Indian territories because of the peculiar conditions and terms of the colonial "settlement" under which the island became an English colony in the seventeenth century. Barrow stressed that in 1651 the Lords in Council and the General Assembly of Barbados issued a unilateral declaration of independence from Oliver Cromwell's anti-royalist regime and in protest against British "Navigation Laws". Barrow noted that the Barbados House of Assembly upheld the 1651 declaration of independence, and he made the case for Barbados's eligibility for sovereign statehood by arguing that the colonization of Barbados was not based on any Order in Council. He emphasized the historical ties, political stability, parliamentary government and other values and institutions that he claimed the British bequeathed to Barbados[1] and which he insisted produced a durable form of democracy that made Barbados suitable for independence and membership in the international community of states.

THE QUESTION OF THEORY: UNIVERSAL HISTORY, SELF-DETERMINATION AND THE WEST INDIAN PROBLEMATIC

In Watson (2008a) I made a case for the appropriateness of a concept of universal history[2] for analysing issues of the racialization of culture, with reference to history, politics, ethnicity and social relations as a whole in the Caribbean. I argued that the experience with self-government as part of decolonization in the West Indies was profoundly affected by the "project of modernity's universal intent", a concept I drew from Susan Buck-Morss, who argues insightfully for "resurrecting the project of universal history from the ashes of modern metaphysics" and employs the concept of "universal history" to refer "more to method than content". Buck-Morss treats "universal history" as "an orientation, a philosophical reflection grounded in concrete material, the conceptual ordering of which sheds light on the political present". She also views "universal history" as a humanistic project that contributes to a sense of "collective, political participation" that imagines a future beyond "custom, or ethnicity, religion or race" and "chips away at the barriers to conceptual understanding and the limits of moral imagination that wall off the wide horizon of the present" (2009, ix, x). I agree with Buck-Morss's refusal to privilege or endorse any Eurocentric "European narrative's claim on universality", mindful of the need to extend the "critical exposure of the untruth of that claim" (2009, 84, note 10; see also Anievas and Nişancioğlu 2015). Buck-Morss also lays the basis for advancing a trenchant critique of all forms of nationalism that is central to my investigation.

William Robinson divides the transformation of the capitalist world economy into periods that include the current phase of capitalist globalization, paying attention to the various moments of state formation that extend to what he calls the nation-state phase of international capitalism (2004, 2014). The West Indian experience with self-determination and sovereign autonomy was characterized by tension and conflict that revealed the problematic relationship between capitalism and sovereignty that extends to the fight for substantive national self-determination, a problem that is part of the legacy of what Buck-Morss calls the project of modernity's universal intent. Jonathan Israel (2006), Jack Goody (2007) and John Agnew (2009) argue that there has not existed any singular legacy from Enlightenment modernity on which we might draw in our search for a relevant, guiding intellectual perspective (Watson 2008a).

In her discussion of the contradictory relationship between capitalism and self-determination, Buck-Morss (2009, 9) says "bourgeois society is unpatriotic, driven to push beyond national limits in trade. Commerce is borderless; its place is the sea. Strictly speaking, the economy and the nation are incompatible. . . . The economy is infinitely expansive; the nation constrains and set bounds." Karl Marx and Frederick Engels drew attention to this problem in the *Manifesto of the Communist Party* ([1848] 1972), when they asserted that the bourgeoisie created a new mode of production for reproducing itself that compelled it to roam the earth, acquiring resources and labour supplies by different means, exploiting labour and producing commodities with the aim of accumulating capital everywhere, a contradictory process that contributed to the breakdown of national one-sidedness and narrow-mindedness and opened up space to think more critically about universal humanity. The global scope of the mission of the bourgeoisie that is bound up with the accumulation of capital suggests that the constraints imposed by the nation-form on the mobility of capital are neither predetermined as geographically fixed nor territorially delimited (Watson 2008c). The point here is that states, sovereignty and power are not organic forms that are tethered to territory; rather, they are institutions which are embedded in power relations, and they exhibit certain "migratory propensities" (Agnew 2009, 48).

The idea that was floated by the West Indian decolonizing elites of a sovereign federation, which the United Kingdom proposed and promoted, based on the right of each unit territory to control the economy – that is, put the economy at the disposal of the state – brought into clear relief the tension that exists between the priorities of capital and those of the nation, as the deepening of the internationalization of capital gathered momentum (Robinson 2004). When the Colonial Office began to promote closer association among the West Indian territories via a federation, the post-1937 generation of West Indian agents of decolonization had to search for ways to deal with the Hegelian[3] "opposition between the force of society and the force of the state, which produces the Janus-faced individual as bourgeois/citoyen" (Buck-Morss 2009, 9, 103, 105–6). Two tendencies and trajectories began to emerge where the force of the state and nation tended to intersect – in this case, the route to an independent federation via regional self-government on the one hand and internal self-government for each territory on the other, leading to sovereign statehood within the British Commonwealth (Parker 2002, 321).

The regional self-government option was complicated by the intractable problem of uneven territorial economic and constitutional development, which was exacerbated by the retardation of the development of the colonies by capitalist imperialism. Lucia Pradella captures the contradiction in the following terms, arguing that together "with exploitation by the national bourgeoisie . . . the working class in less developed countries also suffers from an indirect exploitation by the bourgeoisie in more developed countries". Increases in productivity and "the corresponding decreases in relative wages . . . allow for an increase in real and nominal wages in the more developed country". Consequentially, the "bourgeoisie in the less developed countries" is compelled to forego "a portion of the surplus product" which limits its "possibilities for accumulation. The costs of this disadvantage fall on the working class since capitalists are compelled to increase the absolute surplus value extraction and to lengthen the working day" (2015, 152; see also Lewis 1978). The nature and aims of the colonial project in the West Indian territories, in conjunction with the uneven and combined development that inheres in capitalism, ruled out the development of a national bourgeoisie that could achieve competitiveness in the international economy.

At Montego Bay in 1947, the British set the stage for nurturing the insular prejudices of the territorial elites by allowing each territory to retain decision-making authority over taxation, investment and other revenue-generating activities, a tactical move that laid the basis for creating a weak central (federal) government. There was neither the economic (developed productive forces) nor the political (constitutional parity) basis to support a viable federation, regardless of the number of West Indian territories that would be involved. The territories were closely integrated into the British (imperialist) division of labour (Lewis 1949), based predominantly on monoculture production for export: there was a clear lack of any "deep inner structures" of productive capital to foment regional economic integration. The West Indian elites imagined that self-government via federation would limit the reach of the power of the Colonial Office in the internal affairs of the territories, even though the initiative for federation they embraced originated from Whitehall. More specifically, they were inattentive to the fact that the sovereign power of the imperialist state exceeded the decision-making authority of the local colonial state (Drayton 2016, 3–19 passim).

Eric Williams insisted that a strong federal government was necessary to compel the territories to follow rules that were appropriate for creating the infrastructures for a viable Federation of the West Indies. Grantley Adams complained in 1953 that the weak central governmental structure proposed under the federal constitution resembled "a glorified crown colony" (Wallace 1977, 110). Adams was being habitually inconsistent, as he was not necessarily unhappy with the ambiguity that Whitehall introduced into the closer association debate and on the two paths to self-government.

Susan Buck-Morss poses a number of relevant questions:

> Is it possible to reimagine universal history out of bounds of exclusionary conceptual frames? Can we humans, in a kind of reversal of Hegel, refuse to see ourselves as history's instrument, our particular actions meaningful only when subsumed within some overarching concept as it historically unfolds – even when that concept is human freedom? Can collective subjectivity be imagined as inclusive as humanity itself? Is there a way to universalize history today? (2009, 110–11; see Wilder 2015)

In other words, how might we try to reimagine subjectivity beyond territory bound by the racialization of ethnicity, nation, culture, politics and civilization, which offers only partial frames of our human subjectivity while presupposing the existence of organic ethnicities? Is it possible to think about universal history without thinking of ways to transcend capitalism, nationhood and the sovereign state? As products and agents of modernity, the West Indian leaders did not seem familiar with or concerned about such questions.

Buck-Morss says, "Liberation from the exclusionary loyalties of collective identities is precisely what makes progress possible in history." She has in mind an open-ended political project as part of a continuous process from which we are inclined to recoil because it beckons us to part with certain illusions that make us fearful of "falling off the cultural edge of one's world and its self-understanding" (2009, 149–50). Grantley Adams's defence of the British Empire in 1948, the embrace by West

Indian leaders of the US-led Cold War strategy, the destruction of the CLC, the crisis in British Guiana in 1953, and the decision to abandon the fight for labour rights and working-class politics as part of decolonization suggest that the West Indian leaders failed to reimagine human subjectivity beyond the territorial basis of the "spatial extent of sovereignty" (see Elden 2009). They hardly imagined a world free from strictures associated with ethnicity, nation and territorial citizenship that reflect partial frames of our human reality. The UN model of sovereignty was based on a cosmopolitan, Western notion of universality that reinforced the exclusionary loyalties to territorial identity. West Indian leaders were urged by the United Kingdom to pursue their regional identity within a territorially delimited framework that was ultimately constrained by the illusion of the personhood of the national state. Mary Chamberlain draws attention to ways West Indians grappled with this same problem in her observation that the "major push in all the West Indian-wide organizations calling for independence and federation came from the Eastern Caribbean, with the Trinidadian Charles Petioni and Barbadians such as Richard B. Moore, Leonard Lowe and Reginald Pierpoint prominent among them" (2010, 159).

The two dominant political figures in postwar Barbados – Grantley Herbert Adams and Errol Walton Barrow – confronted certain "human dilemmas" in reaching back to English and British institutions to discover the autochthonous foundations of the constitutional development of Barbados. Implicit in the "autochthonous constitution" concept was the old representative system, the underlying basis for which was the claim that certain "Englishmen had migrated across the Atlantic Ocean in the 17th century, carrying with them 'the rights of free-born Englishmen'. Consequently, the assemblies which had been established first in Virginia in 1619, then in Bermuda and thirdly in Barbados in 1639, could be viewed as part of the heritage of the English settlers in the colonies" (Phillips 1987, 71–72). Through this particular move Adams and Barrow reinforced the myth of British and European universality, which treats much of humanity as different and nominally or juridically equal, but substantively different and inferior. The point here is that Errol Barrow's vision for an independent Barbados came to rest on a notion of universality that was derived from the myth of the British Empire as epitomizing the moral idea of freedom that anchored the culture of negative freedom with which the Western idea of liberty is associated (Patterson 1991).

THE GEOPOLITICS OF SELF-GOVERNMENT IN THE BRITISH CARIBBEAN

During the latter part of the nineteenth century the discussion of federation and its antinomies began to receive considerable attention. In his description of British colonial attempts to organize a Barbados and Windward Islands Confederation in 1875, Sir Fred Phillips stresses that the "Barbadians throughout had been very proud of their constitution which has always been of the representative type and were not prepared to give up that form of government for a federal association" (1977, 8). The Barbadians in question did not include the majority of the population,[4] given the dominance of capitalist private property, property rights, the extremely narrow scope of the economics and politics of the franchise, and political participation and other expressions of power relations (see Welch 1992, 37–39).

Wealthy Barbadian planters and merchants objected to the 1875 proposal to set up a confederation on the grounds that its implementation would downgrade "their constitutional status" and "impoverish the territory since its partners would be nothing but 'poor-relations'" from neighbouring colonies. The Royal Commission dispatched in 1882 to investigate and report on the financial position of the West Indian territories concluded that Barbados had a "fundamentally different constitution and little in common with the other islands and . . . makes no secret of its dislike to be connected with them for purposes of administration" (Cmnd. 3840, 1 [1884], 39–40, quoted in Phillips 1977, 8, 9). The Barbadian planters and merchants were more closely tied to Britain than to the neighbouring colonies in terms of their general business connections, a situation that reflected the comprador practices that formed an important part of the manner in which they reproduced themselves. They were immune to any idea about how a confederal form of regional integration might be made to work to the advantage of all the territories concerned.

The Fergusson/Orr Commission of 1933, which studied the feasibility of a "union of the Windward and Leeward islands under one Governor ... came to the conclusion that each territory should be given the greatest possible measure of local autonomy". The West Indian Royal Commission (Moyne Commission) of 1938 did not support the "extreme proposals" it received "for the grant of immediate and complete self-government based on universal adult suffrage" to the West Indian territories. The Moyne Commission recommended instead that "governments should move slowly in the direction of universal adult suffrage" (WIRC 1940, 26).[5] These and other issues that go back to the 1870s are worth thinking about with reference to how the Federation of the West Indies was created and why it collapsed, with a view to reexamining the misconception that Jamaica wrecked the federation on account of insular nationalism, considering also that territorial nationalism was not unique to Jamaica among the West Indian territories.

The thinking among the West Indian leaders during the inter-war period was that, as federation would be made the prerequisite for self-government in any case, it was necessary for the "political associations of the various islands" to act in concert to make effective demands on the Colonial Office to achieve meaningful progress. The "close connection between the desire for self-government and the desire for federation was to prove a source of weakness for federation when, after the Second World War, the Colonial Office showed itself willing to grant self-government with or without federation". The wishes and aspirations of the leaders of the "political associations" that favoured territorial self-government were far stronger than the sentiment of the merchants and planters, who were cool or indifferent to federation (Mordecai 1968, 18–21 passim). The organization of colonial production and trade connected the merchants and planters of each territory more closely with Britain than with counterparts in neighbouring territories. The separation of the proponents of political federation from ownership of capital and the exercise of economic power led them to the fanciful conclusion that the state could achieve a workable federation as a political project in relative isolation from the determination of economic and capital accumulation priorities.

The Bushe Experiment (1946–48) – introduced under Governor Sir Grattan Bushe of Barbados – outlined the terms for the introduction of internal self-government in the West Indies (Cheltenham 1970; Belle 1988; Emmanuel 1988). The Bushe Experiment reflected recommendations from the report of the Moyne Commission, which did not interpret the 1935–37 upheaval as "a mere blind protest against a worsening of conditions, but as a positive demand for the creation of new conditions that will render possible a better and less restricted life. It is the coexistence of the new demand for better conditions with the unfavourable economic trend that is the crux of the West Indian problem of the present day" (WIRC 1940, 60–61).

Under the Bushe Experiment the introduction of semi-ministerial government in Barbados set the stage for changing the leadership of the House of Assembly and the composition of the Executive Committee.[6] The Hon C. Edwy Talma, an elected member of the Barbados House of Assembly, claimed it was through Grantley Adams that

> Barbados was selected . . . to a great extent and through the generally high standard of education of the average Barbadian, as the experimental ground for conducting the Bushe Experiment, because they felt that if the politicians in Barbados could . . . carry through the work and perform the services, then it was fitting to bring in full internal self-government not only for the West Indies, but for the African possessions. So, Barbados had the honour, with Sir Grantley as the Leader of the Government.[7]

Talma's observations highlighted the British colonial strategy of reinforcing the uneven spatial geography of colonial administration in the West Indies, which also strengthened the myth that Barbadians possessed an innate intellectual superiority over the inhabitants of all other British possessions. Talma seemed patently unaware that the selection of Barbados to supervise the implementation of provisions under the Bushe Experiment was based on fortuitous factors that were deemed helpful to control the pace of decolonization and thereby keep reforms within acceptable and predictable limits.

In his account of "landless emancipation" in Barbados, Sir Hilary Beckles (2004a) points out that what Barbadians lacked in access to geographical expanse after emancipation to support semi-independent propertied small farmers, they compensated for with education. Educational attainment and high comparable literacy rates among Barbadians resulted strictly from fortuitous circumstances that reflected Whitehall's strategy of rationalizing the allocation of resources in ways that favoured Barbados. In the century after emancipation, a form of rudimentary elementary education was set up in Barbados that led to levels and rates of functional literacy (James 2007) that exceeded what obtained in other West Indian territories, where there was greater access to land relative to average population density.

Sir Fred Phillips notes that internal self-government in the West Indian territories was treated as an "intermediate stage of a process leading to full independence" (1977, 84). Stanley DeSmith argues that "it does not appear in the texts of the constitutional instruments. But the explanatory notes appended to the instruments when they are published in London are less reticent and they point to the existence of gradations in the self-governing hierarchy. The constitutions of Jamaica in 1959 and Trinidad and Tobago in 1961 were said to confer 'full internal self-government'" (1964, 55–56; see Drayton 2016). The UK government promoted the idea of a unified West Indian nation as part of an attempt to convince the West Indian leaders that it was better for them to remain with the British than to embrace the Americans, when the United States was pressuring them to free their colonies.

Sir John McPherson, comptroller for development and welfare in the West Indies and co-chair of the Caribbean Commission (CC) British Section, favoured the idea of integrating the West Indian governments into the CC to avoid playing "into the hands of the Americans". McPherson argued that while he was not an apologist for "the British Colonial Empire", he was prepared to go "on the defensive when Colonialism is under discussion with Americans". He accused the Americans of lacking good manners and expressed the hope that "in time they will outgrow their violent and irrational hatred of 'Colonialism' stemming from their inhibitions about their origin as a nation and their self-centred and cock-eyed idealism".[8]

Governor Bushe of Barbados was more direct in expressing official

British concerns about American economic, commercial and geopolitical expansion in the West Indies. He asserted that American

> commercial opportunism is becoming daily more obvious. . . . There have been many illustrations, particularly during the debates on the British loan, of the American desire to acquire the British islands in the Caribbean. Beneath it all there is a growing belief that in the majority of Americans there is a strong fundamental Anglophobia, combined . . . with an inferiority complex which leads them to endeavour to run down and humiliate the British at every opportunity. This is mainly directed at so-called "British Imperialism".[9] (Parker 2002, 328; see also Louis 1977)

Governor Bushe and Sir John McPherson seemed deeply perturbed about the impact and implications of the crisis of the British Empire for the British national and international self-image. Both men expressed their frustrations over Britain's inability to stem the tide of the disintegration of the empire and the implications for the decline of the British ruling class to the status of surrogates of the Americans in the postwar international order (Conway 2015; Louis 1977).

Washington's design for a postwar hegemonic project of liberal internationalism would come to rest on the Atlantic Alliance, the Bretton Woods institutions, the expansion of American capital, Cold War anti-communism, and a closely monitored and regulated division of labour in which the United Nations would be assigned responsibility for supervising self-determination and universal human rights, and with the United States supervising the expansion of international capitalism and the requisite geopolitical and military security strategy (Smith 2003, Agnew 2009, Elden 2009, Parker 2002; Panitch and Gindin 2012; Conway 2015). The US hegemonic strategy preserved certain features of imperialism, with militarism, economic and financial leverage and violence mediating consent and coercion, that are characteristic features of hegemony (Robinson 2004; Agnew 2005).

Morley Ayearst argues that the 1941 destroyer-bases exchange between the United States and the British influenced the liberalization of British colonial policy in the Caribbean. He notes that "President F.D. Roosevelt took . . . personal interest in West Indian developments" and "discussed

Caribbean affairs, including political reforms, with both the British and American members of the Commission" (1960, 135; see Parker 2002, 323–24).[10] The United States became increasingly involved in discussions with Britain over the administration of the Caribbean region in the post-war period. In March 1942 the Anglo-American Caribbean Commission was established as part of a strategy for coordinating the management of affairs in the region (Palmer 2006, 8–9, 20–21, 43; Blanshard 1947; Poole 1951).

The Anglo-American Caribbean Commission morphed into the CC when France and the Kingdom of the Netherlands joined the organization. French delegate Claudel said to Hewitt-Myring during the CC deliberations,

> What the United States wants . . . is domination of the Caribbean. They hate us – you especially, but also the Dutch and ourselves – and they want to get rid of us. . . . And what do they do? They make no attempt to learn of anything we have done for our people. They have messed up their own race relations in a way unequalled in history, and they come and lecture us. . . . And what are they really aiming at? I suppose, a lot of Cubas and Haitis and San Domingos, with men like Trujillo, backed up by American money, and hundreds of prisoners rotting in their jails.[11]

British press officer Philip Hewitt-Myring, who attended the CC conference in St Thomas (US Virgin Islands) in 1946, reported that the "St. Thomas Conference marked a vitally important turning point, not only in the affairs of the Caribbean Commission and its subsidiary bodies but also in the general history of international relations in the Caribbean".[12] Hewitt-Myring's comment on the strategic role of the commission in the Caribbean acknowledges the decisive role the United States was already playing in integrating the Caribbean into the postwar international hegemonic order. Washington looked at inter-American relations, decolonization, freedom, human rights and the British strategy for bringing self-government to the West Indian territories through the lens of the Cold War project. Washington's geopolitical strategy was deployed to secure greater material advantages via investment opportunities, market expansion, military bases, hydrocarbons in Trinidad and Tobago, bauxite in

British Guiana, Jamaica, Haiti and the Dominican Republic, and access to cheap labour supplies and the expansion of its export market. The British imagined that they had a better chance to limit American influence and change the priorities of the CC, provided they could move the West Indies toward federation with enhanced powers of self-government and economic reform.[13]

According to Jason Parker, the

> United States . . . regarded Caribbean federation as a vehicle for decolonization, not least for other areas. From the early 1940s, Charles W. Taussig had supported federation because it extended the logic of the CC: regional co-operation could smooth imperial transition and benefit colonial peoples. Taussig, in contrast to some British counterparts, had . . . seen federation as a virtually irrevocable step towards self-government, and in this he was in agreement with West Indian nationalists, most of whom felt that federation offered at least a halfway-house to independence and economic progress. (2002, 324–25)

The vision the West Indian nationalists harboured of a voice for the working class via federation was furthest from the thinking of American and British authorities, whose positions on the matter differed by degree rather than kind. While the British saw federation as the best option to limit American penetration of the West Indies, the United States saw it as a way to weaken the role Britain would play in the affairs of the Caribbean in the postwar years. The United States was also deepening Britain's integration into the larger hegemonic project of liberal internationalism via membership in the North Atlantic Treaty Organization, the spread of American capital through the Marshall Plan and the geopolitical cover it would provide for Britain's far-flung economic and financial interests (Panitch and Gindin 2012).

West Indians were familiar with the harshness of American Jim Crow from working on US military bases and for American businesses in the Caribbean during the war years or from living in the United States. They earned better wages working for American interests, however, and the presence of American military installations in the region also meant greater employment opportunities for some than were available under the British (Parker 2002, 331–33). There was a growing sentiment in some West Indian political and labour circles that the United States seemed more responsive to the needs of the region than the British (Bolland 2001, 441–49 passim; Horne 2007).

Wynter Crawford, founder of the WINCP, expressed a somewhat similar sentiment in an interview with the governor of Massachusetts during a visit to the United States. Crawford stated that Downing Street was becoming concerned about the

> increasing influence and popularity of the United States in the British Caribbean. Britain cannot fail to be aware that the vast majority of the West Indian people would prefer to link their future destiny with that of America. As a British subject, I offer no apology in making this statement, and to those who disagree with me, I suggest that a plebiscite be taken to determine the issue. With West Indians, it is not so much a question of loyalty to Britain, as it is a question of loyalty to their own bellies.[14]

American capital was deepening its hold on the Caribbean, and US security imperatives were testing the limits of British protectionism – "exclusive preserve" – over strategic resources like oil, bauxite and other raw materials (Parker 2002, 338, 339).

The West Indian decolonizing elite imagined that a political federation that combined strong labour rights for workers with effective colonial state power over the economy offered the best chance of solving the problems then plaguing the region; however, they were divided in their opinions about the real meaning of constitutional and political obstacles to federation. Sir Fred Phillips summed up the various positions on federation expressed by the West Indian delegates assembled at Montego Bay in 1947. Some criticized the idea of throwing together in a single federation colonies that were at different stages in their constitutional development. Others argued that the precondition for any form of federation should be "immediate internal self-government for all the units and dominion status for the federation". Some were prepared to accept whatever Britain could offer, while others "were like anxious bridegrooms wishing the union to be speedily created" (Philips 1977, 21). The West Indian delegates discerned that the British government had left the door wide open for each territory to choose internal self-government with the possibility of independence (with or without federation) and they worked deliberately to keep that door open.

Nigel Bolland argues that the CLC's preoccupation with the issue of constitutional reforms in the West Indies "led the labour organization to neglect the broader development of a strong regional labour confederation and its local components" (2001, 483). The delegates focused on the political and constitutional challenges and paid much less attention to the material, scientific, techno-industrial, commercial and economic dimensions of the problem. By Phillips's account the options that were presented to the West Indian territories did not originate with the two conferences held at Montego Bay in 1947 and 1948. On the eve of the dissolution of the Federation of the West Indies in 1962, the UK government made it clear to Norman Manley that Whitehall would not object to Jamaica's seeking independence alone, a promise Jamaica found hard to ignore, affirming modernity's anti-universalist scourge.

ADAMS, BARROW AND THE POLITICS OF
SOVEREIGNTY IN BARBADOS

In the aftermath of the anti-colonial rebellion of 1935–39 in the West Indies (Bolland 2001, 212–356 passim) Whitehall took every measure to ensure that the changing relations of forces around constitutional and political reform would neither threaten nor undermine the capitalist property relations and rights that had endured since slavery. The survival of capitalist economic hegemony depended also on access to and control of labour supplies (Bolland 2001, 173–95). The BLP and DLP upheld the "historic compromise" on which the strategic dominance of the agro-commercial and mercantile interests was based: the point here is that the differences between Adams's BLP and Barrow's DLP, relative to how they dealt with the dominant forces within the Barbadian state and civil society, were far more technical than substantive.

The state sector expanded, and the state soon became the single largest employer of labour. The growth of the black middle strata would owe much to the expansion of the public bureaucracy and the social democratic approach to housing, education, land use and social welfare issues. The ranks of the black middle strata expanded with the growth and consolidation of the professions, home ownership, tertiary education and the expansion of opportunities in the middle-level managerial ranks. Social democracy was grafted onto the "historic compromise". A relatively small number of individuals from the black political elite and the professions has been integrated into the lower rungs of the capitalist strata (Smith and Smith 2015, 264), almost exclusively in the provision of services. Emigration and remittances contributed to the rising standard of living for growing numbers of the population; remittances did not only help some individuals and families to buy land and meet the franchise eligibility requirement, but also helped to change the social landscape of Barbados in fundamental ways (Chamberlain 2010; James 1998; Richardson 1985).

The BLP and DLP both laid claim to the mantle of socialism, which became largely a politically laden, ideological construct for anchoring a bipartisan political consensus for governing Barbados. The "historic compromise" has been modified over time through a process of flexible accommodation in which the dominant capitalist forces reorganized their business strategies, with the two leading political parties readily accommodating themselves to the imperatives of capitalist economic hegemony.

Grantley Adams studied at Oxford University from 1919 to 1924; he returned to Barbados in 1924 and set about to spread the ideology of Asquithian liberalism, which he embraced during his Oxford days, an ideology on which he built his "political philosophy, social programmes, and economic projects" for Barbados (Phillips 1998, 12).

Anthony De Vere Phillips argues that Adams had rejected socialism "as an ideology appropriate for the transformation of Barbados" by the time he returned to Barbados. Phillips notes that the ideology of British Fabian socialism gained traction in the West Indies partly through the influence of middle-strata individuals who studied in Britain before and after World War II. He argues that many of the "socialist movements led by middle class intellectuals were viewed with considerable suspicion by the working classes", such that "when Grantley Adams went up to Oxford University in 1919 he was not impressed by the heritage, achievements, track record, or future prospects of socialism in Britain or the British Empire" (1998, 12, 14).

Adams rejected the strategies and tactics of Charles Duncan O'Neal's DL and the Garveyite UNIA between 1924 and 1937–38 (Beckles 2004a). Theodore Sealy notes that "Adams was anti-Garvey and Barrow was pro-Garvey. . . . Grantley Adams . . . could not (even years after Garvey was dead) say anything good about that black Jamaican who spread the world philosophy of a new deal for the black man from Africa" (1991, 23–24; see Drayton 2014, 121). Africa and things African-oriented hardly generated any positive resonance with Adams. The Fabian Society promoted social democratic ideals based on highly selective state participation in the economy around particular industries like coal and steel, government participation in certain commercial enterprises, and the abolition of discrimination based on sex and gender, without necessarily getting rid of patriarchy. A plank in the Fabian Society platform was educational reform to promote social change based on delayed subversiveness that was expected to lead to socialism in the long run (Pelling [1953] 1965, 76).

The basic aim of social democracy is not the abolition of capitalism but rather to bring some of the more pronounced contradictions inherent in capitalism within manageable limits, to achieve a modicum of class peace through the role of the state, with a view to making subsuming labour under capital more tolerable. An underlying and flawed assumption of social democracy is that the state exists in an external relation to the fundamental capitalist process and is therefore uniquely positioned to intervene in the economy from outside. Lenin argued compellingly that the "implementation of these forms of state intervention is aimed at effecting economic efficiency and equity without striking at the core of the problem . . . private property and capitalist accumulation of wealth. . . . The result is . . . the maintenance of the capitalist system with the attachment of a welfare appendage" (Lenin [1917] 1972, 78).

Errol Barrow considered himself the inheritor and purveyor of the socialist values and traditions of the DL, to the point of claiming that he was born a socialist (Sealy 1991, 32), in contrast with Adams, who, according to Jean Holder, described himself as a "Right-Wing Socialist" (2015, 61). Adams settled on a career in politics and worked strategically to take over the leadership of the labour and trade union movement to bring the working class under strict control of members of the middle strata like himself and steer it away from the pursuit of any revolutionary socialist or other progressive goals. It was in the heady political circumstances of the period that Adams arrived at a sense of personal self-discovery, when he was forced to modify his Asquithian liberal ideology and tolerate a weaker version of Fabian socialism (Sealy 1991, 23), for reasons that were largely beyond his control.

In a 1968 interview with the magazine the *Bajan*, Adams said he had admired "W.E. Gladstone as the greatest of all Englishmen and was completely imbued with the principles and practices of liberalism because there was no socialism when I was a boy". Phillips says there "was a phase in Adams' political and trade union career . . . when he openly declared for a brand of socialism and the class struggle" (1998, 15; see Hoyos 1972, 96, 106–7; Hoyos 1984, 32–33). In fact, between 1924 and 1937 Adams expressed the view that socialists in Barbados were bent on destruction rather than construction (*Barbados Advocate*, 11 July 1925). Hilary Beckles argues that when Adams was elected to the House of Assembly in 1934 – when members of the DL were sitting members in the House – "his debut represented a triumph for the liberal black middle classes who were now confident that they had found a leader who could withstand the pressures of Garvey's black nationalism and O'Neal's socialism on the one hand and white racism and conservatism on the other" (2004a, 191).

Adams's differences with the capitalist forces were technical rather than substantive. In fact, he was forced by his personal preferences to reach an accommodation with the struggles of the working class and the popular social democratic movement. He continued to reassure the dominant agro-commercial ruling interests that the leaders of the BPL would "keep the workers in check and . . . tell them how stupid apart from being criminal it is to strike when negotiations are the correct way to improve conditions" (Will 1992, 10). Adams's reassurance to the capitalist interests exposed his liberal and opportunist, anti-working-class political outlook.

The anti-colonial eruptions in the British Caribbean during the 1930s directed "attention on working-class politics and stimulated working-class organization, especially into trade unions". A new set of leaders emerged, "either men of working-class origin, or men who were willing to identify themselves with working-class rather than middle-class aspirations". In the process the interests of the middle strata prevailed and subsumed the needs and interests of the working class under their mantle, and though the "full force of this change would not be felt until adult suffrage was attained . . . even in the late thirties these new articulate spokesmen could not be ignored. From then on, the flavour of West Indian politics ceased to be 'Liberal' (in the British party sense) and became labour" (Mordecai 1968, 27; see Bolland 2001, 366–68; Lewis [1939] 1977, 52; Parker 2002, 324).

The Colonial Office had declared that it was "impossible in the modern world for most of the present Colonies in the area to reach full self-government on their own, e.g. it is ludicrous to think of, say, Barbados or British Honduras, with their populations of 200,000 and 60,000 respectively, standing on their own feet in international discussions".[15] The report of the Moyne Commission summarized the aspirations of the new political leadership around the BGWILC[16] as follows:

> Although the question of closer union has remained officially in abeyance since [1933], there is evidence that a lively and growing interest has continued . . . in the many political circles in the West Indies, some of which now advocate . . . wide measures of federation to cover all the British colonies in the Caribbean area. For example, the Guianese and West Indies Labour Congress put before us definite proposals . . . to provide for a federal constitution for the British West Indies. . . . But it is evident that throughout the British West Indies contact is being maintained between those in each Colony who are most interested in securing rapid political progress; and constitutional developments, such as the widening of the franchise, in any area may be found to reinforce the strength of the movement for federation of the whole group.[17]

Progressive and revolutionary ideas, philosophy and theory are designed to raise social and political consciousness toward promoting improvement in the material conditions of the exploited and oppressed. The DL morphed into the BPL, which was formed in 1938, two years after the death of O'Neal. In 1939 the Trade Unions Act was passed in Barbados, granting legal recognition to unions, and in 1941 the BWU registered as a labour organization. In 1940 the BLP, which grew out of the BPL, contested the general election and won five of the twenty-four seats in the House of Assembly. The Conservative Electors' Association, which largely represented the dominant agro-commercial interests, was formed in 1941. In 1942 the BLP contested the election and won four seats to the Conservative Electors' Association's twenty, a clear sign of the power of private capital and the effectiveness of the restrictive property-based franchise in propping up white capitalist political hegemony. The "Old Representative System"[18] in Barbados was based largely on the ownership of private property. At least two other significant developments occurred in 1943 – the reform of the franchise, which granted the right to vote to women who satisfied the property and income criteria for eligibility (Hart 1998, 136), and the further liberalization of trade union legislation (Emmanuel 1988, 94–95).

In 1944 Wynter Crawford and certain other individuals formed the WINCP from defections from the BPL in 1941 (Hart 1998, 143). Universal adult suffrage was introduced in 1951 under the Representation of the People Act (1950). The BLP under Grantley Adams won the first general election under universal adult suffrage in 1951, capturing fifteen of the twenty-four seats in the House of Assembly. The BLP and WINCP became the political parties of "labour"; they also contributed to the fragmentation of the working class along political party lines which extended to political affiliation and ideology.[19] This argument considers the reality of contending interests at the intersection of pro-working-class and anti-working-class outlooks, considering that there was no compelling evidence that the working class was in a position to develop an independent and viable political movement of its own.

Keith Hunte (1988) argues that the DL and the BPL were best positioned to mobilize and politicize the working-class mass when they came on the scene in Barbados. In a relatively short time the working class would be captured by and subsumed under the political parties and the organized labour movement, with the BWU playing a decisive role to that end. The attempts to politicize the working class by individuals like Clennell

Wickham and Clement Payne were compromised by the colonial state and business forces with assistance from black middle-strata leaders (Will 1992; Beckles 2004b).

When the class struggle reaches the point of popular mass political mobilization, as had begun to occur in the wake of the 1935–37 anti-colonial struggles, the dominant social and political forces in West Indian societies resorted to ideological tactics and political action to prevent the working class from strengthening its position, in the guise of promoting democratic socialization and civic values among the polity. In order to protect capitalism, the contradictions between economics and politics must be managed, and a very effective method for mediating those contradictions has been to introduce juridical (deontological, that is, abstract) political equality and freedom via the state in civil society, while preserving economic dependence and material and social inequality. This tactic necessitates fragmentation, disorganization and separation – the separation of direct producers from their means of production, economics from politics, the individual from society, the state from civil society, the state from the market and the national society from international society (Wood 1995; Teschke 2003). It also necessitates the production of philosophical and theoretical ideas and knowledge and ideology that defend so-called objective, value-free knowledge that is assumed to exist independently of knowing subjects without whom such ideas could not be produced in the first place (Jahn 1998, 613–41 passim).

Patrick Emmanuel discusses the "Principal Landmarks" that helped to frame the relationship between the trade union movement and the political parties in Barbados, drawing attention to important changes that were introduced into the island's "constitutional rules", the forms and process of "political mobilization and institutional formation" that occurred in the "non-official political system", the "concrete policy issues" around the struggles between officialdom and the mass struggle and the "ideological dispositions" of the political figures. Some of the changes Emmanuel discusses were fundamental to the formation of the "historic compromise" that informed the "consensus . . . which the BLP and DLP would embrace for governing Barbados" (1988, 94, 95). The terms of the "historic compromise" were set in place in 1946, before the BLP became the majority parliamentary party, five years before universal adult suffrage was introduced, and fifteen years before the DLP won its first victory in the general election of 1961.

The "historic compromise" is best theorized within the context of the Bushe Experiment, which proved effective in mediating the contradictions between economics and politics based on the primacy and sanctity of capitalist private property around party politics, trade union democracy and political decision-making in the halls of power. There was no compelling evidence that the impact of trade union politics and political party competition contributed to the development of working-class consciousness that transcended economism and pragmatism around working conditions and wages. The BWU developed into a professional and highly bureaucratic and authoritarian labour organization that tethered the concerns of the working class to bread-and-butter matters, with hardly any attention to the development of political consciousness among the workers (Bolland 2001, 549–64). Neither Adams nor Frank Walcott showed any interest in developing the BWU into a working-class organization (Mark 1966). The BWU became and remained an agent of Cold War globalization from the late 1940s to the formal end of the Cold War (Watson 2004; Horne 2007).

Richard Cheltenham captures the basic idea of the political consensus that was forged to anchor the "historic compromise"; he argues that not only did the two dominant labour parties in Barbados commit themselves to "accommodate the mercantile/planter interest within a mixed economy", but they also encouraged the creation of "professional associations" by the agro-commercial capitalist interests when they were forced to withdraw from direct political management of the political economy. The capitalists strengthened "the Chamber of Commerce, created the Manufacturers' Association and reinvigorated the Sugar Producers Association and the Barbados Employers' Confederation. The titans of business in Barbados thereby helped to bring an era in local politics to a close, while constructing the scaffolding for a new 'political consensus'" (1970, 252, 254–55), this time under black majority rule (Smith and Smith 2015).

The white ruling strata in Barbados based their opposition to self-government and independence on the assertion that Barrow would undo the "historic compromise", given his publicly expressed socialist convictions, and they missed no opportunity to exploit Grantley Adams's Cold War red-baiting of Barrow and the DLP Opposition.[20] White supremacy as a distinct form and expression of racialized power relations had become the hegemonic ideology, doctrine and strategy for regulating the political economy of Barbados from the vantage point of the agro-commercial capitalist class. White supremacy is best understood as a ruling-class ideology that transcends whiteness as the somatic norm and extends to the norm of political order in society. Where blacks embrace the notion that whites are naturally better at managing the economy, they are not simply buying into hegemonic white supremacy, they are also discounting a long history of the consequences of the historical fact of black separation from ownership of capital in the commanding heights of business and the consequences thereof. The danger here lies in substituting myth for historical fact and accuracy, bearing in mind how myth can displace fact and become normalized at the expense of scientific knowledge. The white capitalist class forces acquired certain rights and privileges (as owners of private property) in the state and civil society that set them above the mass of the population, an absolutely fortuitous outcome.

In one of his heated exchanges with Barrow in the House of Assembly, Adams accused him of disloyalty to the government and declared that in the interest of party loyalty those members who felt they could not "agree with the Government, that they cannot even trust the Government, let them form their own party, the Government will still get on". Adams added fatefully, "If therefore members have any fear, I throw out the challenge, 'Let us have a showdown' and the earlier the better."[21] Barrow and certain other BLP dissidents took Adams at his word: they left the BLP, formed the DLP in 1955, and won state power in 1961.

In 1983, almost three decades after he broke with Adams and the BLP, Barrow provided details about conditions that existed inside the BLP when he joined the party in 1951. He said that under Adams's leadership the BLP was functioning without a systematic and structured programme and lacked any "positive platforms of its own" to inform and guide it in opposition to the ruling class, which he found "whimsical and opportunistic" and problematic for the progression of the relationship between the young people of the party and the leadership. Barrow argued that the BLP "did not take any positive steps as a political party to ameliorate [the working class] and that was one of the principal reasons for the formation of the Democratic Labour Party". He stressed that the "BLP did not address itself to the problems of economic growth and unemployment. . . . A few plasters were put over sores, but nothing was really done to develop the human resources in this country" (*Sunday Sun*, 3 March 1983). Substantively, the BLP and DLP were/are reformist, parties that differ by degree more than kind; they do not merely emphasize their "socialist" credentials, they also reached and follow an established understanding for governing Barbados.

Adams adopted the Cold War tactic of "red-baiting" by accusing Barrow and certain others of being members of a communist cell in Barbados that he claimed was sponsored by Cheddi and Janet Jagan in British Guiana (Horne 2007; Beckles 1990, 184; Drayton 2014, 122).[22] Morley Ayearst argues that the PPP victory in British Guiana "was due not to the ideology of its leaders but to the fact that these leaders were the first to combine the key appeal of the Left with a thorough party organization in the constituencies, a grass-roots campaign unmatched in the colony's history and the support of the strongest and most active labour unions" (1960, 210). Habitually the United States has not permitted facts to interfere with the pursuit of its Cold War agenda. A defining feature of anti-colonial, populist-oriented struggles in the West Indies was the ways in which race, class, nationalism and communism converged. Jason Parker says, "Race and Communism ran through West Indian political developments like nerves under the skin." (2002, 334)

In the aftermath of the 1937 working-class rebellion in Barbados, Grantley Adams, in a calculated move to capture the leadership of the progressive working-class movement in the BWU and the BLP, took to "singing . . . the Red Flag[23] and flaunting the 'hammer and sickle symbols of Bolshevism'" at political events, while eschewing working class autonomy, Marxism and Marxism-Leninism and Communism" (Phillips 1998, 15). This is not to deny that Adams and the BLP implemented reforms that brought basic benefits to the Barbadian working class. Per capita income increased between the end of World War II and the middle of the 1950s

(Worrell 1994–95; Barbados 1945). Adams's biographer F.A. Hoyos says that Adams "adopted the advanced programme recommended by the Caribbean Labour Congress and insisted that the sugar factories of the island should be nationalized, and the sugar plantations cut up and distributed among smallholders" (1972, 130–31). Adams knew that his call for deconstructing the sugar industry would be ignored by London and the plantocracy. The relentless restructuring of the international sugar industry, in the direction of the concentration and centralization of capital, and the deepening of capital-intensive production and the introduction worldwide of sugar substitutes, based on intensive technological innovation, were combining to generate disastrous consequences for Barbados's uncompetitive sugar industry, the survival of which depended on British protectionism and other forms of state subsidies.

BARROW, CONSTITUTIONAL AUTOCHTHONY, BARBADIAN EXCEPTIONALISM AND UNIVERSAL HISTORY

Errol Barrow's declaration that Barbados had to rely on a "metropolitan country for control and leadership and . . . patterns of jurisprudence . . . pattern of constitutional . . . and parliamentary institutions . . . (and) the pattern which has been given to us by the government of the United Kingdom" (Holder 2007, 25, 50) reflected his deeply held view about the factors that determined the constitutional development of Barbados (Phillips 1977, 80; Wheare 1960, 93–95). His seemingly plausible notion of constitutional autochthony betrays his selective reading of history and Barbadian social reality (Drayton 2016, 3, 7). Barrow made some of the most revealing statements about his understanding of the nature of the Barbados Constitution in the speech – "No Loitering on Colonial Premises"[24] – he delivered at the constitutional conference on independence for Barbados in July 1966 at Lancaster House. In his outline of the historical foundation of the political culture of colonial Barbados, he emphasized the "unique" status and character of Barbados as a British colony. He traced Barbados's political culture to its unique "association with the Crown of England",[25] insisting that the colony was founded by "settlement" rather than "by conquest or by purchase . . . at the time when English political institutions experienced their severest strain" (Holder 2007, 65).

The effect of Barrow's assertions was to banish the memory of pre-colonial presence and settlement that Barbados had experienced (Beckles 1990, 1–6), implying that the land was an empty place waiting to be settled by English others. He failed to acknowledge the role of force and violence in the colonial "settlement" of Barbados, eliding the part that was played by displacement, banishment or acts of genocide that characterized the European "settlement" of the Americas (see Stannard 1992). Stuart Elden quotes Pomponius's *Manual* in the *Digest of Justinian* from the period of classical antiquity as follows: "The *territorium* is the sum of the lands within the boundaries of a community [*civitatis*]; which some say is so named because the magistrate of a place has the right of terrifying [*terrendi*], that is, exercising jurisdiction, within its boundaries" (quoted in Elden 2009, v). Edward Said says, "In the history of colonial invasion, maps are always first drawn by the victors, since maps are instruments of conquest, once projected they are implemented. Geography is therefore the art of war" in the absence of "resistance if there is a counter-map and a counter-strategy" (quoted in Elden 2009, v; see Tilly 1985). Barrow is silent about the fact that the development of Barbados as an English colony was based on the labour of enslaved Africans.

Barrow reminded the secretary of state for the colonies that "the English inhabitants of Barbados settled a Parliament for themselves and ... created the Legislative institutions which we have since, without any disturbance, enjoyed" and that anchored "the solid comforts of representative government" that Barbados had experienced during an unbroken period of 327 years from 1639 to 1966 (Holder 2007, 58). He gave the impression that the seventeenth-century English settlers bequeathed to Barbados the preconditions for stability and continuity that would guide the territory into independence.

The question remained of who qualified for and enjoyed the "solid comforts" to which Barrow referred. He did not mention the enslaved Africans and the forms of resistance they waged against the racialized class exploitation, oppression and dehumanization that were employed to enrich the English state and English commercial capitalists. Mary

Chamberlain reminds us that "Barbados had had three major insurgencies – 1816, 1876, 1937 – which were sufficient to give revolutionary teeth to every other generation. But overall, the high levels of population, the lack of land and the totalitarian nature of white dominance had resulted in a nation riddled with hostility but fully versed in reality" (2010, 191).

Barrow's contrivance that the legislative institutions developed "without any disturbance" stretches the imagination, considering that colonial law of property justified the use of coercion, violence and terror to maintain chattel slavery in the service of capitalist expansion. His notion of the colonial founding of Barbados by settlement erroneously equated Barbados with a virginal territory in which the settlers created an original, free society. In fact, the same territory bore the imprint of the sovereign power and terror of the English Crown (Drayton 2016, 7). Barrow's assertions resonate with the self-image of the English, who invented their own origins as a people who sprang from originally free, independent and self-sufficient yeomen who survived miraculously and unsullied by any form of domination before the Norman Conquest, having claimed that they knew only liberty from the outset (Horsman 1981).

Barrow juxtaposed the peculiar form of parliamentary stability in Barbados beginning in 1639 against parliamentary and social and political instability and chaos in England under Oliver Cromwell. He said,

> In 1651, when Englishmen were cowering in their homes under the whip of Cromwell's major-generals, and when they who had lopped off the head of a king sought to enmesh the people of Barbados in their "saintly" tyranny, Barbadians stubbornly defended their respective institutions from Cromwell and in the famous Charter of Barbados which they signed, they ... managed to preserve for three centuries the supremacy of parliaments and the liberty of the subject. (Quoted in Holder 2007, 58)

Barrow identified 1688 as the year when "the parliament of Barbados celebrated its golden jubilee and judges administered the same common and statute law which was under a temporary cloud in England". He continued, "In our country, as in England, the supremacy of Parliament is zealously upheld and a Government of Barbados, like its counterpart in Britain, would never resort to any subterfuge designed to frustrate the clearly expressed desires of a duly elected Parliament" (in Holder 2007, 58). The elected parliament in seventeenth-century England was not based on popular power or representative government, considering that the construction of the body politic rested on the primacy of the ownership of private property. Barrow's real aim was to try to allay the real concerns the United Kingdom (and the United States) had about the likelihood of an independent Barbados led by him and the DLP becoming a socialist "dictatorship" and creating what they imagined to be a security crisis in the Eastern Caribbean (Holder 2007, 58; Sealy 1991, 32; Dear 1992).

Barrow stressed that the people of Barbados under "majority black governments had adopted non-recriminatory and democratic means to break the political power of the local oligarchy" and had achieved "full internal self-government, based on adult suffrage . . . a cabinet system, an independent judiciary, a competent public service, a population which is 98 percent literate – most significant of all, a Treasury which has never needed a grant in aid of administration" (Phillips 1977, 80), in contrast with certain other British colonies. He conveniently invented a narrative of a non-contradictory constitutional and political tradition for Barbados, an ideological assertion that would become part of a template for a deep-seated ethnocentric nationalism he helped to popularize. The point here is that the struggle for any form of democracy is by its nature contradictory, as there are contending interests at stake, and any gains made by the working class are always subject to renegotiation, given that crisis and instability inhere in the capital–wage labour relation.

Sir Fred Phillips shares Barrow's account of Barbados's autochthonous constitution model, arguing that West Indian independence constitutions may not be autochthonous in the formal sense of the term; however, they "can safely be regarded as autochthonous in substance" (1977, 80n9). Phillips reiterated the theme of the "constitutional position of Barbados as a settled colony . . . from the conquered or ceded territories like Trinidad, Grenada or St. Lucia which were subject to the legislative authority of the Queen in Council by virtue of her prerogative powers". Phillips added that from "the inception of its settlement, the sum total of the constitutional status of . . . Barbados was the instruction from the Crown to the settlers by which the summoning of the representative assembly was first authorized as well as the appointment of the Governors by Commission under the Great Seal". In contrast with the

> conquered territories or those which surrendered their legislative competence, the Legislature of Barbados never delegated its powers or took second place to the crown's general prerogative powers in respect of the enactment of legislation affecting the Constitution. This position was to be unilaterally altered by the United Kingdom Government in 1962 by the Imperial Act, the main purpose of which was the dissolution of The West Indies Federation. (1977, 16, 17)

Phillips here discounts the fact that the sovereign power of the British state superseded that of any colonial possession (Lewis 1968, 97; Drayton 2016).

Barrow was deeply concerned by the UK government's enactment of the West Indies Federation Dissolution Act of 1962, which provided "for constitutional changes and any kind of association between one territory and another by Order in Council". He said emphatically, "I reminded the Secretary of State that this might be alright for Jamaica and Trinidad and the Lesser Antilles, but . . . I hoped that the provisions of this West Indies Federation Dissolution Act . . . were not intended to be extended to the territory of Barbados, because we had never been governed by Order-in-Council." He continued, "On the floor of this House I read out on more than one occasion the Secretary of State's reply. . . . Mr. Maudling said on the floor of the House of Commons that the West Indies Dissolution Act was not intended to be used to make constitutional changes in Barbados."[26] Barrow was reawakening the sentiments that were expressed by Barbadian business interests during the 1870s–1880s, in opposition to entangling Barbados in a federation with the constitutionally less developed Windward and Leeward Islands. Neither the comprador capitalists from nineteenth-century Barbados nor Barrow in 1966 devoted necessary time to ponder how the more advanced "representative system" of Barbados might have helped to set the context for the constitutional upgrading of the neighbouring colonies. The record shows that the arc of history tends to bend in the direction of more advanced forces setting the trajectory for upgrading the entire process, a motion that opens space for thinking more seriously about the universality that Susan Buck-Morss (2009) discusses.

Phillips says when the Barbados "Independence Conference convened in London in July 1966, the Conference had before it a draft constitution which had been prepared entirely by the Barbados Government headed by . . . Barrow – a most competent politician. The document had been published in Barbados and accepted by both houses of the Legislature before it was taken to London for approval" (1977, 80).[27] Barrow reminded the secretary of state that

> the Government of Barbados does not accept that any draughtsman or member of a political party in the U.K., no matter how exalted his position may be – he may be the Prime Minister Mr. Harold Wilson himself; it is neither his job nor his duty nor his business to prepare a Constitution for Barbados. The Constitution of Barbados has not only got to be an autonomous constitution, but . . . it has . . . to be an autochthonous constitution – that is, one that has sprung from the land itself.

He chastised the "Neo-colonialists, these long-jacket Uncle Toms . . . in the Opposition Parties" in Barbados for wanting to preserve the misconception that the "people of Barbados are incapable of making decisions for themselves, and that they have to depend on some person of a different complexion to tell them what is good for them".[28]

In a conversation with Theodore Sealy in 1976, Barrow insisted that Grantley Adams was "mixed up" in attempts to discredit his government in 1965 with accusations that he would pursue independence for Barbados alone to create a republic, set up a one-party state and abolish elections, following the publication of a White Paper on Barbados and its place in a federal structure. According to Sealy, Barrow told him that Adams and the conservatives who made up the BLP delegation to the Barbados independence talks in London "opposed everything in the Independence Constitution", and there were things

> which we compromised on which we knew were not consistent with more advanced Constitutions given to countries recently becoming independent. But we wanted to get the thing out, we said we could argue about that point

later. It appears that the Secretary of State, on the advice of the Governor of Barbados, was looking for an excuse to say we could not reach an agreement on Independence and thus to postpone it. (Quoted in Sealy 1991, 32)

The point he is making here has to do with the savings clauses that Drayton discusses.

Barrow expressed his frustration in assertions he made that if the United Kingdom did not grant independence he could invoke the "autochthonous constitution of Barbados" principle to declare independence unilaterally. Douglas Williams (Colonial Office) reminded him that the power and authority of the Crown superseded whatever rights were conveyed in the autochthonous-constitution principle, in a note he penned to a colleague, in which he mentioned that Barrow had made public announcements that he wanted independence for Barbados by September 1966. Williams said, "As far as our lawyers can discover, there is no provision in the Letters Patent or in local legislation for any elections to be held within a specified time after the House is dissolved. Theoretically, therefore, the statutory period could come to an end, the House could dissolve, and Mr. Barrow could remain the Premier of Barbados for life." Williams continued, "I have just been talking to my namesake, who . . . had a long interview with Mr. Cameron Tudor. He tells me Mr. Tudor, speaking on behalf of his master, was adamant that Mr. Barrow would under no circumstances have elections before going to independence, and . . . if the British Government tried to insist on elections he would declare independence – and his membership of the Commonwealth – unilaterally. This is an event which, if it ever happens, I shall look forward to with relish."[29]

Gordon K. Lewis identified part of the dilemma that the operation of imperial power in the colonies presented to colonial governments when he said, "From the mid-Victorian period on up until recently, West Indian government was crown colony government. The constituent parts differed in different colonies, but they all had one feature in common, the common denominator as it were of the system: that the power of the crown in the local legislature, if pressed to its extreme limit, could avail to overcome every resistance that could be made to it" (Lewis 1968, 97; see Drayton 2016, 7; Chamberlain 2010, 157). In fact, there was nothing about Barrow's claim of constitutional autochthony that prevailed over the power of the British Crown in settling matters of the colonial status of territories like Barbados.

Barrow nonetheless asserted: "Any rules which we practise and observe in this country are rules which we have imposed on ourselves by our own free institutions and Acts of this Parliament and by the dint of the settlers in 1627."[30] The alienation of the state from society begins with the invention and superimposition of the state as an alien power of domination on society (Gullí 2010). The state originated therefore as an alien, dictatorial power. The dictatorial and authoritarian character of the state is misconstrued as non-existent in what passes for the democratic body of both the state and the body politic (Watson 2015b). This domination is preserved in liberal democracy, a fact that does not surface in Barrow's conception of colonial law, policy and practice. The transition from colony to sovereignty does not and cannot abolish the nature of the state.

During the Barbados House of Assembly debates on the Public Order Bill 1970, the leader of the Opposition, Tom Adams, drew an important contrast with Barrow's assertion: he said, "Barbadians suffer from having been raised in a Colonial regime; we accept a lower standard of liberty for ourselves than we would if we had been born in England or the United States of America. That is one of the great disadvantages of being a Colonial; you get habits of authoritarianism drilled into you from childhood."[31] Adams is accurate about the authoritarian nature of the colonial state; however, he left unresolved the problem of the dictatorial nature of the state in all class societies.

Gordon Lewis identified the enduring cultural problem that Barrow and Adams ignore when he said, "Nothing could have better illuminated the dangers secreted in the West Indian tendency to embrace uncritically British constitutional conventions, as if a colonial Governor, however liberal, could be reduced to the ornamental status of a constitutional monarch." Lewis added insightfully that "the Barbadian political leadership had allowed its Anglophilism to get the better of its sense of colonial realities" (1968, 239). Like Barrow, Adams also failed to understand that authoritarianism is a built-in feature of all forms of state power.

Liberal notions permeate Barrow's "No Loitering on Colonial Premises" speech delivered at Lancaster House. Stefano Azzarà (2007) notes that Domenico Losurdo argues compellingly that "it was not liberalism that imposed the requirement of universal suffrage in Europe, but rather Jacobinism – the radical tide of the French Revolution". It was in the setting of the French Revolution "that there arose for the first time – with Robespierre and Saint Just – the demand not only for political equality, but also for 'material rights', such as 'the right to life' and 'the right to work'". The seminal point about the right to work has to do with for whom and for what ends one has to work: work does not necessarily have to entail being compelled to sell labour power to reproduce one's existence (Gullí 2010). Azzarà (2007) quotes Losurdo as saying, "Liberalism . . . was distinguished in the revolutionary period by a violent anti-revolutionary argument in support of the Ancien Régime, on the side of the aristocratic classes, and against the principle of 'sovereignty of the people'." Barrow did not discern any contradictory resonances in the classical liberal traditions and institutions that semi-feudal, monarchical England miraculously bequeathed to Barbados during the seventeenth century and continuing into the twentieth century.

Losurdo emphasizes that the "diffusion of liberalism" in conjunction with its specialized "political regime . . . presented itself . . . as a sort of 'Herrenvolk democracy'" and it was hardly "the principle of individual liberty, but, rather, a dialectical mechanism of 'emancipation' and 'de-emancipation' that characterized liberalism" (Azzarà 2007). Losurdo contends that while liberals broadly emphasize individual liberty, they fundamentally lacked "entirely the universal concept of man – the idea of equality – which was to find expression with the French Revolution". The liberal concept of individual liberty characteristically had mainly formal application to the "subordinated classes, whose condition was one of servitude, and who were therefore denied political and civilian rights" (Azzarà 2007).

Sheldon Wolin insists that none of the modern British liberals were egalitarian (2008, 219). He notes that liberal ideology "came to represent an uneasy combination of elements: elected representative government, limited government, equal rights, property rights, and an economy that, when freed from governmental interference and rid of privilege, nevertheless produced inequalities as striking as any in the traditional regimes" (2008, 218; see Wood 1995). Wolin here addresses aspects of the bourgeois democratic revolution when he argues that "there is no political affinity, only a disjunction between democracy and a system that assumes inequality among investors and reproduces inequality as a matter of course, depends on individual self-interest as an incentive, practices a politics of misrepresentation, and hence is inconsistent with such democratic values as sharing, caring, and preserving" (2008, 268–69).

David Theo Goldberg (2002, 4–5) connects classical and modern liberalism with racialization, racism and exclusions. He says:

> As modernity's definitive doctrine of self and society, of morality and politics, liberalism has served to . . . legitimate ideologically, and to rationalize politico-economically prevailing sets of racially ordered conditions and racist exclusions. Classical liberalism (which includes in its range much of the commitments of contemporary conservatism. . . . And . . . racially conceived compromises regarding racist exclusions – ranging from . . . colonial rule and its aftermath . . . have been instrumental in sustaining a consensual dominance of liberalism in modern state formation.

One would be hard pressed to discern any semblance of contradiction in the liberal discourse that Barrow so eagerly embraced in making his case for Barbados's constitutional autochthony. Barrow was painstakingly silent on the antinomies of liberalism when he made the case for independence for Barbados.

ADAMS, BARROW, EXCEPTIONALISM, RACIAL ANGLO-SAXONISM AND BRITISH IMPERIALISM

Grantley Adams was an uncompromising proponent and defender of Barbadian exceptionalism, a theme on which he lectured the Federal House of Representatives, as prime minister of the West Indies Federation (see Duncan 1988). A few years after the Bushe Experiment took effect in 1946, Adams reminded Governor Savage that politicians in the legislature and many people in the electorate felt that three hundred years of representative government and a system of universal education . . . made Barbados more fit to receive the utmost extension of constitutional reform than any other part of the Empire. We are of the considered opinion that this is no mere Barbadian vanity but that Barbados has reached the stage reached by the Canadian, Australian, and South African colonies, when, while remaining colonies, they were advanced to the stage of complete self-government in internal affairs.[32]

Not one of the former British colonies Adams mentioned permitted indigenous people to exercise the human, social and political rights and privileges that the resident Europeans reserved for themselves. Europeans at large traditionally exercised their freedom negatively by denying freedom to diverse others, especially during colonial times: their concept of freedom was heavily racialized and class-inflected (Azzarà 2007; Losurdo 2011).

Adams laid the groundwork for the claims Barrow would also make for Barbadian exceptionalism. The following passage, in which Adams explains why he believed he was knighted, captures the essence of his notion of Barbadian exceptionalism:

I feel sure that whether a man chooses the political course rather than the legal course, any honour that comes to him comes . . . not as an appreciation of his personal service but because he is a member of an organization and a member of a Parliament which has done or tried to do some good for its country. . . . I know these things because I have been told them and I say them at first hand – I know the . . . unique position which Barbados holds among the Caribbean colonies in the eyes of the Colonial Office and the British Government of whatever political complexion. . . .The average Barbadian is always conscious of his superiority to other people of the world; but it is a fact that 300 years of representative institutions have created for us a responsibility and a desire objectively to approach political problems that are . . . inevitably lacking in communities which have not had the advantage of three centuries of unbroken representative government. . . . I know that this honour or any other honour which may be bestowed on me by the British Government . . . or by any international organization, has been due in the political field to the fact that Barbados is absolutely unique among the non-self-governing territories in its unbroken

parliamentary traditions and in the way we have made use of them.
. . . I say that if anything has happened to me on the Trade Union side, it
is due to the fact that there is a similar recognition in the outside world
that Barbados shows as great a success in economic matters as in political
matters, and a greater success than in other colonies.[33]

Adams here ignores the fact that the unbroken parliamentary system
was organized on the basis of domination, racialization, oppression and
inequality. In asserting the "moral epistemology" of British imperialism,
he notes that Barbadians were conscious of their "superiority to other
people of the world",[34] in much the way the English saw themselves
in relation to Europeans and world humanity. The English objected to
being subsumed under a mass called the "Caucasian race" and they
invented the doctrine of "Racial Anglo-Saxonism" to justify the myth of
English racial and cultural exceptionalism and superiority in Europe and
beyond (see Horsman 1981). Adams linked the loyalty of Barbadians to the
British Crown to an imagined innate superiority of its inhabitants,
and he layered the myth of Barbadian superiority and exceptionalism
onto the terrain of British racial and cultural uniqueness. Just as the
British did not view themselves as typical Europeans, Adams projected
the myth about Barbadians as a peculiar group of colonial subjects who
towered above other West Indians and all other colonized people, if not
all of humanity.

Adams is silent about the political settlements that the same British
parliamentary ("container") institutions imposed on their own working
class and on the people whom they colonized, enslaved and oppressed
in the Caribbean. He does not address how patriarchy, the oppression
of women, class exploitation, high-handed liberal authoritarianism and
despotism, racialization and the pernicious and enduring consequences
of capitalist slavery affected the development of the majority of the population of Barbados under the "old representative system". He is silent
about any difficulties the "representative system" created for people like
himself, on entering politics, beginning in the 1930s, and even after he
led the BLP in the House of Assembly into his tenure as the first premier of Barbados. His contributions on the "Trade Union side" included
deliberate action to weaken the Barbados labour movement and destroy

the CLC in the interest of the Anglo-American Cold War project and the business interests, with the effect of preventing the working class from developing into an entity that could defend its own interests (Watson 2004; Hart 2004; Horne 2007).

J. Cameron Tudor's remark that Grantley Adams saw the world through a Barbadian lens and was foremost for and about Barbados (Sealy 1991) is at odds with the facts, unless Tudor understood Barbadian interests as an extension of British interests. In fact, Adams saw Barbados exclusively through the lens of the "moral epistemology" of British imperialism. He sought intentionally to strengthen Barbados's attachment to the British Empire by invoking the notion of Barbados as a rightful piece of Great Britain's overseas property, which gave British interests primary claim to "rightful property income" derived from the labour of Barbadian toilers. Adams always placed the rights and interests of Barbadian workers below private property interests and rights (Will 1992, 66–67; Smith and Smith 2015, 85). Hilary Beckles says, "Adams' entry into the political culture of Barbados as the formulator of conservative opinions in the leading planter journal enhanced his image within the workers' movement as a planter-merchant supporter" (2004a, 190), rather than a committed defender of the interests of the workers or an individual with socialist values or commitments.

John Wickham (1979, 20), the late Barbadian cultural historian, equates "patriotism" with "an expression of acknowledgement of one's cultural heritage, the gift . . . we have received, the qualities and instincts that make us unique, for it is what makes us unique that constitutes our culture". Wickham adopts an organic and romantic notion of culture, as reflected in the highly questionable and unsupportable assertion that culture is unique to each group and "patriotism" is a gift, considering that patriotism is an idea and part of an ideology rather than a quantifiable, empirical phenomenon.

Wickham's problematic notion that patriotism is inherited invokes primordial sentimentalism, encourages the mind to imagine things the way they never were and relies on "retrospective illusions of the national personality" to interpret history (Balibar 1991). Richard Koenigsberg reminds us that a "necessary condition for the espousal of an ideology within a society is the existence of an unconscious fantasy shared by group members. . . . An ideology . . . achieves status and power as an element of culture – insofar as it . . . permits . . . fantasy to be activated upon the stage of society" (2016, 3). Wickham's view of culture and patriotism reminds us of how myth comes into practice and becomes normalized via the habit of equating the institutions and practices humans create in reproducing themselves with expressions of the laws of nature (Agnew 2009). Modern Barbadian culture evolved within an international context, considering that the "particularism of place" is best understood as a specific expression of a complex of inextricably bound domestic and international processes.

ADAMS, THE WEST INDIAN WORKING CLASS
AND THE COLD WAR

Three years after Grantley Adams declared at the founding meeting of the CLC in Barbados in 1945 that the creation of a socialist Caribbean Commonwealth offered the only realistic hope for addressing the myriad problems that plagued the region, the UN General Assembly adopted the Universal Declaration of Human Rights. In the interim it established a special committee to oversee decolonization and self-determination for colonized societies.

The United States and the United Kingdom were among the main opponents of the adoption and implementation of the Universal Declaration of Human Rights. In 1948, the British government chose Adams as a member of the British delegation to a special session of the UN General Assembly that convened in Paris, at which he unapologetically defended British imperialism.[35] Reaction to Adams's speech in Paris from labour unions and anti-imperialist movements throughout the British Empire and beyond was swift and harsh. However, Adams returned to Barbados to a hero's welcome for what anti-working-class elements and monarchists including J. Cameron Tudor interpreted as an outstanding performance (Watson 2004).

It hardly dawned on Adams and other Anglophiles in Barbados that the British Empire had entered a terminal decline. Adams enthusiastically embraced the Cold War project and was uncompromising in his attack on the CLC, which he deliberately helped to destroy, along with any prospect for a strong labour and working-class-oriented organization to take root. He helped to organize and lead an anti-communist cabal of West Indian decolonizing elites that purged the revolutionary elements from the trade union movement and the political parties (Horne 2007; Drayton 2014, 121). One of Adams's main targets was Richard Hart from Jamaica, who had contributed immensely to building bridges between Jamaica and the Eastern Caribbean territories through the trade union and labour movement and beyond, with the CLC playing a strategic role in that process (Hart 2004; Horne 2007).

In 1951, the secretary of state for the colonies was informed that the "authorities should keep in mind the existence of the [CLC] . . . and the possibility that trouble may spread from one colony to another through this agency" (Horne 2007, 165). Taking his orders from London and Washington, Adams called on all West Indian labour unions to withdraw from the World Federation of Trade Unions (WFTU) and join the Cold War–sponsored International Confederation of Free Trade Unions (ICFTU).[36] He also collaborated with the UK government against Cheddi Jagan and the PPP in the constitutional and political crisis in British Guiana that London and Washington orchestrated as part of the Cold War project in the Caribbean (Horne 2007; Watson 2004; Rabe 2005; Palmer 2006). Nigel Bolland argues that "cracks were beginning to appear in the CLC in 1948 between Richard Hart on the left wing and Gomes and Adams on the right, but it was the great split in the international labour movement in 1949, when the superpowers' Cold War rivalry divided the WFTU, that led to the division and destruction of the CLC in the early 1950s" (2001, 483–84, 499).

One of the defining features in the rise of the progressive labour and working-class movement in the West Indies was the principled political stand the leaders of the movement took in defence of self-government to strengthen the advancement of the cause of the working class. Nigel Bolland argues that Cold War politics had a divisive effect on the labour movement in the West Indies as was reflected in the decline and "eventual destruction of the CLC and its replacement by the Caribbean Area Division of the Inter-American Regional Organization of Workers (CADORIT), affiliated to the ICFTU, in 1952" (2001, 498; see Watson 2004). The CLC ceased to be an important political force by 1953, when the Anglo-American Cold War project targeted British Guiana. CADORIT would in due course be replaced by the absolutely compromised, anti-working-class Caribbean Congress of Labour. Britain easily mobilized the leadership of the political parties and the labour unions in the West Indies to support the infamous decision to suspend British Guiana's constitution and dispatch British troops to the territory to remove from office the democratically elected government of Cheddi Jagan and the PPP. The participation of the West Indian leaders in the Cold War–sponsored action against British Guiana set back the struggle around labour rights, self-government and for sovereignty in the West Indies (Horne 2007). Promoting popular democracy was not a priority of the bourgeois democratic revolution in the West Indies.

The United Nations was championing the right of colonized peoples and other dependent non-self-governing societies to self-determination and independence; however, the United Kingdom actively regulated the pace toward self-government in the West Indies and settled for "gradualism in the process of constitutional decolonization, with each unit of the federation retaining its powers except in so far as it specifically surrendered them. . . . Moreover, no period was specified for graduation to dominion status" (Boland 2001, 499; see Mawby 2012). The creation of the Bretton Woods institutions, the UN model for sovereign autonomy, the Marshall Plan, the Atlantic Alliance, the deepening of the internationalization of American capital and the regional defence pacts the United States created were among the main pillars of the postwar liberal international order under the hegemonic leadership of the United States (Panitch and Gindin 2012).

As postwar anti-imperialist and anti-colonial movements asserted themselves on the world stage through forms of resistance including national liberation insurgencies, Western states conveniently misrepresented themselves as embattled, peace-loving, secular democracies that were obliged to use military force and other coercive measures to defend world order and protect freedom against the predations of non-Western states and non-state actors. It was their idea of freedom or the highway. The postwar "Free World" routinely sanctioned and/or employed "force . . . to discipline, or even exterminate, unruly subjects, such as trade unions, indigenous movements, communist parties, or other popular challenges that were pursuing competing political projects" (Barkawi and Laffey 1999, 422; Clymer 2003, 13; Bilgin and Morton 2002).

When the Federation of the West Indies was launched in 1958, the United States was already deeply involved in the West Indies as a source of aid, technical assistance and other support, with strings, for individual territories. For example, Trinidad and Tobago, St Lucia, Antigua, and Jamaica were scheduled to obtain funding for certain infrastructure and economic development projects, and the University College of the West Indies was to receive US funds to augment certain facilities for training as well as for technical assistance and trade education. In 1961 the West Indies Federation federal budget and the Federal Development Loan and Guarantee Fund were targeted to receive a "grant of U.S. $2.5 million from the International Co-operation Administration of the United States Government".[37] On 10 February 1961 the US government and the government of the Federation of the West Indies signed an agreement at Port of Spain, Trinidad, "concerning the United States defence areas in the Federation". Britain "entrusted to the West Indies authority to sign the agreement". The new agreement superseded "all previous agreements under which the United States enjoyed defence facilities in the Federation, and in particular the Leased Bases Agreement of 1941, in so far as that agreement related to leased bases within the Federation".[38]

Charles W. Taussig, who served as head of the CC, US Section, saw the CC as a strategic entity through which the Atlantic allies could collaborate on the "progressive development of dependent peoples toward self-government". Taussig's approach was to pursue those goals through "peace and security in the area and . . . bring about greater education, social welfare, and economic stability" (quoted by Parker 2002, 321, 322). In response to one of Hewitt-Myring's questions about getting facts straight about the British Empire, Taussig told Hewitt-Myring, the British press secretary, at the CC meeting in St Thomas, US Virgin Islands, in 1946, that words like "empire" and "colony" "produce an entirely emotional reaction" in Americans. Taussig stressed that "the American people do seem to have some extraordinary faculty of coming to right conclusions without having to bother about facts".39

Whatever Taussig, who served as President Roosevelt's liberal reformer at the State Department, might have imagined about peace, stability, social welfare, development and anti-colonialism as guiding principles in US foreign policy in the Caribbean, it remains a fact that the geopolitical security imperatives of the US state and the capitalist interests it served trounced justice, which is always a liability where security and the right to exploit are among the priorities of the state. The US hegemonic strategy combined imperialist tactics to achieve much more than traditional imperialism could ever have accomplished, without having to shoulder the cost of owning and managing an empire.

Jason Parker notes that US secretary of war Robert Patterson "confirmed that the colonies were part of the effort to solidify inter-American defense plans, the overriding strategic goal of which was a stable, secure, and friendly flank to the South, not confused by enemy penetration – political, economic, or military" (2002, 322). It would not be left up to West Indian leaders, who were being elected and re-elected under universal adult suffrage, to determine the economic and social priorities they had in mind to respond to the pent-up needs of their societies. For Washington, security always presupposes loyalty, and loyalty is based on fear (Neocleous 2008, 2–3, 81–82).

THE REGIONAL AND INTERNATIONAL POLITICS OF SELF-GOVERNMENT AND FEDERATION

Errol Barrow contested a seat in the federal House of Representatives in 1958 and lost to Florence Daysh; he was also unsuccessful in his bid for a seat in the House of Assembly. He maintained a relatively low profile during the short life of the Federation of the West Indies; however, he did not hide his strong feelings about the causes of the dissolution of the federation. He attributed the "impasse in the Federation" to the "lack of clear thinking and imaginative leadership on the part of the Federal Cabinet", the refusal by "proven" West Indian leaders like Norman Manley,

Alexander Bustamante and Vere Bird to become more actively involved in the federal government, "by seeking election to the Federal House of Representatives" and the failure of the West Indian governments either to "encourage the peoples of British Guiana and British Honduras[40] to join in the federation or to tender advice and assistance to those countries at crucial stages in their political development". For the territorial "federationists" of all political dispositions, the real cause of collapse was the refusal of the UK government to honour the request from the Standing Federation Committee in 1957 to provide £200 million in the form of grants and loans to "set the Federation on its legs".[41]

During a visit by Barrow and Crawford to the British Embassy in Washington, DC, they both spoke unreservedly and undiplomatically with members of the embassy staff about Grantley Adams and the federation. A Mr Hennings, a member of the embassy staff, reported that in the discussion on the constitutional outlook for the Eastern Caribbean with Joseph Sweeney, acting director of the Office of British Commonwealth and North American Affairs at the British Embassy, "Barrow and more particularly Crawford, astonished Sweeney by the firm terms in which they dismissed Grantley Adams as having no part to play in any possible resolution of the present tangled uncertainty." Barrow and Crawford insisted that

> any grouping in the Eastern Caribbean must come about by West Indian initiative; it would be counter-productive for the British or the Americans to believe that they could press such a grouping, and it would be utterly disastrous if either of them thought that any such initiative could be mounted through Adams (for whom in private conversation with me they both spoke in terms of deep contempt). They . . . insisted categorically that the Federal Government must be eliminated from the scene as quickly as possible, and hoped that the Secretary of State's forthcoming visit would not have as its purpose, intended or accidental, the buttressing of Adams' position.[42]

According to Hennings, "Barrow described Adams as "useless, vain, and lazy",[43] and while the State Department "had long accepted that Adams and the Federal Government were losing what authority they . . . ever had . . . that a Barbadian should sweep them aside as encumbrances on the scene in such a downright way was more than a little unexpected".

Barrow was adamant that the federal government had to be abolished and "Adams . . . removed from the scene" to allow Eric Williams to take the "initiative", and he was willing "to commit Barbados under his government . . . to any initiative he [i.e. Williams] might make". Barrow stressed that while the Lewis Report served a useful purpose in getting the smaller islands to see the nature of the sacrifices their leaders would have to make to contribute to the creation of a more viable Eastern Caribbean grouping, it could not be "a basis of discussion because it had been produced under the aegis of the Federal Government, and this was anathema to Eric Williams". Barrow seemed favourably disposed toward Williams's position for "strong central powers" for a federal system; however, he expressed concern about the possible rise of a "Trinidadian imperialism".[44]

Neither the Jamaica Labour Party (JLP) nor the PNP was opposed to the federation. Alexander Bustamante and the JLP held power from 1944 to 1955. Bustamante's "years in Opposition gave him the limelight only when matters of the West Indies Federation came to the fore . . . as this . . . matter of Federation was crucial to his return to power". At the 1947 Montego Bay Conference Bustamante argued that "if Britain wished to get rid of the colonies and put them in a Federation, Britain should put up the millions . . . to finance it. And that remained his theme while he was . . . in the Opposition" (Sealy 1991, 111). Bustamante's insistence that a federation of paupers was unacceptable to Jamaica under any conditions and his declaration that he would support federation provided that it came with the provision for full self-government for each territory (Mordecai 1968, 36) have been cited as grounds for accusing Jamaica of destroying the federation, an unreasonable accusation in light of available evidence.

The JLP ran several candidates for, and won more seats in, the federal parliament than Norman Manley's PNP in the 1958 elections. When Robert Lightbourne, a JLP member in the federal legislature, resigned his seat, which created a vacancy that led to a by-election, Bustamante and the JLP decided against putting forward a candidate to contest the seat, thereby signalling "a total rejection of the whole federal concept" (Sealy 1991, 111), largely because the United Kingdom did not provide the amount of financial resources the federal government requested to run the business of the organization.

Norman Manley spoke like a dedicated federationist and statesman at the 1947 Montego Bay Conference: he said it would be unfortunate if the West Indies should forfeit the

> chance of amalgamation, which is the only hope of a real political destiny, to forge ahead with building nationhood. Here we have it in our grasp. Dare we refuse it and rightly condemn ourselves for all time at the bar of history? Here we are on the sea of destiny, some of us in vessels of a certain size, some huddled in a little craft, a few have accomplished a rudimentary sail to take them along, and here we are offered a boat seaworthy, manned by our own captains and our own crew. If we won't leave our little boats and get into that larger vessel towards the haven we seek, because of our personal ambition, then I say we are condemned and purblind, and history will condemn us. (Quoted by Phillips 1977, 22)

Manley's view, however, was contradicted by the "first and most fundamental" of the resolutions which the Montego Bay delegates adopted and which offered the "first glimpse of the emphasis West Indians have at all times put upon 'states' rights', an approach that . . . bedevilled the federation and all subsequent attempts at regional cooperation and integration ever since". The resolution states: "this Conference, recognizing the desirability of a political federation of the British Caribbean territories, accepts the principle of a federation in which each constituent unit retains complete control over all matters except those specifically assigned to the federal government".[45] Neither Jamaica nor Trinidad and Tobago instructed its delegates at Montego Bay to adopt the same resolution, which reflected the primacy of states' rights.

In *The Economics of Nationhood* (1961), Eric Williams summed up his perspective on what constituted the only appropriate model for a successful federation of the West Indies. He said: "Only powerful and centrally directed economic co-ordination and interdependence can create the true foundation of a nation. Barbados will not unify with British Guiana, or Jamaica with Antigua. They will be knit together only through their common allegiance to a Central Government. Anything else will discredit the conception of a Federation and in the end leave the islands more divided than before" (quoted by Sealy 1991, 193). Williams insisted that the future development of the Federation of the West Indies would depend on the body's discarding its experimental colonial constitution and advancing toward full independence and sovereignty with a declared date for independence. He added, "We must fix a date for the Federation to be independent and the 22nd of April is as good a date as any, so let us fix the 22nd of April and since the Prime Minister of the West Indies cannot get up early in the morning, we can have it at eleven o'clock"[46] (quoted by Sealy 1991, 192).

Under article 15 of the Federation Constitution, the Federal House of Representatives was to consist of forty-five members, distributed as follows: Jamaica seventeen, Trinidad and Tobago ten, Barbados five, two each for Grenada, St Vincent, St Lucia, Dominica, Antigua, St Christopher/ Nevis/Anguilla, and one for Montserrat (Phillips 1977, 36). From Montego Bay (1947) to the dissolution of the federation (1962) and beyond, the preferred model incorporated in its most elementary form the doctrine of states' rights. It seemed to matter very little to the nationalists who acquired formal political control of some of the smallest islands in the world that the federation largely lacked the minimum techno-industrial inner structures of productive capital to support its economic framework and help raise up the weakest members, which relied on grant-in-aid receipts from the UK government.

According to W. Arthur Lewis, "Each territory feels that its further economic and social progress depends to some extent upon local initiatives. . . . Locally elected representatives of the people living in the territory and concerned primarily with its interest, must have the power to take measures for its improvements on their own initiative, without waiting for inspiration from distant centres and without fear of frustration by the opposition of a distant authority" (1961, 2). Neither a concrete sense of a West Indian identity nor a productive, material basis for federation had materialized. The absence of a sense of West Indian national identity was captured in the flight into romantic fancy that certain West Indian leaders took. John Compton (St Lucia) dreamt about moving closer to Canada or the United States (*Barbados Daily News*, 13 April 1962). In response to such musings Errol Barrow declared that "no self-respecting West Indian wants to become part of anybody" (*Manifesto* 1961, 16). The leaders were in broad agreement that adequate financial resources from the UK government were indispensable for the viability of the federation.

The UK government suspended Grenada's constitution and Eric Gairy was forced out of office, an incident that took place in the wake of the collapse of the federation. Gairy appealed to the other West Indian leaders to defend him, and they refused. Gairy decided to withdraw from participating in the deliberations of the Regional Council of Ministers.[47] Herbert Blaize, who replaced Gairy, favoured closer association between Grenada and Trinidad and Tobago. Barrow was highly critical of the UK government for suspending Grenada's constitution, an action he described as punishing an entire society for the misdeeds of an individual leader. Vere Bird of Antigua, historically strong on the prerogative of the unit territory in matters of the location of industry, income taxation, and postal services (Lewis 1965), signed an agreement for a $25 million oil refinery without consulting the leaders of the other territories. Bird's unilateral action carried negative implications for the use of Barbados's oil-refining capacity. Barrow had all along been sceptical of the fiscal and economic viability of the grant-in-aid territories (*Barbados Daily News*, 7 December 1962; Holder 2007).

Vere Bird's position hardened over time: he insisted that unit (territorial) power should be strengthened and expanded at the expense of the federal government. The Barbados Legislative Council argued that Barbados should act in a manner to deny Her Majesty's Government the option of intervening to determine the organization of governmental power at the unit level and thereby take the initiative in matters such as external funding for the non-sovereign federation. Erskine Ward, a member of the Legislative Council, agreed that the funding of the Little Eight was primarily the responsibility of the UK government, and stressed that the primary responsibility of the Barbados government was to the people of Barbados.[48]

At a 23 July 1963 meeting of representatives from Barbados, British Guiana, Jamaica, and Trinidad and Tobago that was held in Trinidad, Barrow reiterated his commitment to "an association with our fellow men and

Governments in the Eastern Caribbean, disdained because of their size and dismissed as insignificant by journalistic phrases like 'Little Eight' and 'Little Seven'" (*Barbados Advocate*, 23 July 1963).[49] Five months later, on 16 December, in Puerto Rico, Barrow said, "My Government has given me a mandate to secure independence before the next election. If it is not granted, it will be declared, because I do not feel that we should have to ask for it" (*Barbados Advocate*, 16 December 1963; Sealy 1991, 32).[50] Four days later, on 20 December, J. Cameron Tudor told the Junior Chamber of Commerce that Barbados had to make important decisions about its political relationship with the Eastern Caribbean territories ("Whither Barbados: Together or Alone", *Barbados Advocate*, 20 December 1963).

London and Washington saw to it that Cheddi Jagan was replaced by Forbes Burnham in British Guiana in 1964 (Palmer 2006, 198–235 passim; Rabe 2005), and Burnham expressed support for a free trade agreement with other British Caribbean countries. Barrow was enthusiastic about broadening the scope of functional cooperation beyond the Little Eight.[51] By early 1965 Barrow stated publicly that "it was easier to find a community of interest with the larger territories than the pettifogging politicians in the Eastern Caribbean". The *Barbados Advocate* editorialized that insularity had got the better of the federation venture and Barbados should "concentrate on our problems at home and plan for eventual independence" (see Cheltenham 1970, 214–17, 218).

Business interests in the territories had been playing a secondary role in the post-federation discussions, largely because the West Indies did not constitute their real market (*Barbados Daily News*, 7 December 1962; Holder 2007). Businesses were interested in the extent to which the new federation initiatives could provide protection from international competition. The report by Dr Carleen O'Loughlin confirmed that without a solid and long-term financial commitment by the United Kingdom there was no hope of creating a viable financial infrastructure for a new federation. The very idea of constructing an independent federation pursuant to the confirmation of "satisfactory assurances about the quantum and the duration of assistance by Her Majesty's Government" was difficult for the UK government to swallow, given its own domestic challenges and also the financial and other expectations that were bound to arise from other British colonies with needs and concerns (Cheltenham 1970, 222). Between 1961 and 1965, the Barbados economy continued to grow, with evidence from investment, production and trade diversification (Barbados 1965). Rising receipts from sugar, on account of higher selling prices, rather than from rising productivity and competitiveness, resulted in improved wages and foreign exchange earnings that benefited the economy. Tourism expanded in terms of arrivals, accommodation, employment, construction and services, including banking, handicrafts, taxi service and revenues. The DLP government invested in economic and social infrastructure, revised the income tax code, expanded the income tax base and thus collected higher revenues. Trade expanded and, though imports continued to outstrip exports, there was a sense that the diversification programme was showing positive results (Worrell 1994–95, 95).

Remittances also helped to improve foreign exchange receipts. Population growth stabilized, owing largely to high levels of net emigration (Cheltenham 1970, 228–31; Worrell 1994–95). There was growing confidence that an improving and expanding economy made the prospect for independence much more encouraging. The regional political landscape looked more propitious with Jamaica and Trinidad and Tobago, both of which became independent in 1962, becoming more involved in functional cooperation in common services such as shipping, meteorology, aviation and higher education. Barbados and British Guiana were trending toward independence and were committed to sharing consular and diplomatic representation to help reduce the foreign service bill (Cheltenham 1970, 232).

Scepticism ran very high among almost all of the Eastern Caribbean leaders over Errol Barrow's "Cessna diplomacy",[52] which was reinforced by a fear that Barbados would try to dominate a federation at the expense of the smaller territories (Mordecai 1968, 442). The "unwillingness of Her Majesty's Government to commit itself on the question of financial aid is . . . regarded as . . . one of the main reasons for the lack of progress with the proposed federation. Another is the inability of the politicians to get on."[53] Dominica's chief minister was suspicious of Barrow's relationship with Trinidad and Tobago, a concern that was compounded by the chief minister's dislike for Eric Williams. St Vincent's Ebenezer Joshua preferred federation over independence for the units; however, he said that while some form of political association was preferable, he was drawn to the "current of world opinion . . . and in particular of opinion at the United Nations" that favoured self-determination. The UK government was well aware that, with or without federation, the remaining islands were not capable of functioning without grants or other economic assistance to render independence viable "in accordance with accepted standards of good government".[54]

St Lucia's chief minister, John Compton, also said he feared domination by Barbados in a federation; however, he indicated that he "favoured association with Windwards, Leewards and Barbados", especially for economic benefits. Grenada's chief minister, Herbert Blaize, was sceptical of Barrow's motives and stressed that Barrow had not approached him on customs union or any other issue. Blaize seemed to favour a federation of the seven (without Barbados) or some form of union with Trinidad and Tobago; however, in the discussion of the West Indian Summit held at the Colonial Office it was reported that a senior Trinidad and Tobago government official was emphatic that Trinidad and Tobago was not interested in any form of unitary statehood with Grenada because its people were not prepared to share their country's wealth with the impoverished Grenada.[55] Undeniably, the leaders of Barbados expected that federation would provide outlets for migration from Barbados: Adams, Barrow and Barbadian leaders at large were strongly committed to freedom of movement throughout the discussion leading up to the federation.

Barrow stressed that from Barbados's perspective the "strongest arguments for a Federation were the freedom of movement that it would have afforded its citizens in seeking job opportunities, and the creation of a wider market that would have allowed her narrow manufacturing base to expand – thus making the island a more powerful magnet of foreign capital". Barrow added that the other compelling argument "to federate was to be seen in the context of the Commonwealth Immigration Act which 'virtually shut the door against our people who have been going to Britain in their thousands looking for remunerative employment'". Echoing Adams and other Barbadians, Barrow said, "I can almost give you an undertaking that with the wider markets which will be created, with Customs Union and Freedom of Movement, I doubt very much whether we will have to go to the British Government asking for loans, because the upsurge of capital which is willing to come into this area for a multiplicity of reasons will preclude us from going to any country asking for loans."[56]

Vere Bird enthusiastically supported full internal self-government to avert deterioration of the "internal security situation"; he also stressed the need for external aid to help improve salaries to strengthen civil service and police morale and avert potential disturbances. Bird favoured a regional approach to public and police services, and he rejected the notion that the main cause of internal security problems and instability arose from subversives and extremists, arguing instead that the problem stemmed from limited resources, small size and poverty. Compton and Barrow met in St Lucia in early August 1964 and signed an agreement to discuss the possibility of forming a customs union.[57]

In a letter dated 31 August 1964, the secretary of state for the colonies, Duncan Sandys, reminded the administrator of Antigua that, in reference to the administrator's dispatch number 156 of 19 June regarding the "request from your Executive Council for full internal self-government to Antigua in January 1965", he was not willing to entertain such an idea as "long as there remains a serious possibility of establishing a federation". Sandys preferred "to see the question of unit constitutional advance in the Leeward and Windward Islands considered in this context", as the Colonial Office was committed to the principle of keeping "constitutional advance among the Leeward and Windward Islands to a uniform pattern".[58]

All of the assessments that the governors and administrators provided stressed administrative inefficiency within the civil service and internal security and police matters in relation to "good government", for which they all agreed Britain's support was indispensable; hence the strong emphasis they placed on the Public Service Commission. Governor John Stow of Barbados insisted on a strong executive power for the Public Service Commission[59] ostensibly to guard against any potential abuse by elected leaders. Commenting on the "role of advisory bodies such as service commissions", Richard Drayton observes that "the 'savings clauses' declare that no regulation or aspect of justice and punishment which was considered lawful in the period before independence shall be judged now to be unlawful relative to any other part of the constitution" (2016, 15).

Barrow admitted that since the prospective benefits of a customs union would tend to favour Barbados, the benefit to Barbados could be offset by allowing freedom of movement within the area. The other leaders were not impressed by Barrow's statement, because West Indian businesses routinely relied on protection for local markets from international competition. Following Barrow's meeting with Compton, the

> merchants of Castries have become opposed to the idea because they fear that they will be dominated by the Barbados mercantile community, that industrialization will be centred in Barbados and . . . as freight rates to Barbados are cheaper than elsewhere in the Eastern Caribbean, commodities will be imported in bulk into Barbados and transshipped . . . to the smaller islands to the benefit of the Barbados merchants and to the disadvantage of the merchants in Castries. . . . Barrow's reported statement about future air services in the Eastern Caribbean has not helped to dispel the suspicion with which he is apparently now viewed.[60]

With respect to Eric Williams's position on the constitutional advance of the Leeward and Windward Islands, N.E. Costar from the British High Commission in Trinidad said, "Dr. Williams has told me that . . . Britain should not concede any further advance towards self-government or independence in any of the separate islands of the Leeward or Windwards." Williams felt that the United Kingdom had been too accommodating and that "we should compel the Leewards and Windwards to come together in a federation, whose viability should be guaranteed by the most lavish financial aid from Britain" as a prerequisite for "Independence and a link with Trinidad". Costar said that Williams was "not . . . very likely to express these views in these kinds of terms in public. He will probably confine his comments to criticism of Britain on the financial aspect, leaving the constitutional aspect unmentioned."[61]

Costar offered the following mixed assessment of Eric Williams:

Dr. Williams is in many ways his main enemy. On the credit side, he is industrious, intelligent, has financial integrity (not universal in the West Indian politician), he espouses the democratic ideas and institutions of the West, and he can . . . show great personal charm, which he uses to good persuasive effect. Against that stand his vanity and conceit and contempt for most of his fellow men. In addition for all his ability, he lacks the skill to administer and put first things first. There is also . . . a streak of a would-be dictator in the man. . . . If they do not agree with him it is, he suggests, because of antagonism to him personally, and an element of personal animosity having crept in, Dr. Williams loses all sense of balance in an argument. . . . Williams found it impossible to be on good terms with hardly anyone whom he cannot boss.[62]

Eric Williams viewed Cheddi Jagan with disdain and contempt on political and ideological grounds. He did not feel that British Guiana should be allowed to become independent under Jagan, whom he blamed for aggravating ethnic problems in the territory in ways that carried potentially negative implications for Trinidad and Tobago.[63] Williams was not alone in his assessment of Jagan's lack of suitability, as certain other leaders in Guiana made similar statements. Williams also volunteered to spy on Jagan for the United States and United Kingdom: his anti-communist outlook made him a potential recruit for the Cold War project (Palmer 2006, 221 ff). Barrow noted that Barbados had been very tolerant in allowing

a big influx of people from a neighbouring island who contributed 50 percent of the crime and prostitution in Barbados when compared to the Government of St Kitts under Chief Minister, Mr. Paul Southwell, who deported St. Lucians, and that of Dr. Eric Williams . . . who had made it clear that an influx of people from the islands was not in the interest of Trinidad where jobs, school places and so on were concerned. (Burke 1966)

Barrow stressed that "not one Chief Minister of the Windward and Leeward Islands said that Barbados was wrong to seek Independence for herself".[64] John Stow, governor of Barbados, commented in his personal report for April 1964 that the draft scheme incorporated "decisions to whittle down the executive powers of the Federation and deprive it of revenue raising power" and represented "a very weak Federation with the real power firmly residing in the units". Stow added, "It is not entirely clear whether Barrow really believes that such a Federation could work. Privately, he has told me that it could not, but since the draft Federal Scheme has been prepared and sponsored by Barbados, the impression is given that Barbados is prepared to go along with it." The governor noted also that Barrow felt that unanimous agreement by the seven was unlikely and even if they could agree "the Federation will be 'frustrated' by Her Majesty's Government not giving the embryo Federation what he would consider 'adequate' funds to make a go of it. What is certain is that he feels strongly that to give any strong lead in favour of a Federation will do him no good politically at present."[65]

The Colonial Office acknowledged that prospects for a federation of the remaining seven territories had dimmed, when Douglas Williams stated that Barrow was expressing pessimism "about the prospect of attaining federation", in light of "the lack of progress", his "casting around for alternative forms of regional cooperation, starting with . . . a customs union", "the broadly differing views of Antigua and St Lucia on the subject, Antigua's request for full internal self-government, and Eric Williams's announcement that a union with Grenada was not in the works 'within the foreseeable future'".[66] Douglas Williams drew the following distinctions between Barbados's level of development and that of the Leeward and Windward Islands:

> In our view . . . Barbados differs from the Leeward and Windward Islands in certain respects. There seems little doubt that, by the standards of the modern world, Barbados could sustain independence on its own. It is financially viable. It might . . . be possible for the U.K. Government safely to contemplate entering into a "Western Samoa"[67] type of relationship with Barbados, should that Government so wish, since . . . Barbados could be expected to conduct its external relations in a way which would not cause the United Kingdom any embarrassment. At the official level . . . we think that if the federation talks break down, we shall have to contemplate granting Barbados separate independence.[68]

The larger implication of Douglas Williams's statement was that the

United States could buy into independence for Barbados on the terms he stated as a spokesman for the UK government. Barrow was satisfied that the UK government had concluded that Barbados had satisfied the requirements for independence. The Colonial Office also gave the green light, and Edward Du Cann, chairman of the British Conservative Party, emphasized that the question of the future of Barbados, including independence, was for Barbadians to decide and that Britain was supportive of Barbados in that regard (Williams 1966). In a comment about the British Caribbean, Barrow levelled a charge that the countries had "mastered the art of not being able to live together in unity" ("Angry Premier Is Restrained", *Barbados Advocate*, 5 January 1966). The leader of the Opposition in Barbados, Ernest Deighton Mottley, said his party, the Barbados National Party, supported the islands of the Eastern Caribbean coming together to deal with economic and other problems; however, his party was not opposed to independence for Barbados ("Federation Is of Greater Advantage", *Barbados Advocate*, 6 January 1966).[69]

The position of the United States was that "whether Barbados becomes independent alone, or within an ECF, we believe it will not request outright assistance from the US, but will expect consideration for soft loans and will again renew its request for the once-promised Peace Corps. These inevitable approaches, we believe, should be received with replies somewhat more concrete than 'sympathetic consideration'" (Kellman 2010, 32). Washington had shown little interest, dating back to the immediate postwar period, in shouldering any of the financial liabilities that Britain was itself reluctant to assume on behalf of the West Indian territories (see Louis 1977). The United States felt that the readiness of Barbados for independence hinged in large measure on Barbados's and the neighbouring islands' "obvious strategic interest to the United States. They are presently in the camp of the West, with democratic institutions and ideals of social justice and parliamentary democracy according to British standards. They have so far not been influenced by outside anti-democratic elements" (quoted in Kellman 2010, 34). The United States held firmly to the tenet that the security of the state must always be paramount and human security and freedom must be treated as secondary. An enduring sovereignty myth is that sovereignty actually resides in the people: if, therefore, the people are sovereign, it must follow that the security of the state necessarily translates into the security of the people (Agnew 2009). The British Caribbean has simply never satisfied the minimum requirements in terms of raw materials, science and technology, research and development, manufacturing and a sizeable population with a labour force that includes complex skill sets that can support production, trade and capital accumulation on the basis of competitive advantage. The entire Caribbean, at the absolute minimum, might begin to meet such requirements on a potentially sustainable basis, a potential that is compromised by the region being divided into so many islands. Barrow engaged in rhetorical flourish about Barbados's right to declare unilateral independence if necessary; however, he waited until he had obtained official sanction from the UK government, the United States, the Opposition, and a number of civil-society entities, before making representation to Whitehall for a constitutional conference on independence.

ASSOCIATED STATEHOOD FOR THE
EASTERN CARIBBEAN POST-FEDERATION

The term "internal self-government" was not part of the terms of reference at the constitutional conferences Her Majesty's Government sponsored between 1943 and 1955; however, during the period 1955 to 1967, of the sixty-seven constitutional conferences that Her Majesty's Government sponsored, twenty-four were about the British Caribbean and "fifteen dealt with steps toward independence". Jamaica, Trinidad and Tobago, British Guiana, and Barbados achieved full internal self-government which fell "short of independence in so far as it implied the absence of full international personality and of Statute of Westminster legal status". The constitutional development process in the West Indies Associated States was so unusual that the term "internal independence" should be coined to apply to their constitutional status to mean "falling short of full independence . . . because legal personality in the international community cannot normally be accorded such States" (DeSmith 1964, 85).

The terms "territorial integrity" and "contingent sovereignty" would appear to have a degree of relevance to the context in which the UK government was attempting to work out issues of self-determination for very small colonies. It began to become clear that no British Caribbean territory had a right to internal self-government, such that any sovereignty that might accrue to any one of them would have to be earned, bearing in mind that the "three . . . elements of earned sovereignty" include "provision for shared sovereignty, measures enabling some type of internal institution building, and negotiations for final status". The indisputable point here is that sovereignty has always been indeterminate – phased, conditional, constrained and subject to degrees of supervision – as sovereignty is historical and therefore inorganic (Elden 2009, 167; see Agnew 2009).

After Jamaica, Trinidad and Tobago, British Guiana, and Barbados became sovereign monarchies under independence acts passed by the House of Commons (see Drayton 2016, 9) the question of the constitutional status of the remaining West Indian territories that were part of the federation[70] had to be revisited. By that time the "seat of constitution-making no longer, in so far as British dependent territories are concerned, [had] its venue only at Whitehall in London", considering that the "Committee of 24 at the United Nations Headquarters . . . is . . . tending to call the tune" (Phillips 1977, 88). The United States was the first state to bring the "idea of associated statehood . . . before the United Nations as far back as 1953", when it "persuaded the General Assembly that it had given Puerto Rico full self-government by way of associated statehood": the General Assembly, under resolution 15 of 14 December 1960, adopted the "free association" principle that linked full self-government to associated statehood.[71]

The United Nations was beginning to define "a new and internationally approved status to substitute for colonial rule". Sir Fred Phillips observes that the

> United Kingdom Government . . . had become alive to the fact that the reaction of United Nations organs must be taken into consideration when considering new constitutions. This was . . . one compelling reason why in 1965 a Constitutional Planning Department was established in the Colonial Office, its responsibilities being "general questions as to future policy, co-ordination of constitutional development . . . assistance to geographical

departments in the introduction of new constitutional patterns including United Nations implications". (Quoted in Phillips 1977, 87, 88)

Phillips (1977, 89) argues that "when the question of the cessation of transmission of information in respect of Puerto Rico under article 73(e) of the charter was being considered, the United Nations General Assembly Resolution – 748 (VIII) included in its preamble the proposition that the general assembly had competence 'to decide whether a non-self-governing territory had or has not attained a full measure of self-government'".[72] Associated statehood therefore became a "new and internationally approved status to substitute for colonial rule in circumstances wherein it was impossible to apply either full independence or integration to a new state" (1977, 89).

The UN General Assembly considered the West Indian Associated States still colonies because the United Nations itself "had no 'presence' to supervise the referendum, which was considered a sine qua non to associated statehood or to observe the elections". The United Kingdom viewed the territories as "States (not Colonies) in association with Britain" even as those "States viewed themselves as internally independent" (Phillips 1977, 91). In his annual report for 1966–67 the UN secretary general said, "I believe it is necessary to note that while universality of membership is most desirable like all concepts it has its limitations and the line has to be drawn somewhere. . . . The Charter itself foresees limitations on United Nations membership." The secretary general stressed that under "Article 4 of the Charter not only must a State be peace-loving . . . it must also . . . be able and willing to carry out the obligations contained in the Charter". The secretary general had "in mind . . . states which have been referred to as 'micro-states', entities which are exceptionally small in area, population and human resources, and which are now emerging as independent states" (quoted by Phillips 1977, 92).

Arthur Lewis wrote in *The Agony of the Eight*: "Federation is the only framework which will guarantee law and order, good government, financial stability, the recruitment and retention of good technical staff, and the ability to attract financial assistance from outside including the power to borrow and including also the kind of stability which attracts private investment. If each little island goes off on its own way, its people must suffer" (1965, 36). Eric Williams had argued very bluntly that "federalism was indicated not only by economic considerations but by every dictate of common sense. . . . The Caribbean, like the whole world, will federate or collapse" (quoted in Wallace 1977, 95–96). Arthur Lewis did not view federation in the West Indies as a political project to validate what had already been achieved through regional integration via economics, finance, science and technology, production, trade, the movement of people and other processes, none of which were achieved by the West Indies; rather, he argued that federation was the political prerequisite to lay a foundation for a potential regional integration strategy for improving the lot of all the territories. Lewis provides a set of axioms and guidelines for policymakers to follow and he discusses the role of international capital in the economic modernization of Caribbean societies; however, his neo-Ricardian economic perspective makes it impossible to grasp and comprehend the spatial character of capitalism, which is an international form of production for private accumulation.

Whitehall expressed additional concerns such as the "difficulty in the West Indian context of divorcing responsibility for external affairs from some aspects of control over domestic policy", mindful of the location of the West Indies in "what is, internationally speaking, a sensitive area", which gives their domestic policies international repercussions of a "fairly serious" nature. The United Kingdom did not see how it could manage their external affairs without some involvement in their domestic affairs, considering the inescapable connection between domestic and international politics. The question of defence and internal security posed problems such as how to exercise "ultimate responsibility for internal security in these territories without any power to deal with those elements which had produced an internal security situation in the first place".[73] The UK government looked at the matter through Cold War security frames. The geopolitical position of the United Kingdom on the West Indies Associated States differed by degree rather than kind from the way it viewed the newly independent states of Barbados, Guyana, Jamaica, and Trinidad and Tobago.

The Colonial Office had reservations about how the Leeward and Windward Islands were handling their finances (budgetary account and capital account) and about having to maintain a "substantial financial responsibility" without "some ultimate means of control" or the "power to cut off aid if scandals develop involving our aid". The UK government was not impressed by the notion that political stability in the territories could compensate for the lack of material resources and other factors. There was a sense that the prospect of any of the islands becoming attractive sites for the flow of money escaping political instability and higher taxes (offshore financial centres) would pose additional security concerns to justify further the need to maintain a presence in them.[74]

The Colonial Office also expressed concern that Eric Williams might have designs on the Windward and Leeward Islands. The British High Commission in Trinidad and Tobago labelled Williams a dictator.[75] It was also reported that William Bramble, chief minister of Montserrat, possessed dictatorial tendencies, and expected the "Police, the Courts, the Public Service Commission and . . . the Government to do his bidding irrespective of General Orders, Financial Instructions, and the Laws". Whitehall noted that Bramble's excesses were curbed only by "the Administrator, Financial Secretary and Crown Attorney". In the absence of that "check . . . the public purse will be used to further party/union affairs; in fact, it will be impossible to differentiate between the party, the union and the government". It was therefore deemed necessary to take additional measures to "minimize the abuses one sees lying ahead".[76]

In the search for a way to balance its responsibility for foreign policy with a degree of control over the internal affairs of the West Indies Associated States, the United Kingdom discussed with some scepticism the so-called Samoan solution as one possible option for addressing and possibly resolving certain regional security problems that affected those territories.[77] Signs of the mistrust, cynicism and insecurity that had been rampant among the leaders were expressed largely in the dislike for Eric Williams (Mordecai 1968, 442) and scepticism about Barrow's intentions. Williams was adamant that the UK government should force the remaining territories to federate, as they would never do so of their own volition, and he noted that without integration most countries would face a dismal future.

The Colonial Office felt strongly that in geopolitical terms "Cuba . . .

made the Eastern Caribbean a highly sensitive political and strategic area" and "most of the leading politicians would be prepared to flirt with Mao, or Fidel, or anyone else if they could announce that they had been driven to this unwelcome course by the parsimoniousness of Britain or the United States". It was suggested that the United Kingdom, the United States and Canada should be brought in "as equal partners in any plan for the economic development of the area"[78] to try to keep communists from making any headway. Clearly, Cold War security concerns were decisive in the framing of the strategy for constitutional advance and economic modernization in the Windward and Leeward Islands.

CONCLUSION

Attempts by the United Kingdom to promote closer association among the West Indian territories started before World War II; however, the postwar efforts were based on much more than the administrative and financial exigencies of empire, and highlighted the crisis of British imperialism and the slow collapse of the British Empire, which signalled the end of Britain's role as a dominant world power (Conway 2015). The US strategy for replacing traditional imperialism with an international hegemonic "model" of world order that anchored the Cold War project brought into clear relief the United Kingdom's increasingly subordinate role in the Caribbean. The United Kingdom was therefore compelled by dint of circumstances beyond its control to search for ways to provide the decaying imperialist order with a credible soft landing. The United States viewed the creation of the CC as part of the postwar hegemonic political settlement into which it integrated Britain, France and the Netherlands, in line with its security priorities, with which they reluctantly but understandably adjusted their own priorities.

The Cold War project involved preventing political parties and labour unions with socialist-oriented, working-class positions from winning state power, which extended to defeating and destroying the CLC. The Cold War in the Caribbean began with the West Indies rather than with the Cuban Revolution, as was seen from the late 1940s around the labour movement and working-class struggles that extended from Jamaica to British Guiana.

The ideological side of the struggle – anti-communism – clouded the more fundamental aspects, which included free and unrestricted access to strategic materials like oil and bauxite in the Caribbean. The United Kingdom and other European powers became the core beneficiaries of the hegemonic strategy, and they acted predictably to realign the territories with US Cold War security priorities even before British Guiana (1953), Guatemala (1954) and the Cuban Revolution (1959).

The West Indian territories looked to the UN model of self-determination and sovereign autonomy to give legitimacy to their claims for self-determination; however, the United Kingdom left the option open to them from the outset, beginning in 1947 at Montego Bay. The West Indian territories failed, however, to appreciate that the UN model was not designed to permit decolonizing territories and newly independent states to exercise sovereignty according to their peculiar nationalist interpretation. The UN model favoured the expansion of capitalism, which is at variance with the achievement of substantive self-determination. All major geopolitical initiatives the United States undertook in Latin America and the Caribbean from the Monroe Doctrine onward highlighted the contingent nature of the sovereignty of other states from the US security angle. The US insistence that the exercise of sovereignty must be aligned with and subsumed under its security imperatives, based on the idea that for the United States to be safe at home it must feel secure abroad, dates back at least to the Monroe Doctrine.

Mary Chamberlain notes that the

> arguments for some form of regional self-government through federation had been put on hold during the war, but they were not dead. . . . The Bases Destroyers Agreement had been negotiated with no reference to, or consultation with, local interests, reminding the region of its colonial status and its powerlessness to manage its own interests. It was also a reminder of the powerlessness of the British government in the face of American interests – and of the nascent threat posed by the United States as an imperial successor to Britain. (2010, 157)

The United Kingdom adopted an ambiguous approach to self-government in the West Indies that put the two options of territorial primacy and a weak federation on the table, with a nod to the former; however, the West Indian territories would have settled for a federation with a strong central government if the UK government had presented it as the only viable option and with a commitment to finance the venture on a sustainable basis (see Mordecai 1968, 32–33). By 1961 Norman Manley had been assured by the Colonial Office that membership in the federation did not rule out independence for Jamaica, at the very moment when the federation was proceeding with the plans the United Kingdom had approved for it to become a sovereign entity.

Barbados represents an interesting case, with Grantley Adams and Errol Barrow insisting on the territory's unique constitutional origin and cultural trajectory among West Indian territories and embracing the "representative system" with claims of constitutional autochthony and exceptionalism. Adams asserted Barbadian exceptionalism, which Barrow strategically embraced and exploited to buttress the case he made for independence for Barbados. Barrow argued that the constitutional path Barbados followed in becoming a British colony made independence an immanent factor such that, in his opinion, neither of the two options for self-government offered by the United Kingdom necessarily imposed constitutional constraints on his government's right and ability to write its independence constitution or declare independence.

Hardly appreciated and never accounted for is that self-government and sovereignty exposed the fundamental incompatibility between capitalism on the one hand and self-determination and sovereign autonomy on the other. The outcome of the West Indies federal experiment confirmed that the idea of self-government and independence for each territory rested on values that were derived through the anti-universalist norms of Western secular modernity. The UN model of sovereign autonomy was built on the same Eurocentric foundation of state-centric power politics, anti-historical and romantic conceptions of state sovereignty and the incompatibility between capitalism and self-determination.

The Cold War was hardly an alien imposition that was foisted on the Caribbean region, but very much part of the postwar liberal (international) hegemonic order into which the Caribbean was largely integrated. The geopolitical trajectory of the Cuban Revolution has been constrained by the same reality. Dialectically, capitalism connects the world in ways that lay the preconditions for the pursuit of our universal humanity, by treating the nation-form as a means to an end; however, the capitalist approach to global integration reproduces contradictions including all manner of inequalities, violence, instability, disorganization and alienation around capital accumulation and state power and domination that make it difficult for us to live as full humans. The Western response has been to attempt to neutralize the anti-imperialist class struggles that unfolded around labour rights, working-class interests, decolonization and sovereignty. The destruction of the CLC by Grantley Adams and the majority of West Indian agents of Cold War globalization was part of the international liberal offensive against the making of universal history in the Caribbean, and the region continues to bear the deep scars from that offensive.

4.

THE CONTRADICTIONS OF SELF-DETERMINATION
DECOLONIZATION, THE COLD WAR AND CLASS STRUGGLES

THIS CHAPTER EXAMINES THE ROLE THE Cold War project played in shaping the trajectory of decolonization in the West Indies from the 1940s to the dissolution of the Federation of the West Indies. The chapter seeks also to answer questions arising from the implications of the crisis of British imperialism and the disintegration of the British Empire for decolonization struggles in the West Indies. It examines the environment in which Errol Barrow developed into a political leader in Barbados and the West Indies. More specifically, how did the integration of the United Kingdom into the postwar hegemonic order the United States constructed affect the United Kingdom's ability to manage decolonization in the British Caribbean? How did the United Kingdom's acceptance of the idea that the US security interests in the Caribbean would be paramount in shaping its Caribbean policy condition its approach to questions of self-determination and sovereign autonomy for the West Indian territories? To what extent did the Cold War project complicate the constitutional and political situation for the West Indian territories, with reference to the making and dissolution of the Federation of the West Indies? Did the Cold War project play any particular role in determining how the UN model for self-determination and independence influenced thinking on approaches to self-government in the West Indian territories? Did the aspirations of the post-1937 generation of West Indian labour and political leaders follow the vision they had in the aftermath of the 1935–37 rebellions? Did the decolonizing elite in the West Indies embrace Cold War designs around the restructuring of the economic and geopolitical arrangements for managing the international capitalist order? What role did Barbados play in the processes and the outcomes? How did the development of the working class affect and how was it affected by the larger regional and international processes?

The Cold War project was decisive in shaping the entire process toward self-determination in the West Indies, leading up to independence. Before the Cuban Revolution, Cuba did not offer a pretext for the Cold War to shape decolonization in the West Indies. The Cold War was brought frontally into the West Indies in British Guiana approximately six years before the Cuban Revolution came to power. When revolutionary Cuba nationalized foreign-owned assets in Cuba, the United States insisted that the Cubans had to be punished for nationalizing capitalist private property, on the basis of the ideological claim that private property in the means of production (and, by extension, the right to exploit and reproduce inequality and poverty) is the indispensable and irreducible foundation of human civilization and progress. The implication here is that the right to exploit is sacrosanct and antecedent to all other historical rights, a claim that is absolutely without merit. The changing geopolitical context in which Cuba established close economic, geopolitical and strategic links with the Soviet Union was exploited by the United States to change the international relations dynamics in the Western Hemisphere and worldwide.

Kenneth Thompson argues that the United States cast its containment strategy in "universalist and indiscriminate terms without being measured by the historic foreign policy constraints of the interests and power of the nations that were directly concerned. The driving force of containment in Asia was collective security and this invited disregard and contempt for a clear-eyed recognition of containment's limitations on the borders of China and the Soviet Union" (1981, 212).

FROM IMPERIALISM TO AMERICAN HEGEMONY: CONTAINMENT AND WEST INDIAN RADICALISM

George Lamming argues that his arrival in Trinidad in 1946 at nineteen, to work as a teacher,[1] was a "freedom moment" that brought him face to face with "a family of islands" in each household and made him aware that the West Indies already constituted a sub-universal entity that was "federated by blood". Lamming's concept of a "sub-universal entity" resonates with Susan Buck-Morss's concept of universal history and suggests that Lamming saw the West Indies within the broader context of international human experience, with reference to the struggles against colonial and imperialist oppression, exploitation and alienation. In Trinidad Lamming joined in the intellectual cultural milieu provided by the Readers' and Writers' Club, where he met and interacted with Marxists like Clifford Sealy, Jack Kelshall, Alfred Mendes and other "very explicitly Marxist, unapologetically . . . Marxist, or learning to be Marxist" individuals (Scott 2002, 90, 94, 100).[2]

Many West Indians had begun to organize along progressive political lines before anti-colonial rebellions erupted during the 1930s. Walter Rodney argues that in the case of British Guiana, it was much earlier, "in the late nineteenth century that the modern political economy of Guyana took shape", through spontaneous activities and struggles that accompanied the formation of the working class in the colony and the trade union movement that became part of that process (1981, 221, 219). Before the 1930s, British and American authorities were expressing concern over radical nationalist, progressive and revolutionary political and ideological tendencies in West Indian societies. Frank Furedi stresses that London and Washington discerned a high degree of black racial and nationalist consciousness among the West Indian populations, and expressed reservations about the rise of left-wing political tendencies within the fledgling working classes. Furedi points out that the British and American authorities were particularly alarmed by the very high level of racial consciousness in the West Indies around the Italian invasion of Ethiopia (1998, 198–205 passim).

The impact of Marcus Garvey's UNIA in the West Indies was significant, and it was typical for progressive forces to combine nationalist and socialist ideas in the emerging working-class discourse and political movement (Beckles 2004a). Beginning in the late nineteenth century and continuing into the twentieth, workers in colonies such as Antigua and Barbados created friendly societies, lodges and other self-help entities which they drew upon to meet certain financial and even political ends (Bolland 2001, 333; Beckles 2004a).

The British Guiana Labour Union was founded in 1919 and the Guianese and West Indian Federation of Trade Unions and Labour Parties was created in 1926. The BGWILC announced that it aimed to "transfer political and economic power from the small class of capitalists to the West Indian working class". There was discussion of the "nationalization of key industries, particularly oil and sugar" with a view to revolutionize the relationship "between man and man – between capital and labour", as the basis for achieving "happiness" and "freedom". The BGWILC played an important role in the adoption of a regional approach to labour and trade union organizing and labour politics in the West Indies. Before the creation of the BGWILC, the Guianese and West Indian Federation of Trade Unions and Labour Parties proposed self-government under a "strong federal government" and a "federal labour organization", with a provision for locating labour rights at the centre of any federal government (Bolland 2001, 336, 478; see Horne 2007).

In 1945 the West Indies hosted the BGWILC and delegates from a number of other British Caribbean countries for a conference in Barbados. The CLC was created out of the 1945 conference in Barbados. Jamaica sent delegates to the 1945 CLC meetings, which was the "first time there was direct contact between labour organizations in Jamaica and those of the Eastern Caribbean and Guyana". Echoing the sentiment for nationalization and public ownership of certain resources and industries in the West Indian territories, Grantley Adams "urged the delegates to declare a policy on land tenure, advocating the nationalization of the sugar industry and the abolition of the private ownership of large units of land" (Bolland 2001, 475, 478, 480).

Two decades before the CLC was formed, Charles Duncan O'Neal and others founded the socialist-oriented DL in Barbados in 1924. The PNP was established in Jamaica in 1938, after the Jamaican Progressive League was founded in New York. The Marxist forces within the PNP agreed to follow the party's nationalist orientation "while preserving their own separate identity as leaders of a socialist movement within the broad anti-imperialist front" (Bolland 2001, 329). The founding of the PNP elicited negative reactions from US consular agents in Kingston, and the British government and the United States had been monitoring the tendencies within the fledgling working-class formations from Jamaica to British Guiana before formal measures for decolonization were introduced in the aftermath of the working-class rebellions in the West Indies between 1935 and 1937 (Bolland 2001, 212–356 passim).

Norman Manley did not object to the PNP's wearing a socialist label. According to Theodore Sealy, "Manley and the People's National Party declared themselves formally to be socialists" even though it included "all elements, right, left and centre, but after Sir Stafford Cripps had given it a socialist tint in his inaugural speech, the left wingers gained more and more ground inside the Party". Sealy notes that when he asked Manley about the wisdom of adding "another massive purpose – socialism – to that programme" he responded, "You know, this war that is on, after this war, the world is going to be a socialist world, so we might as well be pre-pared for it" (quoted in Sealy 1991, 162). In British Guiana Cheddi Jagan and a number of his associates, including certain Marxists, formed the Political Affairs Committee in 1944 with an ostensibly Marxist-oriented working-class orientation and appeal. The Political Affairs Committee was the precursor of the PPP, which was founded in 1950 (Bolland 2001).

[The] British labour movement's involvement in influencing its Caribbean counterparts began in 1925 when Crichlow of the British Guiana Labour Union participated in the British Commonwealth Labour conference in London and in 1926 when F.O. Roberts attended the British Guiana and West Indies Labour Conference hosted by the British Guiana Labour Union. Lord Passfield, the Fabian socialist, who became Secretary of State for the Colonies in the second Labour government in 1929 . . . showed a commitment to reforming the archaic labour laws in the West Indies. (Bolland 2001, 359)

Most West Indians who participated in the labour and trade union movement were enthusiastic about the activities they undertook to improve the lot of the West Indian population. Nigel Bolland remarks, however, that they "had too much faith in what they thought the British Labour Party would achieve on behalf of the Caribbean working people" (2001, 359).

Grantley Adams was forced to make certain concessions to the progressive and revolutionary forces within the BWU and beyond, by including the "singing of the Red Flag and flaunting of the 'hammer and sickle' symbols of Bolshevism" at political events, while masking his contempt for Marxism and Marxism-Leninism and communism (Phillips 1998, 19n12; Hoyos 1972, 130–31). Albert Gomes of Trinidad observed that local "cinema audiences generously cheered appearances of Hitler and Mussolini; and . . . when the Russians . . . repulsed Nazi invasion, Stalin became a figure of awe and veneration among the masses. . . . When Hitler seemed to be succeeding, they experienced a feeling of satisfaction that someone was getting the better of the English", a sentiment that was shared by "trade unionists who had profound ideological reasons for hating the Hitlers and Mussolinis of this world" (1974, 57, quoted in Horne 2007, 54).

Grantley Adams "frequently expressed his admiration for Soviet Russia . . . during the . . . Second World War". Throughout the European colonies in the Caribbean there was a recognition that German brutality and European imperialism shared certain racial and cultural characteristics (Horne 2007, 54; Phillips 1998) of global white supremacy. The optimism that the growing presence of the Americans in the West Indies would represent a positive development for the population subsided when Jim Crow began to exact its toll around the American military bases and beyond (Horne 2007, 54; Bolland 2001, 479).

In the aftermath of the 1930s rebellions in the West Indies (Hart 1998, 120–34 passim), the British government, mindful of the implications of the outcome of World War II for British and European imperialism, proposed closer association among the West Indian territories as a way to manage the anticipated contradictions arising from decolonization in an orderly manner. Britain's interest in closer association was conditioned by a need to rationalize the management of colonial affairs and limit what Whitehall interpreted as growing US intrusion into the West Indies.[3] Britain's eagerness to promote self-government for the West Indies in the speediest possible fashion within a federal framework[4] was conditioned by the changing international situation, of which the anti-colonial struggles formed but one important variable.

AMERICAN EXPANSION IN THE CARIBBEAN: THE COLD WAR FOUNDATIONS OF DECOLONIZATION IN THE WEST INDIAN TERRITORIES

Christopher Layne argues in relation to the American liberal doctrine of Wilsonianism that "primacy and empire . . . infuse American grand strategy with . . . the crusading mentality and self-righteousness" (2006, 132). When the nineteenth-century Jeffersonian "Empire of Liberty" project was conceived, the American ruling class imbued its expansionist motives and actions with a "divine providence" logic that was assumed to have miraculously invested the United States with the right to supervise the advancement of world humanity. The point here is that whenever the United States intervenes in other countries, militarily or otherwise, at any cost, in pursuit of its expansionist security interests, it self-righteously assumes that it automatically acts in the best interests of humanity, for which the world ought to show its gratitude. This hubris has conditioned a putative American exceptionalism and a sense of indispensability (Marqusee 2007, 115–16; Teschke 2003, 39). This particular neo-Wilsonian self-image resonates with Thomas Jefferson's assertion that the US Constitution was uniquely designed for self-government and expansion (Foner 2002; Landau 1987).
    Layne says,

> Wilsonianism always has been based on the fear that unless the United States can remake the world in its ideological image . . . unless American ideology is preeminent globally, the United States might have to accept curtailed political liberties and economic regimentation at home in order to ensure its security in an ideologically hostile world. This is why U.S. foreign policy rests on the assumption that political and economic liberalism cannot flourish at home unless they are safe abroad.

Layne stresses that this "fundamental pathology in American liberalism" registers an eagerness to suppress, by pre-emptive measures, "alternative ideologies" (2006, 133; see Ninkovich 1994, 53). The US-led post-imperialist (hegemonic) Cold War project has certain antecedents in the neo-Jeffersonian and Wilsonian logic. Layne's otherwise useful account comes across as largely subjective in failing to account for the fact that capitalism is an international form of production, and capital accumulation is a global process that requires a global geopolitical strategy for keeping the world open to and safe for capital, for which the US security strategy is designed.

Tarak Barkawi and Mark Laffey (1999) argue convincingly that there is no compelling evidence to support the ideological assertion that liberalism is a force for peace in the world. In fact, "Wilsonian Democracy" contributes to global instability, insecurity and indeterminacy and "permanent or semipermanent war", and also makes the pursuit of global justice secondary to the quest for state security (Layne 2006, 134; see Johnson 2004, 153). The US Strategic Command politicizes America's use of its military power, justifies the threat to use nuclear weapons and portrays the United States as less than "fully rational and cool-headed" (quoted in Chomsky 2000, 6, 7; see Johnson 2004, 168, 181). The United States pursues absolute global capitalist domination with a view to Americanize globalization and achieve "full spectrum dominance", via the undisputed military and other forms of control of land, sea, air and space. It is on this basis that the US hegemonic grand strategy exhibits an imperial bearing; however, neither the Americanization of globalization nor the achievement of an American global empire is within the reach of the American ruling class (Agnew 2009; Robinson 2004, 2014).

The spread of American capital in the Caribbean, beginning before World War II, helped to upgrade the general material, economic and technological conditions in the region and improve the average productivity of labour over time, foremost in the interest of capital. Samuel Farber notes that the "various reciprocity and other economic treaties in force, in various forms, from 1902 until the early 1960s" between the United States and Cuba intensified the integration of the Cuban economy into the US political economy from the early twentieth century (Farber 2006,

9). The construction of the Panama Canal under American capitalist auspices created employment opportunities for large numbers of workers from the West Indies and other Caribbean territories and beyond. After the completion of the Panama Canal many West Indians migrated from Panama to Central America (Costa Rica and Nicaragua) and to Cuba and the Dominican Republic as agricultural wage labourers, in step with the movement of American capital. The construction of the Panama Canal, with its Jim Crow cultural (social and economic) horrors and tragedies for the West Indian labourers and others (Richardson 1985; Newton 1984; Vitalis 2000; Senior 2014), made it possible for those migrant workers to contribute significant amounts of remittances that helped to improve the lot of rural and urban working-class households, filled colonial coffers, and contributed to the rise of the early twentieth-century black middle strata in places like Barbados (Chamberlain 2010) and Jamaica, the two West Indian colonies that contributed the bulk of the black immigrant labour force to Panama.

By World War I, American companies like Kaiser Alumina had been trying to secure control of bauxite resources in British Guiana. By the end of World War II, Reynolds Metals was actively seeking access to Jamaica's bauxite resources, to the consternation of the UK state and British capitalist interests. In 1945 Walter Rice, vice president and general counsel for Reynolds Metals Company (Richmond, Virginia), expressed concern that mining legislation might be enacted in Jamaica "which would require processing of the bauxite either through the alumina stage or through the production of the metal itself, within the British Empire. Any such restriction would be ruinous to us since we are looking to Jamaica as a source of ore in the near future." Rice described Jamaica's bauxite deposits as "one of the most important ore bodies discovered in any part of the world in the past few years. They are particularly important to the United States because of their location" (quoted in Horne 2007, 93). Washington made it clear to the United Kingdom that its Cold War national-security priorities would have to take precedence over any British interest, a message the United Kingdom could hardly disregard (Parker 2002).

American agricultural interests had already secured a firm footing in banana export production in Jamaica. Long before tourism and commercial banking gained hold in the West Indies, American capitalist interests and official US influence had developed in those colonies and in the wider Caribbean. The introduction of American capital into Jamaican export agriculture before World War II helped to modify the production structure of the largely agrarian economy. By 1937, bananas accounted for 55 per cent of the value of domestic exports from Jamaica, with sugar contributing around 18 per cent. By the time Kaiser Alumina and Reynolds Aluminum (American companies) and ALCOA (Canada) had set up their extractive operations in British Guiana and Jamaica, the production structures of those colonies had begun to change, with a small industrial working class emerging (Horne 2007, 11). From 1943 to 1947, around "116,124 agricultural and industrial workers recruited in the West Indies worked in the United States, earning approximately $100,000,000 of which $40,000,000 was remitted to the West Indian states" (Horne 2007, 9).

The construction of American military installations in Antigua, Trinidad and British Guiana during World War II helped to weaken the grip the planter-merchant interests held over the bulk of the population. When "the U.S flag rose in Antigua on the first day of spring 1941", Washington moved "from the wings to center stage in Antiguan life". The American military bases in the Caribbean "immediately became an enormous labor market" (Horne 2007, 52, 53). Horne quotes J.W. Cowling's comments on the harrowing conditions of forced labour in the British colonies during World War II. Cowling contrasted the pervasiveness of anti-forced-labour propaganda that wartime Britain asserted against the impositions that Germany levied against "inhabitants in the occupied territories" with the silence that accompanied "the arbitrary resumption of forced labour . . . (to win the war) in our colonies . . . often for the benefit of private employers". Horne notes that "Washington, in offering wages, represented something of an improvement over London, which at times winked at bondage" (2007, 52, 53; see Cowling 1943, 3).

The spread of American capital in the West Indies helped to widen the general environment in which working-class struggles developed around the nationalist political parties and the labour and trade union movement. The "contradictory impact" of the slow decline of planter dominance in the West Indian colonies "gave a palpable boost to labor organizing and to the idea that the majority should rule", and the introduction of American Jim Crow racial discrimination, "racist militancy" and racial violence into the Caribbean helped to strengthen a preexisting "antiracist and progressive militancy that helped drive labor organizing – and ultimately, independence" (Horne 2007, 12; see Bolland 2001, 479). Horne argues that the experience of West Indians with American Jim Crow contributed to the rise of new forms of resistance among West Indians at home and in the United States, where they joined forces with black Americans in struggles against racialized oppression.

Ellen Wood locates the roots of authoritarianism in the liberal institutions that replaced the absolutism of the ancien régime in early modern Europe. Wood points out that John Locke asserted "the primacy of private property over political jurisdictions in the colonies" and produced a labour theory of property and property rights that rested on extracting and appropriating surplus labour from slaves, indentured workers, other contract labourers and wage labourers, and also served the needs of empire. Locke's labour theory of property justified colonial expropriation and the genocidal removal of the Amerindians and others not simply "by the right to rule, nor even simply the right to appropriate, but by the right, indeed the obligation, to produce exchange-value" which is the life blood of capitalism (Wood 2003, 98, 99).

Marx explained that "the realm of freedom . . . begins only where labour which is determined by necessity and of mundane considerations ceases", which means that freedom "lies beyond the sphere of actual material production" ([1894] 1967, 820). Wood argues that because "capitalist class exploitation takes the form of a market relation, it cannot easily be justified by invoking hierarchies of civic or legal status, such as the relation between feudal lords and serfs. Instead, the relation between capital and labour is typically presented as a contractual relation between legally free and equal individuals" (2003, 100–101). In fact, "reliance on purely economic modes of exploitation, and the suppression of extra-economic identities and hierarchies . . . made capitalism compatible with ideologies of civic freedom and equality in a way that non-capitalist class systems never were". Such liberal ideologies "can even be mobilized to justify the capitalist system, as the epitome of freedom and equality". Inevitably, however, "when ideologies of civic freedom and equality confronted the realities of imperialism and slavery, the effect was to place a new premium on racism, as a substitute for all the extra-economic identities that capitalism had displaced" (Wood 2003, 100–101). Kenan Malik clarifies the problem with the untenable assertion by Enlightenment liberals that race is the source of inequality in capitalist societies. Malik responded that it is the economic (capitalist) organization of society that leads to the racial classification of humankind. Malik said, "It is not 'race' that gives rise to inequality but inequality that gives rise to race", the point being that the "ambiguous attitude to race . . . arises from an ambivalent attitude to equality" (1996, 39).

SELF-GOVERNMENT AND ECONOMIC RELATIONS BETWEEN US AND BRITISH CARIBBEAN TERRITORIES

In 1947 the US Congress passed the National Security Act and the Taft-Hartley Act, two laws that were strategic in shaping the character of the Cold War project and carried negative implications for working-class struggles in the United States and internationally, including territories that were embarking on decolonization as well as newly independent states. Other shaping factors included the crisis of European imperialism, the postwar geopolitical impact and influence of the Soviet Union in Central Europe and beyond, the upsurge in national liberation struggles in the "Third World", and the United States-led strategy to intensify the internationalization of capital and capitalism (Arrighi 1982). The United States went about building up the geopolitical institutions and multilateral organizations to give international capitalism a post-imperialist character.

The Inter-American Treaty of Reciprocal Mutual Assistance (Rio Treaty) of 1947 was part of the international security arrangements the United States forged: in Europe (the North Atlantic Treaty Organization), the Middle East and west Asia (the Central Treaty Organization), Southeast Asia Treaty Organization, and Oceania (ANZUS: Australia, New Zealand and United States). Those security arrangements are best understood by looking beyond the ideological rhetoric about containing or rolling back international communism. In Latin America, the United States conjured up images of an existential Soviet threat: in 1947 the Central Intelligence Agency claimed exaggeratedly that "Communist undercover penetration of strategic sectors of the various economies is already such as to permit the USSR, by merely giving the necessary orders (1) to withhold from the US its normal peacetime flow of strategic raw materials from Latin America, and (2) to precipitate economic crises in several key Latin American countries" (CIA 1947, quoted in Westad 2005, 146).

The military security pacts the United States organized were designed to control or defeat a range of oppositional forces ranging from nationalist to revolutionary and communist entities that would seek to control or roll back the spread of international capitalism and its geopolitical arrangements – including Iran (1952), Korea (1950s), British Guiana (1953), Guatemala (1954), Cuba (from 1959), and Vietnam and Southeast Asia (1960s–70s). Large-scale West Indian immigration to the United Kingdom had a positive impact on the colonies in terms of foreign-exchange receipts and family life via remittances; blunted the sharp economic and social edges of population growth and high unemployment; helped to improve the standard of living for many; and warded off political instability. The capital accumulation strategy advocated by W. Arthur Lewis – dubbed by his New World critics "industrialization by invitation" (see Watson 2008c) – favoured light manufacturing, tourism, and commercial banking and non-bank financial activities. The US farm labour programme created temporary jobs for contract (agricultural) workers from the West Indies to work in the United States.

When the Federation of the West Indies came into effect in 1958, US assistance programmes to West Indian countries had expanded to a reasonable extent (Parker 2002; Horne 2007). The growth of labour unions and political parties in the West Indies had the effect of compounding the fragmentation of the working class and its political movements that the capitalist division of labour initiates. Nigel Bolland argues that in the West Indian territories

> political and ideological pressures sharply divided many labour move-
> ments and political parties supported by labour organizations. Most cat-

astrophic, from the perspective of the growing labour movement and the struggle for democracy and independence in the British Caribbean, was its effect on the CLC . . . which seemed to offer the possibility of a popular basis for a federation of socialist-oriented nations. Within a few years the CLC was eviscerated by internal rivalries fed by the Cold War. (2001, 474)

The classic case was the form that labour politics assumed in Jamaica, with the Bustamante Industrial Trade Union allied with the JLP, and the National Workers Union in alliance with the PNP.

The fracturing of the working-class movement in the West Indies along trade union and political party lines was influenced by the approach the British Trades Union Congress adopted to deal with labour organizing that extended to waging class struggle. The Trades Union Congress approach was compatible with the interests of certain middle-strata leaders in the West Indies – men like Grantley Adams (Barbados), Albert Gomes (Trinidad) and Vivian Henry (Jamaica) – who fought to keep politics (political parties and control of state power) and economics (trade unions and economic concerns of workers and capital accumulation) separate nominally in organizational and institutional terms (Bolland 2001, 476–77, 478). The strategy rested on a division of labour that disarmed the working class, reinforced the power of capital in the state and economy, and assumed that formal political freedom and juridical equality under the bourgeois democratic revolution represented the endpoint of the realization of freedom and democracy in capitalist society. Those leaders seemed unmindful that under liberal capitalism, political freedom coincides with economic dependence and inequality for the working class, which is compelled to reproduce capital – its opposite – as the necessary precondition of its own material reproduction.

Richard Hart understood that the approach of the Colonial Office to West Indian federation was designed to reproduce the colonies as suppliers of mainly primary commodities to the UK market. Bolland emphasizes that the labour and political forces that "constituted the CLC in its first years represented a socialist spectrum from social democrats of Fabian complexion to Marxists who wanted working-class control and regional economic planning", a vision that helped to shape the idea for a united "regional labour movement . . . connected . . . with the aspiration towards democracy, independence and a socialist Caribbean federation" (2001, 480–81).

The United States took the initiative to see that the training of technocrats, labour leaders, police and other military and security personnel and others took place increasingly within new bilateral and multilateral arrangements. CADORIT[5] – the Caribbean division of the Latin American Regional Organization of Workers – began to have a decisive impact on the development of labour unions such as the BWU and others across the West Indies and beyond (Watson 2004). The United States was not interested in replicating the old European-dominated order based on inter-imperialist rivalry: Washington integrated the former imperialist states and their dependencies into a new US-led multilateral hegemonic framework.

THE COLD WAR PROJECT: GEOPOLITICAL STRATEGY, CAPITAL ACCUMULATION AND SELF-DETERMINATION

Thomas Hammond argues that the Cold War between the communist world and the non-communist world was an "intense conflict especially between the Soviet Union and the United States that started after World War II". Hammond notes that it was "called 'cold' because it . . . involved fighting between Soviet and American troops by almost every means other than direct armed conflict" and the use of nuclear weapons. Hammond adds that it

> involved massive propaganda war, sometimes becoming quite virulent. It has . . . meant a frantic race to see which side could develop the most terrible weapons of mass destruction. The Cold War has seen competition throughout the world from friends and allies . . . It has been . . . a war on almost all fronts, a war for influence throughout the world in which both sides have used radio broadcasts, propaganda pamphlets, espionage, subversion, and sabotage,

as well as a "war among historians" and other scholars and intellectuals "over how the Cold War got started, whether or not it was inevitable, and . . . who bears the main responsibility for starting it" (1982, 3, 4).

George Kennan, architect of the US Cold War strategy and a US ambassador to the Soviet Union, insisted that the expansion and strengthening of US power and security interests worldwide via the Cold War project required the United States to "cease to talk about vague and unreal objectives such as human rights, the raising of living standards, and democratization". Kennan declared that the day was "not far off when we are going to have to deal in straight power concepts. . . . It is better to have a strong regime in power than a liberal government if it is indulgent and relaxed and penetrated by Communists" (George Kennan, February 1947, quoted in Landau 1987, 33; see Barkawi and Laffey 1999). In Kennan's words, bourgeois democratic values like freedom, justice and individual rights must always be subsumed under US national security priorities (see Neocleous 2008).

Kennan made his assertions at precisely the moment when a large portion of global humanity was raising its expectations of self-determination, freedom and independence under the banner of sovereign autonomy. Kennan's writings on the Cold War cast security and justice in binary terms, with the security of the US state taking precedence over justice and human security. The bulk of American scholarship on the Cold War and US security issues "attempted to delegitimize domestic Third World revolutions or radical movements on the grounds that they were Soviet-inspired or Soviet-sponsored" (Westad 2005, 3). When stripped of its ideological veneer about a struggle between liberal freedom and totalitarian unfreedom, the Cold War could be seen as a US$6 trillion project the United States executed to restructure, expand and solidify the economic, geopolitical, jurisprudential and ideological dimensions of international capitalism under its hegemonic guidance.

I refer to the Cold War as a project because it was not limited to a series of discrete events or programmes or policies, but was an integral part of a much larger planned and executed strategic process to remake the postwar international order in keeping with the hegemonic vision of the United States. The notion that the Cold War was essentially an expression of interstate competition between two "superpowers" remains an enduring state-centric oversimplification. The Cold War architects[6] emphasized ideology to mask the real aims and motives behind it, in a move that was intended to shift attention away from the reality of international class struggles and to interstate conflict, with states misrepresented as conscious human actors.

In Odd Arne Westad's view, the American "empire of liberty" and the Soviet "empire of justice" were based on deeply held ideological views and "criticisms of early twentieth-century European imperialist practices". Westad insists that "some of the extraordinary brutality of Cold War interventions . . . can only be explained by Soviet and American identification with the people they sought to defend" (2005, 5, 38, 72). Under the "empire of liberty" philosophy, freedom, liberty, democracy and justice presuppose the right to exploit, which rests on the subsumption of labour under capital and compels labour to produce capital, whereas the "empire of justice" anticipates bringing to an end the need for labour to produce capital, which is its opposite. Marx pointedly observed that freedom for the working class and society at large commences only where the law of value and necessity cease to determine human possibilities ([1894] 1967, 820).

The United States had no intention of leaving it to West Indian leaders, who were elected on the basis of universal adult suffrage, to devise and implement development programmes to improve the lot of the working-class masses and determine the national and international priorities of public policy. From the outset the United States conflated its material and geopolitical interests with a self-serving, moral self-image of American exceptionalism, to which it imputed the grand myth of divine providence to justify a strategy for simultaneously ruling at home and abroad. The United States consistently masks its use of force and violence with a moral justification drawn from the neo-Jeffersonian theme of the "empire of liberty" and from the Wilsonian "crusading mentality and self-righteousness" (Layne 2006, 132; see Marqusee 2007, 115–16; Marqusee 2003, 39; Harvey 1989, 35; Westad 2005, 397).

The success of the project of the postwar internationalization of capital required societies undergoing decolonization to adjust their development strategies, expectations and aspirations to the requirements of the Cold War project. It imposed liberal international discipline on the West Indian political parties, governments and the labour and trade union organizations and their activities which extended to the working class and the exercise of state power. Cold War notions of freedom and democracy were employed to determine which governments qualified to borrow in the international financial market, to promote "development" based on the priorities of private capital accumulation (Westad 2005, 152–57; see Parker 2002; Robinson 2004).

The Kennan formula was part of the Truman Doctrine of containment and counter-revolution (see Jagan 1972). The promises the decolonizing elites made to the colonized populations in the West Indies in return for supporting the populist, nationalist agendas they trumpeted had to satisfy Washington's imperatives of security and capital accumulation. Liberal zones of peace and non-liberal zones of war, which characterize the Western-dominated territorially fragmented world, are mutually constitutive of the international capitalist world order (Barkawi and Laffey 1999, 422).

Philip Hewitt-Myring, the press officer for the British section of the CC, meetings held in St Thomas, US Virgin Islands, claimed that the Americans hatched a conspiracy against the British. Hewitt-Myring accused members of the American section of the CC of engaging in "conduct that had so often proved to be due simply to native boorishness or mere ineptitude", purveyors of "silly little deceits that were constantly practised by the United States Section". Hewitt-Myring was suspicious that the Americans would try to use the CC to insist on the decoloniza-tion of Europe's Caribbean colonies by invoking chapter 11 of article 73 of the UN Charter – "Declaration Regarding Non-Self-Governing Ter-ritories". Charles Taussig, who headed the American section of the CC, read from a speech by President Truman that emphasized US support for the UN Charter to see to the "progressive development of the peoples of the region in . . . economic, educational, and social matters". Hewitt-Myring claims that soon after he met Charles Taussig in Washington he "began to realize that . . . Taussig had an acute dislike of Britain and all she stood for".[7]

The hegemonic post-imperialist character of the US strategy could be discerned in the lead role the United States played in developing the postwar multilateral strategy for managing the international "system" –

notably the Atlantic Charter; the Bretton Woods institutions (the United Nations, the International Monetary Fund and World Bank); and the regional security pacts.[8] The United States used the Taft-Hartley Act (1947), the National Security Act (1947), McCarthyism and the leadership of the American Federation of Labor and Congress of Industrial Organizations to batter the American working class and combat labour radicalism at home and to wage hostilities against anti-colonial and anti-imperialist nationalist and revolutionary assertiveness abroad (Radosh 1969).

Sir John Mordecai argued that the West Indian leaders discovered that they could use federation "in order to realize their nationalist aspirations and were willing to pay something for it" (1968, 33; see Hart 1998, 140–51 passim). He noted, however, that the Kingston Labour Congress of 1947 "made federation its sole theme and agreed unanimously upon a memorandum and a comprehensively outlined draft federal constitution, for presentation at Montego Bay. The memorandum demanded 'a Federation providing for responsible government equivalent to Dominion Status'", and a "Federation at Dominion status from the start" was what "Manley, Adams and Gomes had solemnly agreed beforehand to press for resolution, which others were also pledged to support" (Mordecai 1968, 35).

Secretary of State for the Colonies Arthur Creech Jones, however, summoned the 1947 Montego Bay meeting (Mordecai 1968, 34) for reasons that had more to do with imperatives of the unfolding Cold War project than with integrating the West Indies into a form of closer association that could lead to a potentially viable federation. The Cold War project came to rest on a formidable combination of forces for which the West Indian radical and progressive forces were no match. Mordecai identified two profound ways the change would affect the situation. He notes that it

> began to erode one of the principal reasons why the political leaders wanted federation. They had assumed that self-government would not be given to each island separately, but would be conceded only to a federation. Hence part of the emotion attached to federation was due to its being seen as a necessary prelude to self-government. As the leaders now began to find that they could have self-government in their own legislatures, federation was not so necessary.

Substantively, "federation began to be seen as an obstacle to the local leader fully controlling the affairs of his own island". In effect, the "desire for self-government . . . began to work against federation, instead of in its favour" (1968, 32–33).

By the early 1950s the West Indian nationalist leaders were sceptical of the prospect of private foreign capital playing the dominant role in financing the economic modernization of the territories, on the ground that this would deepen imperialist control over the region. They preferred to borrow from multilateral lending institutions like the World Bank, unaware that such institutions were created to serve as bulwarks of international capitalism and to bring the priorities of newly independent states and colonies in line with its imperatives. Che Guevara delivered a speech in 1965 titled "The Death of Imperialism and the Birth of a Moral World" at the Afro-Asian Solidarity Conference in Algiers, in which he argued that the anti-imperialist struggle was "not unconnected with the struggle against backwardness and poverty. Both are stages in a single journey toward the creation of a new society that is rich and just at the same time" (quoted by Westad 2005, 398).

Guevara stressed that it would be necessary to employ the most advanced technology possible in order to "win the battle of development". He added, "We cannot start at the bottom of humanity's long ascent from feudalism to the atomic age of automation. . . . There must be a great leap forward . . . in the great factories and also in a suitably developed agriculture" (quoted by Westad 2005, 398). Guevara appreciated that the post-capitalist transformation of the world could not be achieved by maintaining the backwardness of the productive forces, poverty and injustice in the Afro-Asian countries. In contrast, the economic modernization the United States and the European powers had in mind for the Caribbean region did not involve a comprehensive transformation of the productive powers of labour and of industry, science, and technology. The Caribbean area was being integrated into the postwar international division of labour as producers of mainly raw materials to complement the requirements of the international capitalist accumulation process, while ideologically exploiting a so-called Soviet threat, in effect reinforcing the combined and unequal development that is characteristic of the fundamental capitalist process (Mészáros 2008, 120; Westad 2005, 403; Anievas and Nişancioğlu 2015; Pradella 2015). Westad argues against the neo-Wilsonian tendency to conflate American "power with morality", which is a deceptive practice that has been dominant among scholars who are in the habit of equating the United States with "a force for good in the world" and concluding "that an inherent morality is both the cause and principle for America's international role". Such "a near-sighted conclusion can only be explained in ideological terms – the identification of the vision of the future that Washington represents is so strong that the moral qualities of that vision outshine all other aspects". The fact that the "United States . . . is an immensely attractive society for many people around the world does not excuse the violence with which it has attempted to influence the world, especially in Asia, Africa, and Latin America" (2005, 403–4; see Thompson 1981, 6–7). Violence is the armour of bourgeois democracy, as coercion is the armour of liberal hegemony.

THE CRISIS OF IMPERIALISM, THE COLD WAR AND THE DEMISE OF THE CLC

The split in the CLC between 1948 and 1952 resulted from a deliberate political and ideological orchestration that was designed to weaken, isolate and defeat the fledgling progressive forces in the West Indian labour and working-class movement, from Jamaica to British Guiana, a development that severely reduced and compromised any role the working class would play in the decolonization process. The divisions within the CLC were compounded by inter-territorial bickering, attacks by the right-wing types like Albert Gomes (Trinidad and Tobago), who accused the CLC of being infested with communists and of being a "totalitarian" force arrayed against freedom, and the lack of financial resources (Horne 2007, 11, 12–13; Drayton 2014, 122). The creation of the Cold War–inspired ICFTU had the intended effect of weakening and demoralizing the WFTU and deepening the fissures in the international working-class and trade union movement.

The WFTU was dominated "at the executive level . . . by British and

French unions" that worked systematically to subordinate the needs and interests of colonized peoples to those of a decaying imperialist system (Bolland 2001, 490). The WFTU also followed the liberal strategy of separating economics from politics in the European trade union movement, a move that also extended to its proposals for change in the colonies. The rise of the ICFTU confirmed that the European bourgeoisie remained concerned that their trade union movements had failed to destroy the intense resistance in the colonies to separating politics from the labour movement. In 1949 the Colonial Office instructed the governors of the West Indies to take the necessary steps, including the provision of financial assistance, to steer the "Colonial trade union bodies . . . where possible to the new non-Communist Organization" – the ICFTU (Bolland 2001, 490–91).

The eight West Indian delegates who attended the ICFTU conference in London in December 1949 represented around 23,000 members of trade unions which happened to be the largest and most powerful unions in the British Caribbean. The delegates included Adams (Barbados), Middleton (Belize), Chase (British Guiana), Bradshaw (St Kitts), Mitchell (Grenada), LeBlanc (Dominica), Charles (St Lucia) and Alexander of the St Lucia Seamen and Waterfront Workers Trade Union (Bolland 2001, 497). Their presence and participation signalled the open embrace of anti-communism by the West Indian trade union and political leadership, and their effective integration into an emerging "Cold War globalization" (Watson 2004 passim).

Soon thereafter the US-sponsored and dominated CADORIT began to run offices in the West Indies and call the shots in setting the priorities and direction for the trade union movement and realign broader working-class priorities with trade union democracy. The link between the Latin American Regional Organization of Workers and CADORIT was forged by Serafino Romualdi through the American Federation of Labor, with the aim of destroying the CLC. Grantley Adams and Frank Walcott, leaders of the BWU, consciously participated in helping to bring CADORIT into the West Indies to help promote anti-communism in the working class and trade union movement in all the territories (Watson 2004). Largely, the leading civil society entities in the West Indies – the middle-strata-dominated political parties, the media, religious bodies, most of the trade unions – and the colonial governments, with the exception of the Jagans and the PPP in British Guiana – were relentless in their condemnation of any labour unions and leaders that continued their affiliation with the CLC and the WFTU.

In Jamaica, Norman Manley formed the National Workers Union not simply to compete with the Bustamante Industrial Trade Union, but to finish off the Jamaica Trade Union Council, a move that brought him support from Adams, who was instrumental in facilitating the admission of the National Workers Union into the ICFTU (Hoyos 1974, 177; Bolland 2001, 503). The support they received from the American Federation of Labor, the Latin American Regional Organization of Workers and the British Trades Union Congress bolstered the confidence with which Adams and Manley acted to complete the destruction of the CLC in the service of advancing anti-working-class Cold War politics in the West Indies.

Richard Hart and a number of his colleagues launched a last-ditch effort to create a new confederation of British Caribbean trade unions that would "embrace all unions in the region regardless of their international affiliations" with the WFTU or the ICFTU (Bolland 2001, 505, 506). In response to the request from Hart and the other CLC stalwarts to form such an organization, the anti-communist and anti-working-class Adams (and his cohorts) insisted that the ICFTU was the only legitimate international affiliation with which he was prepared to collaborate, considering that CADORIT had set up operations in Barbados in 1952. The haemorrhaging of the CLC continued apace – the few remaining WFTU-affiliated unions withdrew; what remained of the CLC's leadership dwindled; the organization found it increasingly difficult to raise funds to continue its work; and it became impossible to organize any activities to bring the membership together to address policy issues and plan political strategy. The final shot across the bow of the CLC was the launching of the American-led Cold War offensive against the PPP government and the suspension of the Constitution of Guyana in 1953. Bolland describes the offensive against British Guiana as the "defeat of the last left leaders who had supported Hart in the CLC. The CLC became defunct without having been formally dissolved" (2001, 506).

The leadership of the political parties and trade unions in the West Indies had endorsed and accepted the UK prescriptions in 1948 for self-government and federation. By 1952 the CLC model for a federation with a strong and sovereign central government gave way to a model that was based on the primacy of territorially based collective identity (insular nationalist self-government) which was consistent with UK and US security interests. It therefore became much easier to apply the anti-communist litmus test to restrict travel by the "left labour"-oriented political leaders in the West Indian territories. The anti-communist liberal momentum intensified with the banning of certain individuals and literature deemed to be of communist and Marxist persuasion. The battered CLC was gasping for its last breath just as the McCarthyite witch-hunt was exacting a heavy toll on the progressive New York-based United Caribbean American Council, which played an important role in financing CLC activities and providing other support (Bolland 2001, 499–500).

In Jamaica, the PNP took advantage of anti-communist hysteria to expel its left wing, drawing clear lines between the Fabian socialists (social democrats) and the right-wing allies on the one hand and the more Marxist-oriented left on the other. Bolland notes that certain West Indian politicians and union leaders added a twist to their habitual authoritarianism by going so far as to "label their opponents as communists" to get rid of them and assert their anti-communist bona fides. Many progressive labour leaders tried to defend the rights of those deemed subversives; however, the right-wing labour leaders succeeded in splitting the labour movement in a move that set the stage for the destruction of the CLC (2001, 501).

Labour politics in the West Indies acquired a political character that rested on the subordination of the trade unions and the working class to the political parties and private capital, a peculiar relationship that bolstered the position of the party leadership and union leadership at the expense of the working class. As the Cold War intensified, political parties from Jamaica to British Guiana redoubled their efforts to reduce the labour unions and their political work to their appendages. The collapse of the CLC and the "purge of the left wing of the PNP" in Jamaica in 1952 reflected the impact the Cold War was already having on the broad spectrum of working-class life in the West Indies (Bolland 2001, 495, 497). It thus became open season on workers from other territories, who were targeted as illegal immigrants and accused of depriving nationals of jobs and other services[9] – a move that shifted appropriate attention from capitalism and its contradictions.

At the time when Richard Hart was declared an "undesirable visitor" to Trinidad and Tobago he "had already been designated representative of the Federated Workers Trade Union in arbitration proceedings which were pending". Trinidad and Tobago's governor did not issue an explanation for designating Hart an "undesirable visitor" and the action he took to deny him entry. The governor claimed he was acting "according to law and in the best interest of the country" (Bolland 2001, 495). Hart had been invited by the Trinidad Trades Union Council to participate as its assessor in an arbitration tribunal which was set up to deal with a dispute in the coconut industry. The governor's autocratic way of dealing with interterritorial travel by certain individuals was indicative of the contempt in which the leaders of the Cold War project held the Universal Declaration of Human Rights and its human-rights provisions.

There is no point, however, in attempting to exaggerate the CLC's potential to realize its goals in the unfavourable environment in which it had to operate (Bolland 2001, 473–509; Horne 2007 passim). It was not possible for the dedicated and progressive forces in the West Indies to use the CLC to construct viable socialist societies in the region, for reasons that included chronic economic, political and other constraints during the time of the CLC, with or without the destabilization and frontal opposition from the Cold War project.[10] In 1948, Grantley Adams, leader of the BLP and the BWU and a founding member of the CLC, was selected by the UK government as one of its delegates to a special session of the United Nations in Paris. Adams went on the attack as Britain's mouthpiece to defend a dying British imperialism and denounce the Soviet Union, communism and the progressive and revolutionary forces in the anti-imperialist labour movements in the colonies. British secretary of state for the colonies Arthur Creech Jones expressed confidence that Adams could be trusted to defend the British position on decolonization (Watson 2004).

The Fabian Society responded enthusiastically to Adams's selection to join the British delegation, citing his leadership of the Barbados House of Assembly, his stature in the CLC, his expressed opinion that his inclusion in the delegation confirmed "Britain's willingness to give colonials more say in their own affairs" and his confidence in the Labour government's readiness to "grant complete responsibility as soon as the colonies are in a position to take it". The Fabian Society's statement stressed that Adams was "anxious . . . to avoid increased intervention from the outside and is implacably opposed to all attempts to place the colonies under the supervision of the United Nations". Adams also expressed strong scepticism about the "practical contributions" of the United Nations to the "advancement and welfare of the Trust Territory peoples", implying that his motive was to protect the colonies from the negative impact of Cold War power politics (Hoyos 1974, 133–34, 138). Adams openly supported keeping the colonies and especially the working classes under the yoke of a dying imperialism: his utterance betrayed his reactionary, anti-universalist outlook and delighted his handlers at Whitehall (Bolland 2001, 486).

Adams spoke disparagingly about the reactions of his anti-imperialist critics to his shocking and disreputable performance in Paris (Bolland 2001, 487); he was far more interested in bolstering his personal and political legacy with the knighthood that the United Kingdom would soon bestow upon him, in 1952. His confidence was boosted also by the enthusiastic welcome he received when he returned to Barbados from the Paris meeting. Gerald Horne says, "Three columns of trade unionists formed a guard of honor at the airport, and on the triumphal procession from the airport to Bridgetown . . . the path was lined with cheering masses. Squads of bicycles led the way and more than fifty cars followed" (2007, 111). Adams's biographer, F.A. Hoyos, says there were "cheers of thousands and tens of thousands shouted hosannas". There was participation by a cross-section of the population: "at the Garrison Savannah . . . the crowds became so dense that the procession was brought to a halt" because "the streets at time became impassable" (1963, 141).

Whatever sense of pride and euphoria those who shouted their "hosannas" in celebration of Adams's defence of imperialism might have felt about his performance in Paris, they hardly understood that his defence of the "moral epistemology" of British and European imperialism would bolster Britain's self-appointed right to inflict unmitigated violence on Kenya's Kikuyu people, who were fighting for the right to control their land in the Mau Mau rebellion (Elkins 2005). Adams's Paris speech also emboldened the United Kingdom to disregard the 1948 Universal Declaration of Human Rights.

Richard Hart responded to Adams's performance in Paris by drawing attention to the significance of the struggle for self-government in the West Indies and expressing disappointment at Adams's betrayal of the "workers' movements in other parts of the colonial empire where the hand of imperialism is . . . falling more heavily and viciously than anything we can conceive from our experience". Hart added that the "President of the Caribbean Labour Congress has, on one of the most important issues of the time, thrown away the golden opportunity to be the champion of the cause of colonial peoples everywhere struggling for freedom" (quoted in Bolland 2001, 487; originally in *CLC Monthly Bulletin*, September–October 1948). As expected, the Trinidadian Albert Gomes defended Adams by red-baiting Hart, accusing him of exhibiting Nazi tendencies and reminding him that he was "Secretary of a Labour Congress, not head of the Politburo or butcher of a concentration camp". Gomes did not spare the National Association for the Advancement of Colored People (NAACP) and the American Committee of West Indian Federation in New York, which had provided unstinting financial, moral and political support to the CLC and the decolonization movement in the West Indies (Horne 2007, 113, 114).

The British Empire was in permanent retreat; however, Anglophiles like Adams, Gomes and Bustamante waxed nostalgic in appealing to colonials to rally around the Union Jack. Gomes said, "We need the greatest possible solidarity . . . between Britain, her Commonwealth and her colonies, together with her allies, in order to meet the Soviet threat of slavery disguised as salvation." He asserted that the success of the CLC would require "an effective insecticide with which to deal with the verminous elements" because "there is no place for Communism in the West Indies". Grenada's T.A. Marryshow came to Hart's defence by reminding Gomes that he had "no following whatsoever among the masses" (see Horne 2007, 113, 114). Adams occasionally criticized white supremacy, of which he was a victim in Barbados, without providing an informed critique of the pernicious ideology.[11]

In contrast with Adams's way of dealing with racial discrimination and class exploitation in Barbados, Errol Barrow was forthright. He equated the "vested interests" in Barbados – a reference to white economic interests – with "mercenaries", and "white bastards in the Congo who shot down black people". Journalist Willie Burke summarized Barrow's position in the following terms: "The people in Barbados who had money had no cultural standards . . . and they had no use for nine-tenths of the people of the island. . . . He said they felt they were in a position of prestige entrenched by the mother country which was always ready to come to their rescue" (Burke 1966).[12] In his "No Loitering on Colonial Premises" speech at Lancaster House in 1966, Barrow reminded the British that their "colonial system was designed not to promote free institutions, but to safeguard imperial interests" (see Holder 2007, 67). Barrow was self-confident and did not cower in the face of the racism and other obstacles presented by the white capitalist forces that dominated Barbadian society. His class background, his first-hand experience of participating in World War II and his legal training undergirded his resolve often to speak unreservedly where Adams and many others would defer.

Adams joined Albert Gomes in red-baiting Hart by accusing him of being a mouthpiece for Moscow; he also insisted that it was time to rescue the CLC ship of West Indian labour from Moscow's "cabin boy", whom he described as "this wretched, rash, intruding – Comrade" who was acting in a "completely unwise, precipitous and irresponsible" manner (Horne 2007, 112, 113). Adams's defence of the "moral epistemology" of imperialism was informed partly by the white supremacist notion that decolonization without British supervision would be disastrous for colonized people. Adams knew he could count on support and backing from Norman Manley and the PNP and Bustamante and the JLP (Horne 2007, 112, 116; see Mordecai 1968, 34).

Paul Blanshard from the US Consulate in Kingston compared Busta-mante to the "fascist stereotype in many particulars". Blanshard found "the reaction of the upper classes of Jamaica to Bustamante . . . quite similar to the early reaction of European upper classes to Hitler and Mussolini" and argued that "Bustamante's incipient alliance with the upper classes could easily be transformed overnight into a fascist dictatorship" (Horne 2007, 116). Bustamante's anti-communist and anti-working-class approach was legendary in Jamaica, and his heavy-handed style[13] was characteristically authoritarian and resonated not only with Washington's hostility toward progressive labour and trade union politics in the West Indies, but also with its scepticism toward the working-class politics and labour struggles that it criminalized and treated harshly as a rule. As US-based capital continued to make further inroads in Jamaica and the wider Caribbean, it was necessary to find ways to discipline the unruly agents of labour and the working class at large in the West Indies, as part of the process of making the region available to and safe for capital (Bolland 2001, 487; see Robinson 2004).

Substantively, the West Indian decolonizing elite did not base its ideological positions on any disappointment with the Communist International, with special reference to racism or the failure of the Soviet Union to defend the interests of the working class, broader anti-imperialist struggles in the Caribbean or the colonial regions at large. Organic intellectuals like George Padmore and others who broke with the international communist movement, or Marcus Garvey, who rejected socialism as a constraint on human freedom and extolled the virtues of Christianity, were equally dismissed or rejected by the likes of Grantley Adams. In fact, Adams, Manley, Bustamante and others saw Cheddi Jagan, Richard Hart and their allies as misguided communists who were hostile to the liberal international (Cold War) order which they defended. The British warned West Indian trade unionists and politicians from as early as the 1930s to be wary of the European Left and the Soviet Union. As early as the 1920s and 1930s Adams insisted that socialism had nothing to offer the West Indies, and he derided Charles Duncan O'Neal and the DL and kept his distance from the organization and its members in the House of Assembly. He did not approve of the strike as a political weapon that the working class could or should use to force capitalists to negotiate over wages, working conditions or any other valid grievances.

The constraints the Cold War imposed on the space that was available to West Indian leaders to act in the world are best understood as part of a much larger global process. Part of the aim of this study is to expose the pitfalls of nationalism and nationalist consciousness that read sovereignty, states and power in technical terms as ends in themselves. In contrast, I understand those forms as expressions of social relations that are part of the larger struggle for a "universal history" of which the nation-state is a part rather than a definitive outcome. To repeat Buck-Morss, what is needed is a "humanistic project" that contributes to a sense of "collective, political participation" that imagines a future beyond "custom, or ethnicity, religion or race" or nationhood and that "chips away at the barriers to conceptual understanding and the limits of moral imagination that wall off the wide horizon of the present" (Buck-Morss 2009, ix, x). It is imperative to think much more critically and imaginatively about the deterministic ways in which nationalist consciousness constrains the discourse on independence and sovereignty in the Caribbean.

LABOUR, DECOLONIZATION AND RACE-INFLECTED CLASS STRUGGLES

Jason Parker notes that an important feature of anti-colonial, populist-oriented struggles in the West Indies was the way race, class, nationalism and communism intersected (2002, 334). US consular staff in Jamaica linked the PNP and its supporters to communism, and the State Department advised its diplomatic and consular officials to "be alert to the 'distinction between Social Democratic [sic] and Communists'" (Horne 2007, 53). Leaders of the Caribbean People's Alliance (CPA) and the Caribbean Christian Socialist Party (CCSP) in Barbados declared that they were prepared to wear the label of "communist" that the colonial state authorities pinned on them for fighting against exploitation at home and publicly condemning apartheid and the repressive and racist policies the British adopted in crushing the Mau Mau rebellion in Kenya (Furedi 1998).

Washington responded to West Indian labour leaders flaunting what it considered to be "symbols of wartime Soviet solidarity. . . . Much of this concern . . . focused on Jamaica which contained some of the most militant unions and most resolute Marxists and had the added advantage of having one of their compatriots – Ferdinand Smith – serving as second in command of one of the most powerful U.S. unions, the National Maritime Union, which had true transcontinental reach" (Horne 2007, 105–6; see Munroe 1978). US consular staff in Jamaica reported to Washington in white supremacist ways on the nature and extent of what they saw as "anti-white" sentiment among the population and felt strongly about the prospect of "very serious trouble . . . definitely brewing among a very large percentage of the native population". The growth of black racial consciousness and pride and any semblance of black criticism of racialized class exploitation and oppression were partly in response to the embedded white supremacist, Jim Crow outlook of US consular officials, as reflected in the tone of dispatches from British territories to the State Department (Horne 2007, 53, 89–90).

Frank Furedi argues that his examination of anti-colonial and anti-racist struggles in the British Caribbean territories of Barbados, Antigua, British Guiana, Jamaica, and Trinidad and Tobago did not unearth any evidence of blacks trying to pull down whites or acting as jealous colonial subjects. Furedi suggests that the colonial authorities and their organic intellectuals fixated on liberal themes of race and skin colour, routinely blaming the "native people" and the "native" press for whipping up anti-white racial sentiment. Furedi concludes that the Anglo-American strategy equated the "key problem facing American diplomacy" in the Caribbean in reference to the crisis in British Guiana with a problem of racial consciousness (1998, 202–5 passim; Horne 2007, 95), which was symptomatic of a highly subjective liberal (psychological) reading and interpretation of a much deeper structural problem (Reed Jr 2013). London and Washington were also deeply concerned about the political implications of the impact of the UNIA movement in the Caribbean (James 1998). The United States equated anti-racist and anti-capitalist reactions by colonial people with communist-inspired designs, and portrayed revolutionary struggles as irrational, undermined their legitimacy and subjected them to ridicule. The liberal Anglo-American psychological approach to addressing racist oppression under international capitalism was intentionally designed to reduce oppression to a residual psychological factor that lacked any historically rooted and mediated material connections with liberalism and capitalism (see Reed Jr 2013).

The roots of West Indian progressive organizing and activist political work in the African diaspora predate the Cold War, as there were "progressive links" between Caribbean nationals in the United States and their homelands a while before the CLC was founded. Gerald Horne points out that

> Caribbean migrants raised thousands of dollars for the financially strapped CLC and constituted a domestic US lobby on their behalf. Not least because of the economic misery that gripped the islands during the 1930s – which also propelled a wave of strikes – migrants from the British West Indies poured into Harlem . . . where they organized the Jamaica Progressive League, the West Indies National Council, and other groups that took a decided interest in their homeland. (2007, 4; see also Chamberlain 2010, 157–58; James 1998)

As early as 1927 the NAACP journal implored the West Indian people to build an earnest movement to federate the islands. When Paul Robeson visited Jamaica in 1948, he attracted an estimated fifty thousand people to one concert. Robeson told the Jamaicans assembled there that "nothing could be more important than the establishment of an independent Negro country to the south of us" as it could "help show the way to Negro peoples in Africa" and impress upon "Negro Americans" to "join with their West Indian brothers" (*Daily Gleaner*, 10 September 1947, quoted in Horne 2007, 4),[14] thereby signalling his anti-white-supremacist, internationalist values. West Indian migrants in the United States "were a vector for Bolshevism, influencing the Communist International on the so-called Negro Question, not least since West Indians were 'simultaneously more nationalistic, class conscious and internationally minded than were American-born blacks'" (Horne 2007, 5; see James 1998; Reid [1939] 1970).

Horne notes that the "radicalism in Harlem and the British West Indies was mutually reinforcing and it was Washington's task to disrupt if not quarantine this trend". Washington was deeply concerned about the work that certain "Negro Communists" in places like Harlem were doing "for the establishment of a Negro-dominated Socialist Commonwealth in the British West Indies". The United States was very troubled that the NAACP "asked its venerable . . . founder and self-proclaimed socialist, W.E.B. Du Bois, to return as a kind of foreign minister to coordinate the group's activity in the realm of global affairs, notably leading a massive push for decolonization in places like the British West Indies" (Horne 2007, 106–7). The international parameters of the concept of a socialist Caribbean Commonwealth that Grantley Adams introduced at the CLC founding conference in 1945[15] in Barbados seemed to have been prefigured in African diaspora progressive discourses and action.

The expansion and deepening of capitalism in the United States attracted large numbers of people from the Caribbean to America; the political and other links that were forged among some of those immigrants and with their homelands were instrumental in the development of the work of the CLC in the West Indies, including the new forms of social and political consciousness and financial and other contributions that benefited the decolonization struggles. There emerged in New York genuine excitement that a strong CLC as the defender of workers' rights and an eventual West Indian federation could emerge as a "colored independent entity" with the potential to become "an alternative power center – which if aligned with the global left which was its wont – could provide potent bolstering for African Americans" (Horne 2007, 90).

Dixiecrats became alarmed at the prospect of black West Indians and black Americans building close ties in support of an independent, federated West Indies with the potential to bolster international support for the cause of the Negro in America. The growing "influence of those who had spent time in the United States illustrated the downside for colonialism when Washington began to supplant London as the major power in the region" (Horne 2007, 109, 91; see Dray 2002, 406–56 passim). London was mindful of the spread of Communist influence in black American and West Indian organizations and noted the ability of those groupings to exert significant ideological influence in the West Indies, as well as the impact of the financial contributions that African Americans and others made to the coffers of the CLC and other labour organizations (Horne 2007, 91, 92). A British source opined that "in the future . . . we shall find more and more Communist Negro politicians seeking to enter our Colonies and . . . sooner or later we shall have to start admitting them with the best grace we can muster. Refusing an application of this type is merely postponing the evil day" (see Horne 2007, 92).[16]

The matter of black American and West Indian radicals and communists in the United States strengthening political ties with groups that were fighting for self-determination in West Indian territories was part of the dialectic of the postwar internationalization of the Caribbean within the orbit of international capitalism. Anti-American nationalist sentimentalism among West Indian Anglophiles was difficult to ignore. The *Daily Gleaner* (Jamaica) reminded West Indian colonial subjects that they were "strongly pro-British" and "prefer the equality that obtains throughout the British Empire to the discriminatory status that obtains in America" (in Horne 2007, 93). The *Daily Gleaner* also lamented the toll Jim Crow exacted from West Indian toilers in the United States and in the region, and spoke about the uncertainty that closer economic, industrial and cultural integration with the United States was bound to produce in the region. The *Daily Gleaner* had absolutely no realistic alternative to offer the chronically unemployed, hungry and oppressed West Indian workers who flocked to the United States, where their labour power would be more highly exploited, for higher average wages, and the prospects of their standard of living improving in a highly charged, racialized capitalist environment.

US diplomat Charles Whitaker said, "A strongly federated West Indies might be to the detriment of American interests" because a "federated West Indies might make stronger demands for the return of the bases and these demands might carry more weight than the scattered demands of a few loosely organized labour groups as is the case at the present time", with the CLC in mind. The *Saturday Evening Post* provided coverage of a debate in the United States on the likelihood of the West Indian territories becoming a "liability if acquired by the United States" as a way to derail the federation project (Horne 2007, 97). Robert Bradshaw (St Kitts) interpreted closer West Indian unity as a way to combat a "rapacious U.S. imperialism", as he believed that Washington was a "menace to the British West Indies and . . . a direct stumbling block in the pathway of progress in which we are rapidly moving toward the goal of political federation" (see Horne 2007, 104, 105). Bradshaw had first-hand experience with Jim Crow, having lived in the United States for a number of years, and he was familiar with the ideas about annexation that circulated in US imperialist discourses dating back to the nineteenth century.

As late as 1940 and prior to the Destroyers for Bases Deal between the United States and Britain, Senator John Miller of Arkansas exhorted the United States to seize "Bermuda, Bahamas, and all islands of the West Indies owned by England, France, Netherlands", and suggested that battleships should be dispatched to do the job (see Horne 2007, 104). Horne argues that evidence from US consular dispatches revealed a high level of official US concern over the prospects of unity between labour and socialist organizations stretching from Panama to the West Indies (Horne 2007, 106). On October 8, 1945, Norman Manley addressed the NAACP board in New York in the following terms: "We in Jamaica, a very small part of the British Empire, nevertheless occupy today a position of strategic importance in the general colonial struggle." Manley expressed the view that West Indians were "looking to Jamaica for leadership". He discussed the international significance and implications of "the results of the West Indian experiment", adding that the "status of coloured people the world over must be affected by the achievements of the West Indian people and by their success or failure as a people" (in Horne 2007, 108). Manley, Paul Robeson and W.E.B. Du Bois appeared to have shared similar views of the potential of the West Indies in the larger international struggles against racism, oppression and exploitation. Three years later, at the Montego Bay Conference, on closer association Manley and other West Indian delegates succumbed to the British insistence on setting up a weak federation and sabotaging the CLC.

In 1947 the US consul in Trinidad informed Washington that sympathetic American Negroes were supporting efforts for "increased autonomy for the British West Indies or eventual federation". The US consul attached a "sheaf of articles from regional newspapers documenting this concern, including a story about a visit of Barbados's Grantley Adams to the United States and his attempt to form a pro-federation group that included White,[17] Robeson, the contralto Marion Anderson and others"

(Horne 2007, 110). Certain West Indian leaders were looking at the decolonization movement as part of a larger process of international change. Certain prominent black Americans were involved in the formation and development of the international consciousness that took hold in the Caribbean and recognized that their struggles were an integral part of the larger quest for universal history (Chamberlain 2010, 158–59; Buck-Morss 2009).

The pace of political change quickened, as was reflected in the strengthening of the relationship between the NAACP and the CLC. However,

> a Cold War was descending that forced a split in both the CLC and the NAACP on a right-left axis, with the former pole – which was embodied by White and Grantley Adams of Barbados in the first place – moving at warp speed to place distance between themselves and those to their left, men such as Du Bois and Richard Hart. A Cold War had descended that ultimately was to weaken what had been a generally united movement for sovereignty, federation, and labor rights. (Horne 2007, 110)

It was becoming clear that contradictions arising from the economics and geopolitics of the Cold War project were upending the international solidarity that took centre stage in the West Indies–NAACP alliance.

Viable economic integration among any grouping of countries requires deep inner structures of capital, and a sense of the geographical area as constituting a viable market, as a segment of the world market. Contextually, de jure provisions such as a federal constitution and the distribution of powers between the federal government and the unit territories simply do not and cannot suffice to produce substantive regional integration. The West Indies simply did not possess the wherewithal to satisfy the criteria for a potentially viable regional economic integration project; for all practical purposes the federal experiment began as a top-heavy political project that the United Kingdom and the United States were promoting primarily to make it easier to control the subregion within their security environment.

In the imagination of West Indian leaders, the Caribbean Sea stood as an obstacle as well as a strategic communications vector, partly on account of the long history of relative territorial isolation that resulted from the division of the region along linguistic, cultural and other lines. The United Kingdom emerged from World War II severely battered, and saw the colonial possessions as sources of primary goods for rebuilding its economy in a postwar international order. The eagerness with which throngs of predominantly unskilled and semi-skilled rural and urban working-class people flocked to the United Kingdom, and many to the United States, in search of employment and other opportunities to improve their standard of living and that of their families, confirmed that the colonial economy simply could not productively absorb large numbers of professional, technical and kindred workers; there was more than plausible support for the claim that imperialism retarded the development of the colonies (Lewis 1978).

Eric Williams argued in *The Economics of Nationhood* that the Federation of the West Indies would have to discard its experimental colonial constitution and move boldly toward full independence and sovereignty (Sealy 1991, 193). In contrast, just when the federal government was making plans for independence, Washington advised the United Kingdom to rethink its plan for the federation to proceed to independence, to which Whitehall responded by increasing the powers of the governor general, Lord Hailes, and centralizing decision-making authority in his office. Reginald Maudling, secretary of state for the colonies, advised "Her Majesty to amend the Federal Constitution by Order in Council . . . to enable Governor General (with my approval) to act contrary to advice of his Ministers and to refuse assent to a Bill where previously he would have been bound to assent if so advised by his Ministers. The amendments will also give Governor General certain powers of authorizing and meeting expenditures."[18]

Mary Chamberlain points out that "although the Governor General would be expected to take the advice of the Council, he had reserve powers to override it and to reserve action on various categories for the British government, including defence and foreign affairs" (2010, 159). Maudling's proposal carried much broader implications for the federation: it meant shifting upward and outward to Her Majesty's representative the authority to make critical budgetary and other decisions about a federation that was constitutionally authorized to proceed to independence.

The United States "managed to impose its vision, which privileged the idea of targeting those perceived as the agents of Moscow. The problem for the region was that these perceived agents also happened to be the staunchest advocates of labor rights to rescue the common man and woman from the snares of poverty" (Horne 2007, 126). The omnibus labour unions and populist political parties appealed to the deprived masses by promising to ameliorate the squalor and misery they endured. It was therefore quite understandable that the vast majority of the people believed that the struggle for "sovereignty and labour rights" would yield the results they anticipated. In fact, the task proved herculean, as Whitehall and Washington saw to it that neither the decolonizing elites nor their mass base would be permitted to determine the broad context in which the priorities would be set, and the skirmishes and battles fought.

BRITISH GUIANA, BARBADOS AND THE
DESTRUCTION OF THE CLC

There emerged in British Guiana the making of a tradition of radical and progressive labour politics, as witnessed by the growth of a trade union movement during the 1920s that reached out to the other West Indian territories to help build a progressive regional labour and trade union movement based on the primacy of labour rights. The crisis that erupted in British Guiana in 1953 was therefore not an isolated occurrence. The polarization of labour and the working class along racialized ethnic lines in British Guiana followed in the wake of the destruction in 1952 of the CLC, which represented the only hope for a model for labour hegemony. British Guiana would soon learn that the Cold War–inspired strategy for capital accumulation and geopolitical security would define the acceptable parameters of economic reform, self-determination, democracy and sovereignty for all West Indian governments to follow within the framework of the bourgeois democratic revolution. The "ordering" of the process towards independence would therefore be strategically managed from London (Mawby 2012).

Stephen Rabe covers political developments in British Guiana between 1953 and 1969, with attention to the contradictory roles that the United

Kingdom, the United States and certain domestic forces played in the process. Rabe discusses the ways the United Kingdom and the United States – mainly via CADORIT, the American Federation of Labor and Congress of Industrial Organizations, and US and British intelligence agencies and other entities – employed Cold War intrigue to divide the Guyanese population along ethnic lines, by employing "race-inflected" tactics that carried major economic, political and psychological consequences for the society (2005, 34, 36; see Radosh 1969).

According to Rabe, British prime minister Harold Macmillan and President Kennedy viewed "the Anglo-American relationship as an interdependent one". Rabe argues that British "foreign officers wrote of their 'awkward' role mediating between the State Department and the Colonial Office", which did not initially agree that "the United States had legitimate regional security concerns" that deserved a higher priority than the future of British Guiana. British prime ministers Winston Churchill, Clement Attlee and Harold Macmillan embraced the new hegemonic paradigm through which Britain came to depend on the United States to protect its interests around the world, an arrangement from which the United Kingdom and its leading capitalist strata stood to benefit considerably (2005, 97, 102, 108; Conway 2015).

Rabe is sceptical of the claim that anti-communism was an adequate organizing concept for explaining British Guiana's geopolitical predicament. He analyses official British and American sources to show that John Kennedy and Lyndon Johnson exaggerated the links between Cheddi Jagan and the PPP and Cuba in the aftermath of the Cuban Revolution (2005, 117–18). He also notes that Jagan was not in any position to confront or defeat the onslaught by British and American state agencies and non-state organizations – the CIA and British counterparts, business interests, labour unions and religious organizations – that collaborated with local forces in the territory to make it impossible for his government to maintain political stability and control. Four British governors who served in Guiana – Alfred Savage, Patrick Renison, Ralph Grey and Richard Luyt – along with Colonial Office technocrats, several British parliamentarians and members of the British Labour Party, US diplomats, CIA staff and a number of British and Canadian business interests, expressed scepticism about official British and US interpretations of Jagan's intentions: it was not sufficient to shift the balance in favour of Jagan and the PPP, in the face of especially American intransigence (Rabe 2005, 177, 179). For Rabe, while the United Kingdom and the United States did not trust Burnham, whom they viewed as a racist and demagogic, corrupt, populist authoritarian and a Machiavellian personality, they were convinced that Jagan was ideologically dogmatic and politically unreliable, a perspective that weighed more heavily with them than Burnham's liabilities: the United States cast Jagan as part of the larger puzzle with Moscow (2005, 152–55, 179).[19] István Mészáros argues that one of the "most favored ways of making U.S. interests prevail has always been the overthrow of unpalatable governments and the imposition of dictators totally dependent on the new master, so as to rule the countries in question through these well-controlled dictators" (2008, 119). Burnham was not necessarily "well-controlled"; however, the United Kingdom and the United States viewed him as the lesser of the two problems.

Rabe connects the proportional-representation electoral strategy that the Americans called on the United Kingdom to set up in British Guiana with the Cold War tactic of fostering instability in certain vulnerable societies, by fostering ethnic and other divisions in pursuit of security ends (Watson 2004, 108; Radosh 1969). Eric Williams objected strongly to introducing proportional representation in British Guiana, given the implications it carried for ethnic politics in Trinidad and Tobago (Palmer 2006). Other West Indian leaders generally supported the United Kingdom's decision to punish the Guianese society by suspending the territory's constitution and putting troops in the territory in 1953. West Indian collaboration with the United Kingdom and United States against Jagan indicated that the offensive against the CLC had succeeded in undermining the fledgling working-class solidarity in the West Indies. Adams and Walcott in Barbados, Manley and Bustamante in Jamaica, Albert Gomes in Trinidad and several others openly joined in Anglo-American political and ideological offensives against Jagan and the PPP in British Guiana.[20]

Rabe's assertion that Cold War violence violated the "sacred principles of U.S. foreign relations" (2005, 175–76) does not only resonate with Wilsonian myths about the predetermined moral and ethical basis of

American values and institutions, it also fails to appreciate the necessity of force and violence in the production of the postwar liberal international hegemonic order (Barkawi and Laffey 1999). Rabe's attempt to separate liberal democratic practices from Cold War violence suggests that he discounts the importance of the role that coercion and violence played in the production of American hegemony. He criticizes the execution of the Cold War project in Guiana while embracing its geopolitical and normative framework. Having failed to provide a critique of the system he criticizes, he ends up embracing a moral equivalency that plagues liberal (mainstream) interpretations of social reality. Rabe also seems inattentive to the extent of the integration of the West Indian territories into the Cold War project (Horne 2007; Watson 2007).

It is necessary to look more closely at the role that Adams's BLP government and Walcott's BWU played against Jagan and British Guiana, with attention to the making of the CLC crisis. The following passage highlights the role that Adams and the majority of the other West Indian leaders played in collaborating with the British and Americans in a move to crush the social democratic, socialist-oriented project that Jagan and the PPP[21] launched in British Guiana. Gerald Horne says:

> As the second half of the twentieth century unfolded, the British West Indies was on the cusp of immense change. Riveting struggles had compelled the commencement of adult suffrage . . . which slowly was bringing to power forces that embodied the labor-left ideal of the Caribbean Labour Congress (CLC) – namely the Jagans – though London would retain ultimate power for some years to come. Yet since Grantley Adams had cast down the gauntlet in Paris, the CLC itself had been under siege. The contrasting trends found it hard to coexist, and ultimately Barbados was to prevail over Jagan of British Guiana as a regional force, not least since Washington placed its weighty thumb on the scales of history. (2007, 173; see Bolland 2001, 485)

In 1952, the PNP expelled the Marxist left from its ranks over assertions about a communist conspiracy, to the utter satisfaction of London and Washington. The vote to expel the Marxist left from the PNP party congress was 128–75 for expulsion, which showed that the Hart faction had respectable support. The future of the West Indies Federation was foretold in the events of 1948–53 that laid the foundation for the neocolonial model of sovereign autonomy that would become the norm in the Commonwealth Caribbean.

By the early 1950s, when CLC-affiliated unions and political parties in the West Indian colonies were expressing their opposition to the apartheid regime in South Africa, the BLP, under Adams's guidance, "backed the investment of the government's 'surplus' in the polecat economy" (Horne 2007, 174) of South Africa. In June 1952, a bill was laid before the Barbados House of Assembly that authorized the accountant general, in consultation with the secretary of state for the colonies, to "invest all or any part of the Fund in any securities of, or guaranteed by, the Government of any part of the British Commonwealth, or in such other securities as the Accountant General, with the approval of the Secretary of State, may in his discretion select".[22] A number of parliamentarians, including Wynter Crawford, E.D. Mottley and Errol Barrow, objected to the investment of any part of the fund in South Africa, which implemented apartheid in 1948, the same year the United Nations adopted the Universal Declaration of Human Rights.

Adams argued that while it was fitting for members of the House of Assembly to allow the "Head of the Executive to know that we do not desire to see any Barbados money invested in South Africa", every colonial government "has those instructions" that prevent it from passing "discriminatory legislation of this sort". Mottley and Crawford insisted that it was up to the members of the House to act courageously and pass the amendment anyhow.[23] London and Washington found every creative method to protect the apartheid regime from appropriate exposure in order to bolster white supremacist solidarity and because South Africa was a profitable site of international capitalism and a reliable pillar of anti-communism in the Cold War. No effort was being spared to weaken the regional political base of the militant anti-apartheid trade unions and political parties in the West Indies (Horne 2007, 169, 170). Adams's response to investing government funds accumulated in Barbados in South Africa was an extension of his stand in Paris on imperialism, and represented an attack on the Universal Declaration of Human Rights and against progressive and revolutionary struggles for human rights worldwide.

It was typical of Adams to insist on the primacy of imperial prerogatives over the wishes and needs of the colonial populations. He consistently followed the logic of hegemony in anticipating Whitehall's expectations and pre-empting unfavourable reaction, essentially engaging in self-monitoring and self-regulating conduct that frustrated the more enlightened members of the BLP. In the matter of British Guiana, Adams enthusiastically endorsed the Cold War strategy for undermining the Jagan government; however, during his tenure as prime minister of the federation (1958–62), when the UK government dissolved the federation, Adams opportunistically accused Britain of mishandling the Guiana crisis. During the debate in the Federal House of Representatives on the dissolution of the federation, he said, "Conditions in British Guiana show how attempts to reach hasty decisions leave the peoples of the Eastern Caribbean in a defenceless position."[24]

During the early 1960s the United States continued to claim that race, political instability, the need to forestall the emergence of a second Cuba and to pre-empt the spread of communism into South America were too important to allow Jagan room to experiment with any social democratic political economy initiatives (Rabe 2005, 112–25; Horne 2007, 163–65, 169). The United States also favoured the removal of any and all British military installations in the Caribbean to strengthen its own hegemonic control over the region. On the question of the forging of a defence posture by the Federation of the West Indies, Washington declared that any attempt to write "a Federal Defense Plan with no knowledge of the US Forces in the Caribbean would be difficult and valueless".[25]

The United States propagated the reductionist notion of biological race over social class in dealing with historically determined differences between Afro- and Indo-Guyanese people. Cheddi Jagan conceded as much when he said "the main cause . . . for the suspension of our Constitution was pressure from the government of the United States", and the ways the United States and the United Kingdom "deliberately fomented racial disturbances in order to prevent the transfer of full powers" to the PPP. Jagan also accused Forbes Burnham of entering into "alliances with conservative and racist elements" with the effect of causing the "class struggle" to appear "as Indians against Africans and Mixed" (Jagan 1972, 138, 177, 288, 300; see also Fraser 2007, 114–16).[26]

Among the reasons the United Kingdom offered for removing Jagan and the PPP from power was that "London authorities were worrying nervously that British Guiana was not only reviving the fortunes of the CLC left-labour model but was becoming a beachhead for the dreaded communist foe in a sensitively strategic region". In 1951 Whitehall was advised to "keep in mind the existence of the [CLC] . . . and the possibility that trouble may spread from one Colony to another through this agency" (Horne 2007, 165). Targeting, neutralizing and ultimately destroying the CLC was part of the larger Anglo-American strategy from the founding of the organization, and steps were being taken, through the action against British Guiana, to ensure that the CLC would not be revived in British Guiana or the other territories.

CUBA, THE WEST INDIES AND THE COLD WAR

The United States has been driven by an uncontrollable zeal to integrate Cuba into its political economy and geostrategic framework, beginning with the Monroe Doctrine. Thomas Jefferson made the following declaration in 1823: "We will oppose, with all of our means, the forcible interposition of any other power, as auxiliary, stipendiary, or under any other form or pretext, and most especially, [Cuba's] transfer to any power by conquest, cession, or acquisition in any other way." In 1840, Secretary of State John Forsyth declared that the United States would take all steps, regardless of risk, to prevent Spain from transferring Cuba to "any other power" on any basis and "for any reason". A decade later Secretary of State John Clayton stressed that the United States would view as a "signal for war" any move by Spain to cede Cuba "to any other power than the United States" (quoted in Pérez Jr 1998, 49).

At the time of the War of 1898, when the discourse on imperialism in the United States had reached a feverish pitch, Yale University law professor Theodore Woolsey asserted that for the United States to take control of Central America to secure the interoceanic Panama Canal and guarantee the security of the eastern approach to the canal, it would be necessary to bring Cuba under its control (see Pérez Jr 1998, 49). In 1902, US senator Stephen Elkins echoed Woolsey's sentiment, when he said he wished for the day when

> Cuba shall become a part of the American union and the isthmian canal shall be completed, which is now assured, Porto Rico [sic], Cuba, Hawaii and the Philippines shall be outposts of the great republic, standing guard over American interests in the track of the world's commerce in its triumphant march around the globe. . . . This splendid chain of island possessions, reaching half-way around the world would not be complete without Cuba, the gem of the Antilles. (Pérez Jr 1998, 49)[27]

Secretaries of State Forsyth and Clayton, Senator Elkins and Professor Woolsey each raised the myth of the Jeffersonian "empire of liberty" (Foner 2002, 63–64) to the status of a law of nature, in defence of America's self-appointed "right" to determine Cuba's destiny and its capacity to exercise its sovereignty (see also Watson 2015b, 57–60).

Before the Cuban Revolution became ascendant in 1959, the discussion of Cuba in relation to the West Indies turned on issues such as the need for West Indian sugar-producing territories to modernize their production infrastructure in the hope of competing with Cuban sugar exports,[28] and with the economic and financial implications of the return of West Indian migrants from Cuba[29] in mind. During the decade before the Cuban Revolution, when Cuba remained a solid economic and commercial outpost of American capitalism and the US geopolitical sphere, there was hardly any discussion of Cold War concerns that connected Cuba with the West Indies.

At the time, the United States declared that the West Indian territories had to be subsumed under its postwar security strategy, which was approximately fifteen years before the Cuban Revolution came to power. The Cuban Revolution represented another critical shift in the international relations of the Caribbean. No sooner had the Cuban Revolution taken place than most West Indian leaders began to accuse Jagan of introducing big-power politics into the Caribbean with his pro-communist rhetoric, for declaring his intention to move British Guiana close to Cuba and the

USSR and for refusing to acknowledge that Guyana was located in the US geopolitical sphere. The United States rejected Jagan's assertion that India had accepted aid from Russia while maintaining its "neutrality" (Rabe 2005, 133). In 1955 Washington dismissed nonalignment as an immoral geopolitical position.

Bustamante sent a message to the secretary of state for the colonies supporting the United Kingdom sending troops into British Guiana and suspending the colony's constitution (Palmer 2006, 203–7; Sealy 1991, 112–13). Dominica sent a message to the US secretary of state, Dean Rusk, expressing its "appreciation of the firm stand taken by President Kennedy in relation to . . . events in Cuba". Dominica lacked any authority as a British territory to sign the message, which was signed by David Ormsby-Gore, the British ambassador to the United States.[30]

The Federation of the West Indies was dissolved in April 1962 and the Cuban Missile Crisis erupted that October. Long before then, the UK government, following the US position, expressed grave concern about the security implications of an independent West Indies federation.[31] When the Caribbean Committee of the Alliance for Progress was created in response to the Cuban Revolution taking power, the UK government argued that it was necessary to move cautiously to avoid giving the impression that London was acting in a neocolonial way, with independent Jamaica and Trinidad and Tobago in mind. The United Kingdom was a member neither of the Organization of American States nor of the Alliance for Progress.[32]

Eric Williams was ideologically and pragmatically anti-communist and imagined that he could play an effective foreign policy role as a Caribbean regional leader. Colin Palmer notes that Williams

> had sought to reassure U.S. officials that he could assist them on matters relating to Soviet influence in British Guiana and Cuba. He told the American ambassador in Cairo . . . that he had advised the Soviet Ambassador to the United Kingdom that his government should not involve itself so deeply in the internal affairs of Cuba and British Guiana. Obviously taking the side of the United States, Williams also said that he wanted the State Department to inform him about the extent of Soviet support for

the Jagan government. He promised that he would use this information against Jagan . . . in British Guiana. (Palmer 2006, 207–11, 212)

The United Kingdom described the Cuban Missile Crisis as the "Emergency in Cuba". Measures were taken to get West Indian governments to follow British prescriptions for dealing with revolutionary Cuba. For example, D.A. Murphy of the Colonial Office said:

> I was able by oral communication to get Barrow, the Permanent Secretary, Ministry of Communications, to send a telegram to the Cubans cancelling the permission given to them, and advising them to submit their application through the normal diplomatic channels. I have asked Barrow to see to it that future requests from both Cuba and the Soviet bloc should be dealt with in accordance with the instructions contained in your nonpersonal telegrams 337 and 340, and I am confident that this will be done.

The Cuban authorities submitted a "formal note seeking permission for one Ilyushin 18 carrying ten Soviet technicians . . . to overfly Gambia and British Guiana en route from Prague, Algiers, Dakar, Recife, Port of Spain, Havana".[33] The United Kingdom claimed there was reason for concern about a Soviet aircraft flying over West Indian territories.

The Commonwealth Relations Office remarked that the Russians concluded:

> the doctrine and programme of the Cuban Government, as set out . . . in the Second Declaration of Havana, are based on wrong thinking. They see in it Chinese influence and do not believe it sufficiently well founded on the concept of co-existence. The re-education of senior members of the Cuban Government has therefore been entrusted to Mikoyan [the Soviet first deputy prime minister] to be carried out within the framework of the present negotiations and in addition to his immediate task of ensuring that no Cuban decision is made which would upset the possibility of the Moscow/Washington agreements. . . . Fidel Castro himself has to be tamed and taught to think globally and not merely as a Cuban patriot and the liberator of the oppressed peoples of Latin America.[34]

It did not come as a surprise, therefore, that a year after the abortive

Bay of Pigs invasion of Cuba in 1961, the United States tried to take over Cuba by military force (Pérez Jr 1998, 49). The United States fabricated "justifiable grievances" for military intervention against Cuba, alleging that "Cuban rashness and irresponsibility . . . directed at . . . the United States" posed a threat to "peace in the Western Hemisphere" that merited a pre-emptive act of "overt intervention" (Ruppert 2003, 9, 228). The 1962 Northwood document that set forth the "Justification for US Military Intervention in Cuba"[35] provides unambiguous evidence that the United States deliberately fabricated ways to destabilize Cuba and intervene militarily to destroy the revolutionary Cuban state in pursuit of unattainable absolute global supremacy.

Jamaica, Trinidad and Tobago, and other West Indian territories fell in line with the US and UK strategy for dealing with the "Cuban Missile Crisis". The Commonwealth Relations Office stated, on the question of Soviet missiles in Cuba, that "Mr. Krushchev himself agreed to verification by the United Nations of the dismantling and removal to the Soviet Union of the Soviet missile installations in Cuba", notwithstanding Fidel Castro's defiant speech in which he said he would "never allow United Nations inspection". The Commonwealth Relations Office statement concludes, "There can be no question of a deal involving other questions e.g. the United States base at Guantanamo as proposed by Castro. The only real issue at stake is the liquidation of the Soviet threat." Understandably, the UK government did not lose sight of the economic, financial and commercial benefits that certain British capitalist entities realized from trading with Cuba, the "Emergency in Cuba" notwithstanding.[36]

The decision by Downing Street to follow the US lead on the Cuban Missile Crisis helped to confirm that the United States had established its hegemony over the Caribbean. In the wake of the crisis, the UK government readily coordinated with Washington on all security measures deemed relevant for the West Indies and the newly independent countries of Jamaica and Trinidad and Tobago. Forbes Burnham was installed in power in Guyana in 1964 to ensure that Jagan would not lead Guyana to independence, a decision that Eric Williams enthusiastically supported (Palmer 2006).

In early 1966 the UK government resolved that Barbados, in spite of being "dependent almost entirely on its sugar crop, which without the substantial subsidy now received from Britain would have to be sold at the depressed world price", was ready for independence. Douglas Williams (of the Colonial Office) stressed the importance of getting the Americans and Canadians on board to help provide the necessary assistance to ensure political stability in Barbados and the Leeward and Windward Islands, and save them from "communist infiltration from Cuba and South America". Douglas Williams concluded,

> Undoubtedly Barbados is entitled to its freedom and had well earned its right to independence. It has a fine record of financial integrity, liberal Parliamentary practice and general stability and its constitutional progress toward self-government has over the past centuries been marked by gradual and well-timed steps forward. It is to be hoped that its final step to achieve Commonwealth status will be reached in an equally calm atmosphere of mutual co-operation and understanding. ("The Barbados Case for Independence", *Daily Telegraph*, 10 January 1966)[37]

Grantley Adams's BLP, Errol Barrow's DLP and Frank Walcott's BWU embraced the "historic compromise" and upheld the political consensus that helped Barrow to steer the colonial ship clear of entanglements that smacked of political and economic radicalism.

BARBADOS, ANTI-COMMUNISM AND THE DESTRUCTION OF THE CLC

Grantley Adams and Frank Walcott ran the BWU for a number of years from within the BLP; however, the BWU did not become an arm of the BLP in ways that were reminiscent of how Vere Bird (Antigua), Robert Bradshaw (St Kitts) and Bustamante subordinated organized labour to their respective political parties. Francis Mark notes that by 1953–54 the top two leaders of the BWU were from the working class – McDonald Blunt as president general and Walcott as general secretary. Mark stresses that the "willingness of the Union to emancipate itself from the traditional concept of the need for middle-class leadership was probably the reason for the pace and direction of its development after 1954", after which "the

organization . . . demonstrated an increasing degree of professionaliza-
tion and specialization, which makes it almost unique among Unions
in the area" (Mark 1966, 155).[38]

Hilary Beckles argues that Adams's "formidable power . . . over the
organized labour movement, also carried within it the seeds of internal
opposition to his leadership. . . . Walcott agreed with Adams on the removal
of radicals from the Union, the so-called 'Iron Curtain group'." Beckles
emphasizes that Adams had begun by purging the BPL of "radicals" during the early 1940s and expressed his "intention to do likewise with the
Barbados Workers' Union and the Barbados Labour Party" (2004b, 47,
48; see 1990, 83). The roles Adams and Walcott played in dismantling the
CLC and bringing the unions in the various West Indian territories into
the ICFTU also negatively affected the labour movement in Barbados. In
1952, Adams took steps to disband the London branch of the CLC and
dissolve the entire CLC organization. Richard Hart, who defiantly opposed
Adams's move to dissolve the CLC, mentions that Adams proposed uni-
laterally to "hold a Council meeting instead of a Full Congress" because
he did not have the support of the affiliate organizations of the CLC.
Hart informed Adams that the Antigua Trades and Labour Union, the
Trades Union Congress of British Guiana (including the British Guiana
Labour Union), the PPP of British Guiana, Trinidad and Tobago's Trade
Union Council, the People's Political Party of St Vincent, and the Trade
Union Congress of Jamaica were in favour of convening a full congress,
while only the PNP of Jamaica wanted a council meeting to address the
matter (Horne 2007, 177, 178).

Hart accused Adams of resorting to autocratic, authoritarian and
opportunist measures to split the CLC and the trade unions and the
"national movements in the Caribbean consistent with the policy of the
ICFTU". He interpreted Adams's actions "as an attempt to overthrow the
settled policy of the CLC that the matter of the international affiliation of
each member organization of the CLC was its own concern" (quoted by
Horne 2007, 178). Adams and Walcott refused to compromise. In June
1952, the BWU held a conference at Hastings House in Barbados under
the sponsorship of Serafino Romualdi, the anti-communist assistant
secretary general of the regional body of the ICFTU. Seventeen trade

unions from Barbados, British Guiana, Grenada, British Honduras and Suriname were represented (Horne 2007, 178–79).

Assistant secretary of state for the colonies Sir George Steel attended the conference and provided the meeting room and other facilities of the Colonial Development and Welfare Organization. The Barbados press reported that Grantley Adams was taking the initiative to get rid of the communist elements that were threatening the CLC and posing grave security risks to the West Indies. Richard Hart (Jamaica), Cheddi Jagan (British Guiana), John La Rose (Trinidad and Tobago), Ebenezer Joshua (St Vincent), Wynter Crawford (Barbados), Eric Gairy (Grenada), Vere Bird (Antigua), Alexander Bustamante (Jamaica), W. Arthur Lewis (St Lucia) and a number of others visited Barbados in a futile attempt to save the CLC from certain destruction. They failed. The split in the CLC occurred in the fall of the same year (Horne 2007, 178–79) and the organization officially disappeared. The ghost of the CLC would continue to haunt the West Indian decolonization experience, from federation to independence.

During the 1950s and thereafter British governors in Barbados sent monthly reports to the Colonial Office on political and other activities in Barbados.[39] A review of the contents of the monthly reports for a number of years shows that the governor's office conducted extensive surveillance for the Colonial Office, and worked closely with the Barbados Government Post Office to intercept all material that entered the territory destined for individuals who were associated or affiliated with progressive political organizations. The extensive intelligence work done by the governor was part of Cold War surveillance activities in the West Indies.

In 1954, the governor of Barbados forwarded to the Colonial Office a copy of two specific resolutions the CPA passed because the vestry of St Michael refused to permit it to hold a public meeting in Queen's Park in Bridgetown. The CPA forwarded the resolutions to the secretary of state for the colonies, without asking the secretary of state to take any action. The resolutions drew attention to the authoritarian tradition of the local colonial state and stressed that the St Michael vestry was deny-ing the CPA permission to exercise its "democratic right of holding a public meeting in a public place, namely, Queen's Park". The CPA also described the action of the vestry as a "betrayal of British justice and . . .

not short of an open discrimination against a democratic and legally constituted body which would like to express itself for and on behalf of the Barbadian public in a lawful and democratic manner". The CPA stressed that the action had the effect of "denying . . . the rate payers of St. Michael the uses of Queen's Park (a public place vested in the rate payers of St. Michael)". The letter was signed by C. Leroy Brathwaite, Carlton A. Gill, L.B. Brathwaite, and Ulric (Olrick) Grant.[40] The governor informed the secretary of state for the colonies on the CPA and its resolutions, in keeping with the authoritarian colonial tradition, as follows: "When the general political outlook of the leading lights of the so-called Caribbean People's Alliance is recalled, I consider that the Vestry acted wisely in refusing permission for the use of the Park by the Party." The CPA, which identified itself as a socialist organization, also referred to its spokesmen as loyal and law-abiding "British Subjects" who were running their socialist entity in conformity with the pro-imperialist values of the Fabian Society.[41] The CPA seemed unmindful that authoritarianism was built into the modus operandi of the colonial state as an organ of British imperialism.

According to the *Political Report of the Governor for the Month of December 1953*, Wynter Crawford addressed a meeting of about "300 persons, mainly of the middle and lower classes", at which he said that anybody who criticized or challenged the BLP or the action of the British government in Kenya was called a communist and, that being so, "Well, I am a Communist."[42] Crawford was one of the most politically conscious, astute and forthright social democratic politicians in Barbados; he also demonstrated a keen awareness and appreciation of developments and events in the Caribbean region, in Africa and the wider world. In February 1954 the governor reported: "The inaugural outdoor meeting of the Caribbean Christian Socialist Party . . . was held on the 26th and attracted about 300 persons. The chief speakers were Ulric [*sic*] Grant, the two Brathwaites, and C. C. Gill." C.L. Brathwaite ended his speech by asking, "What's wrong with a Communist so long as he means good to you?" and concluded with: "Long live Cheddi Jagan – Long live Burnham. They are great West Indian leaders", which was "received with loud applause".[43]

The governor's monthly report routinely provided detailed reports about the literature that entered the territory destined for the CPA. For example, it was mentioned that "on the 10th Grant received 50 copies of the 'W.F.T.U. Movement' for February 1st–15th'". The report for May 1954 observed that "C.A. Gill, President of the Caribbean Christian Socialist Party, had an invitation to attend a Caribbean Labour Congress Conference in London during June", and Ulrick Grant received about two dozen copies of the CLC publication for April–May under the title "British Honduras Special Issue".⁴⁴ Grant, one of the leaders of the 1937 rebellion, later collaborated with "Richard Hart, a secretary of the Caribbean Labour Congress, from whom, the Special Branch alleged, he was 'receiving quantities of Communist literature'". Richard Drayton credits Grant, Gill and other Barbadian radicals with promoting the idea of forming a new political party that became the DLP, which "was from its origins a nationalist and reformist party, with radicals like Grant agreeing, as they had a generation earlier with the BLP, to yield leadership to more respectable (and conservative) figures" (2014, 123). The deference which progressives like Grant showed to the middle-strata leaders made it much easier for them to control the working class and steer its programmes away from more radical directions.

Cecilia Karch's critical observation on the pitfalls of middle-strata leadership and the implications for the working class is worth quoting at length:

> [The] black middle class embraced the prevailing ideological system; many were proponents of Empire. The majority sought access to the system; they did not seek to destroy it. Status as a middle class and their dependency on the paternalism of the oligarchy, and the colonial system, blunted the nationalist . . . spirit of black middle income groups and go a long way in explaining the recent political history of the island. Individuals from this class, not the class as a class, became political leaders and spokesmen for the majority population. (Quoted in Beckles 2004b, 147)⁴⁵

C.L.R. James (1962) warned of the pitfalls of middle-class leadership and the implications for progressive change in the West Indies. Ulrick Grant displayed keen insights into the exploitative and oppressive nature of the capitalist order in Barbados during and after the 1937 rebellion, and he drew attention to the special relationship that existed between the dominant capitalist forces and the local colonial state. He argued that "if unrest starts in Barbados the capitalistic element will be responsible for it. We will have to fight for what we want but not with sticks . . . (unless) . . . we have to" (Beckles 2004b, 200–201).

In the report for March 1954 the governor mentioned that Barrow during the exchanges said Adams had told friends of Barrow's in the Colonial Office that certain members of the Labour Party were communists. Barrow also said he had friends at the Colonial Office and anything that was said "there about him was . . . known to him in seven days". In addition to Barrow, A.E.S. "T.T." Lewis was branded one of the "chief rebels in the Labour Party".[46] E.L. Cozier (1981), former columnist and lifelong friend of Lewis, wrote that Lewis "considered himself . . . a Socialist, and in those far-off days . . . would not have been offended at being called Communist".

The *Political Report* for June 1954 noted that J. Cameron Tudor joined the CCSP without issuing any public announcement to that effect. The same report mentions that speakers at the CCSP meeting "criticized the Government, and the Premier, and . . . British Colonial Policy", and a number of them said "there was nothing wrong with Communism, or being called Communist as all who the British Colonial System controlled were so branded". The report mentioned also that

C.A. Gill received a letter from Ashton Chase in British Guiana in which he advised the officials of the Caribbean Christian Socialist Party to continue their "progressive movement and stating that the P.P.P. in British Guiana would not stop its campaign". C.A. Gill also received from John La Rose copies of "Freedom", the news organ of the West Indian Independence Party in Trinidad, and from Mrs. Jagan a number of copies of "Thunder", the organ of the P.P.P. of British Guiana.

The CCSP also "received 200 petition forms from the Caribbean Labour Congress (London Branch), relating to the imprisonment of members of the P.P.P."[47] in British Guiana.

According to the *Political Report* for September 1954, Olrick (Ulrick) Grant received twelve copies of the "World Trade Union Movement No.

13" (September 1954), in addition to copies of a "biography prepared by the Marx-Engels-Lenin Institute, The 'History of the Communist Party of the Soviet Union'".[48] Grantley Adams adamantly defended his anti-working-class "right-wing socialist" credentials; understandably, those with socialist credentials who were to the left of his right-wing perspective were easy targets of his red-baiting, as in the case of Errol Barrow. The governor's report did not mention Adams's assertions about his personal socialist outlook; however, there were frequent negative references to the socialism the CCSP espoused, as most of its spokesmen openly said they did not see anything wrong with the communist label.

The governor's monthly reports to the secretary of state for the colonies also highlighted the scope and extent of the dissension and looming crisis within the BLP from early in the 1950s. The main issues noted in those reports included the poor performance of BLP ministers in Parliament,[49] the activities of the rebel faction within the BLP (Barrow and others), the systematic attacks on the BLP administration by Frank Walcott of the BWU, though Walcott voted consistently with the government party, Walcott's deep personal and political rift with Adams and the consistent voting against the BLP government by Crawford and O.T. Allder. Contributing to the rift between Adams and certain other BLP members were his unyielding vitriolic attacks against the rebel factions whom he branded members of a "Communist cell".

The references to the CCSP should also be read with respect to the formation of the DLP in 1955.[50] The report of the governor for April 1955 states, "Behind the scenes discussions regarding the formation of a 'Third party' of the Left led up to the launching of the 'Democratic Labour Party'." Among the officeholders in the DLP were former members of the CCSP – L.B. Brathwaite and C.A. Gill, and T.T. Lewis, the long-time "rebellious Labour Party back-bencher", among several others. Among the names that had been considered for the new political party was the "People's Labour Party". The report mentioned that the "Caribbean Christian Socialist Party seems to have been virtually absorbed in the new Party". The *Barbados Advocate* editorialized that "a strong opposition is essential for good government and to have a party composed of young and vigorous men can only have a beneficial result of keeping the majority Party on its toes and is a sign of the strength of Barbadian democracy".[51] Wynter Crawford had not yet joined the DLP; however, his newspaper, the *Observer*, published the DLP's avowed aims and objects. Predictably, the *Beacon*, the organ of the BLP, heaped abuse on the founders of the DLP.[52]

The DLP represented itself as "socialist in theory, characterized by a demand for a reduction in the degree of social inequality; democratization of resource ownership, socialist reforms in the area of education, public health and social security, and diversification of the economy away from the plantation-mercantile axis" (Beckles 2004b, 52). Peter Morgan, a close associate and confidant of Barrow and one of his cabinet members, said there were many in the local business community who were convinced that Barrow was a communist (Morgan 1994).

The *Political Report* for January 1955 states, "The Caribbean Christian Socialist Party showed few signs of activity during the month. . . . Very little Communist literature came in during the month, but Grant is said to have received a letter from one Ted Brake, a member of the British Communist Party understood to be in China, who has put him in touch with an unnamed 'prominent member' of the British Communist Party." The report continued, "The 'Observer' continues to publish anti-British Mau Mau news items, the most obnoxious being one entitled 'Kenya prisoner threatened with burial alive. Woman Lowered into Refuse Pit.'" Caroline Elkins (2005) provides extensive coverage and documentation of the atrocities the civilized British carried out, including summary executions of Kikuyu people, in the anti-Mau Mau campaign. The British equated the Kikuyu, who were waging resistance against the expropriation of their land, with savages, a typical liberal ploy to justify barbarism draped in the mantle of Western freedom and civilization mediated by capitalism, and the large-scale dispossession of the weak, who were deprived of the means with which to defend and protect themselves. Wynter Crawford used the *Observer* newspaper to keep the reading public informed of what was going on in Kenya, by connecting the United Kingdom's anti-Mau Mau campaign to its opposition to implementing the principles of the Universal Declaration of Human Rights in the colonies. The *Observer* highlighted the incidence of racist oppression and violence in British colonial practice and reported on developments in the anti-colonial and anti-imperialist struggles in the West Indies and beyond.[53]

The political reports for March and April 1955 mentioned efforts by one Mrs Weekes to "whip up enthusiasm for a Women's Political Party. . . . It is as yet uncertain what connections, if any, this political group has with the Barbados Women's Alliance or the Caribbean Women's Alliance."[54] This might have been the earliest recorded mention of a group of women in Barbados who expressed an interest in forming a political organization or political party after the introduction of universal adult suffrage. Women played significant roles in the 1937 rebellion, but their contributions were routinely reduced to footnotes or excluded from the historical record altogether. Traditionally women were discouraged from running for political office and from adopting any independent political positions on major issues affecting the society, owing to its deeply rooted patriarchal prejudices.

Reflecting Cold War priorities, the governor not only labelled the literature that arrived for members of the CCSP as "Communist literature", but also called for close monitoring of the activities of WFTU operatives in the colonies to determine the extent of left-wing influence and the role radicals were playing in the trade union movement.[55] According to the *Political Report* for February 1955,

> On the 1st February the Premier, in the course of a heated exchange with Mr. E.W. Barrow, a rebel back-bencher, in the House of Assembly, informed the House that the Administration was in possession of definite information that a Communist cell was in existence in Barbados and that a member of the House of Assembly . . . (he is generally believed to have had Mr. Tudor in mind) was actively engaged in the activities of the cell.

The premier said he "had not referred to Mr. Barrow, but maintained that . . . it was his duty to give early warning that there was a Communist cell in Barbados". The *Barbados Advocate* called for a "tough line being taken with possible Communist infiltration", while expressing "surprise at the manner in which the disclosure had been made and demanded that 'the danger be faced with a sense of statesmanship instead of vague and casual statements'". As was typical of Adams's authoritarian style, the premier made the allegations "without the prior knowledge of the Administration".[56]

The *Political Report* for February 1955 stressed that the CCSP had established political contacts with communist organizations in Europe, and stated: "Small quantities of Communist literature came in during the month, including some copies of a publication by the Women's International Democratic Federation entitled 'Unity of the Defense of Our Rights, of Our Children, of Peace' and a copy of 'Democratic German Report' dated 21 January, sent from Berlin."[57] The term "socialism" had been appropriated and bandied about by political parties and movements that spanned the ideological spectrum in Barbados. For example, a member of the planter-merchant class, E.K. Walcott, who also served as attorney general, declared that his party, the Conservative Electors' Association, which reinvented itself as the Progressive Conservative Party[58] in 1956, when the number of eligible voters dramatically increased and the electorate mobilized behind the BLP, was no less socialist. Walcott said, in a gross display of ignorance of what socialism stands for,

> when we on this side are accused of not being Socialists, we have practised socialism more so than those who now call themselves Socialists. We are conscientious believers in our socialism. . . . We bought . . . land many years ago and sought to give people access to the beaches and . . . to get the Governor-in-Executive-Committee to acquire . . . . land at Sandy Lane whether that offended his friends or not. . . . The amount paid into the Labour Welfare Fund up to the year 1950 was in the vicinity of $1,250,000 of which $300,000 was put aside for playing fields and $750,000 was reserved for housing of which the sum of $325,000 has been released, and last year we put into that Fund, sums of money aggregating over another million dollars.[59]

Walcott equated socialism with state acquisition of certain lands and public spending on necessary welfare programmes that were designed to strengthen capitalism's social infrastructure. His idea that providing public access to beaches was a socialist act ignores the fact that the provision of public (social) goods is necessary for the development of civil society and the need to broaden the scope and reach of the public domain and social welfare development. He failed to appreciate that it is the role of the state in capitalist society to subsidize capitalist activities by using public funds to create the scientific, technical, industrial and social infrastructure required for reproducing the working class as labourers for capital to boost capitalist production, increase productivity and thereby increase the rate of exploitation, without capitalists directly financing those requirements.

A significant development in 1955, in the wake of Hurricane Janet, which devastated parts of Barbados, revealed that the position of the newly formed DLP on the split in the WFTU and its impact on the CLC was not substantively different from the BLP's. According to the governor's report for January 1956, J. Cameron Tudor explained that C.A. Gill, the former assistant secretary of the DLP, had been clandestinely communicating with "officials of the Caribbean Labour Congress (London Branch) including Billy Strachan and other well-known Communists, and had received gifts of money and clothing for hurricane relief from them without the knowledge or consent of the officials of the Party". Tudor issued a press statement in which he publicly condemned Gill's actions, emphasized that he had acted without the DLP's knowledge, and stressed that the DLP would not have "approved the source of such gifts and that the Council of the Party took a serious view of the matter". Tudor stressed that "it was not in the interest of the DLP to be tarred . . . with the Communist brush". It would not be farfetched to conclude that Tudor was echoing the sentiments of Errol Barrow and other DLP leaders on the CLC and on communism. Tudor put the ideological concerns of the DLP ahead of the material needs of Barbadians who were suffering from the devastation that Hurricane Janet caused when he castigated Gill for accepting funds and clothing from the CLC London branch. The socialism espoused by leaders of the BLP and the new DLP was equally anti-communist and predictably pro-labour, but anti-working-class.

There were tensions between Frank Walcott, the chairman of the administrative committee of CADORIT, and L.J. Marcano, CADORIT's executive secretary. Walcott reportedly objected to Marcano's assertion that the ICFTU was "more concerned with fighting Communism than furthering the aims of Trade Unions". Walcott responded by forwarding "an adverse report to the ICFTU on Mr. Marcano's morals". Marcano apparently viewed Walcott as a bully.[60] The term "bully" is often used as a synonym for "authoritarian".

Each report by the Barbados Intelligence Committee for the five months from June to October 1956 mentioned that there was little or no "Communist literature" arriving in the island and "no signs that the known Communist sympathizers are taking any active part in the Election Campaign" of that year. In November 1956 Ulrick (Olrick) Grant reportedly received "Communist literature" from the WFTU, mainly "an issue that devoted much of its space to the Suez Crisis" and also "a number of copies of the 'Information Bulletin'", a pamphlet published by the Women's International Democratic Federation, for September 1956. This was viewed as being in marked contrast with the flow of information in June 1955, when Gill, then assistant secretary of the DLP, was "understood to have received 12 copies of Dr. Jagan's 'Forbidden Freedom' from Mrs. Jagan", and Grant "received 24 copies of the C.L.C. publication (formerly 'Caribbean News') for March–April and . . . May, and about 12 copies of the W.F.T.U. Fortnightly Review and single copies of other W.F.T.U. publications".[61] Clearly, the Governor's Office kept close tabs on what progressives in Barbados were receiving, reading and disseminating to members of the public, implying that it was dangerous for the working class to be exposed to unconventional political ideas.

The relationship between Walcott and Premier Adams deteriorated for a number of reasons. Adams was the Oxford University-educated son of a headmaster from the middle strata; in contrast, Walcott's social origin was in the agro-proletariat. The social, academic and intellectual chasm that separated the two men made it impossible for Adams to treat Walcott as his equal, which bothered Walcott. Adams refused to offer Walcott a ministerial portfolio in his government. Walcott resigned as secretary of the BLP in 1954, stopped attending party meetings the same year, and intensified his criticism of the performance of BLP ministers in the House of Assembly. Adams revealed his vindictive and dictatorial side when BLP members objected to his announcement that he would drop Walcott from the party ticket in 1956, when Walcott was away from the island. According to the monthly intelligence reports for July and

August 1956, when BLP members requested that the "matter . . . be put to a vote, Mr. Adams declared that it was his decision not to support Mr. Walcott as a candidate in any constituency".

Walcott's attacks on BLP government ministers showed his independence as general secretary of the BWU. Voting with the Progressive Conservative Party in the House was not an option for Walcott, given the long history of the oppressive, racist and exploitative relationship between the agro-commercial (merchant-planter) strata and the black working-class majority from which most of the BWU membership was drawn. The economic and political gradualism of the BLP government notwithstanding, certain economic and social improvements were introduced following the implementation of universal adult suffrage (Worrell 1994–95), and the broad mass of the working population had high expectations that the BWU and the BLP would implement policies and programmes to improve their lives.

The BWU had grown in numbers and strength without real competition, and Walcott's pragmatic and economistic trade union approach involved forming alliances with those who looked out for organized labour; he used the BWU to help shape the political consensus that was taking shape around the "historic compromise" (Cheltenham 1970, 252, 254–55; Emmanuel 1988). The differences between Adams and Walcott were not permitted to interfere with their collaboration to keep the working-class movement in line with Cold War expectations. When the planter-merchant forces in Barbados lost direct control of political power in the House, they did what ruling strata do to protect their interests, including the right to exploit. They strengthened and increased the number of their private-sector organizations to offset any disadvantages they anticipated from the introduction of universal adult suffrage. They had little to fear, as the "historic compromise" was designed to disarm the working class in part by subsuming its interests under parliamentary government.

The formation of the CPA and the CCSP suggested that the two entities were not impressed by the socialist rhetoric that Adams and the BLP were wont to utter. The fact that the CCSP morphed into the DLP in 1955 showed that the anti-communist social democrats succeeded in isolating the progressive forces that emerged on their left. Adams's way of waging ideological warfare against the "rebel" faction inside the BLP exposed his pro–Cold War commitment and set the stage for the split in the BLP in 1955. When Barrow and the DLP won the 1961 general election, they adopted a strategy of accelerating the pace of change in ways that boosted opportunities for the dominant capitalist interests, while keeping the expectations of the working class in line with the BWU trade union democracy.

The 1950s was a decade of rising class struggle, as was seen in developments in the sugar industry. The sugar workers' wildcat strike in 1958 took a severe toll on them (Sutton 2005; Bolland 2001). The international sugar industry was undergoing relentless restructuring, and the local industry continued to falter because it simply lacked an internationally competitive productive base, which was the situation for a long time. Britain introduced the Commonwealth Sugar Agreement in 1950 to guarantee access to sugar from the colonies and to rationalize the allocation of very limited capital to rebuild its domestic industrial base and manage the fallout from the restructuring of the international sugar industry. There was a high degree of tension, confusion and mistrust among sugar workers in Barbados. The BWU and the BLP were at loggerheads over how to respond to the workers' demand that the windfall from sugar exports be paid directly to them rather than being set aside in a sugar-worker provident fund for a rainy day. The impoverished workers were caught between the sugar producers, the BLP government and the BWU and DLP (Mark 1966; Sutton 2005).

The prevailing conditions favoured the rise of progressive organizations like the CPA and the CCSP; however, Frank Walcott collaborated with Adams to expel the radicals from the BWU, just as Adams succeeded in expelling progressives from the BPL and the BLP. The BWU continued to define the central problems facing the working class as bread-and-butter issues; this way of separating economics from politics made it difficult for the majority of the population to appreciate the real connections between the social, economic and political issues within the class struggle that the CLC was created to address, and because of which it was destroyed by Adams, Walcott and others in keeping with broader Cold War designs.

CONCLUSION

A tradition of nationalist-directed anti-colonial, anti-imperialist and anti-racist labour politics tethered to popular democratic struggles took root in the West Indian territories before World War II and played a role in the working-class rebellions of the 1930s. Broadly, the leaders and followers in the social and political movements described themselves as loyal subjects of the British Empire, which suggests that their anti-colonialism was rhetorically anti-imperialist, but hardly anti-British. The mainstream political parties and labour unions understood imperialism as a form of external imposition that could be banished by attaining self-government and independence. They did not understand imperialism for what it was – international capitalism at a particular historical juncture, as Lenin and other Marxists accurately portrayed it. What emerges as strikingly perplexing is how the overwhelming majority of the leaders of the labour and trade union movement and the political parties that adopted the socialist label for themselves and their organizations were also anti-Marxist and anti-communist zealots: they predictably morphed into comrades-in-arms of the Cold War.

The range of dominant ideological and political tendencies that dominated in the West Indies attracted the attention of the United States before the outbreak of the Cold War. When the CLC was formed in 1945, the United States was already expanding its economic and geopolitical presence in the region. The demands for labour rights and a federation with a strong central government working toward independence surfaced in a rather unfavourable geopolitical environment. The United States responded to the pending collapse of European imperialism by devising a hegemonic (multilateralist) strategy that involved the integration of the United Kingdom, France, the Netherlands and other European states, which simplified the task of coordinating geopolitical policies for the Caribbean that put at a serious disadvantage the fight for decolonization and sovereignty that progressives waged. A major setback for the CLC was that it operated in a highly fragmented region dominated by imperialism, which made it extremely difficult to build a regional front among more or less isolated territories and what Grantley Adams called a "united Socialist Caribbean Commonwealth", at the founding CLC conference in Barbados in 1945.

The small numbers of Marxists and "Communists" operated in an environment where prevailing social and material conditions made it very difficult to develop and anchor a rigorous scientific understanding of international capitalism and socialism. There was hardly any understanding that capitalism and state sovereignty make the fight for substantive self-determination hard to achieve. The decolonizing elite embraced nationalism and predictably juxtaposed colonialism and imperialism against independence, viewing the pursuit of formal sovereignty as their ultimate goal, a patently ideological position that imposes a closure on history and therefore on the quest for our universal humanity.

The political parties and trade unions in the West Indies embraced an omnibus populism that proved effective in capturing and subsuming the fledgling working-class movements and bringing them under their control. Populists appeal directly to the "people" as an undifferentiated mass, while ignoring the objective, durable class inequalities, with capitalists running the economy, politicians in control of politics and labour unions looking out for the bread-and-butter concerns of workers. Whatever interest the West Indian leaders declared they had in social justice and peace, they soon sacrificed it at the altar of the Cold War project, with its quid pro quo blandishments of aid and "development assistance", in return for playing the anti-communist card in support of the US national security project. They thus became self-monitoring and self-regulating defenders of American hegemony. The West Indian territories operated fully within the institutional framework of Western "high modernity", with nationalism conditioning decolonization and self-determination, and with sovereign autonomy romanticized as the end point of freedom, crowned by the achievement of membership in the international community of sovereign states.

Failure to question the claim of universality embedded in Western secular modernity has kept the seminal question of the real meaning of universal history, as an open-ended, non-totalizable, dialectical process, at bay. The selfless and admirable ways in which certain West Indians and African Americans in New York participated in the fight for labour rights and self-government in the region put the question of the search for our universal humanity at centre stage. The choice the West Indian leaders made invites the conclusion that they did their part to secure the reproduction of the fragmented world which is the stalking ground for big-power chauvinism and other ways of promoting instability and insecurity in the name of state security and at the expense of human security.

The counter-revolutionary way the United States responded to the Cuban Revolution radically redefined and reconfigured hemisphere international relations and geopolitics by making the region and the wider world more unstable and insecure. The US pursuit of an unattainable, absolute global supremacy was evident in the way it exploited anti-communist ideology to weaken British Guiana and threaten and isolate Cuba. The right to exploit for the ends of private capital accumulation exposes the fault lines between self-determination and capitalism, confirming that capitalism is organized against the realization of substantive democracy, and state sovereignty always rests on some form of domination, exclusion and insecurity. It was and remains romantic to claim that the populist aims and objectives of the anti-imperialist political leaders in the West Indies could secure the labour rights, freedom and sovereignty that the working-class masses thought would be realized, if they put their confidence in and rallied behind the decolonizing elite and give them a mandate to rule democratically on their behalf.

5.

HISTORIC COMPROMISE AND POLITICAL CONSENSUS IN BARBADOS

ONE OF THE IMPORTANT CONCERNS TO BE addressed in this chapter is the plausible notion that the creation of the DLP in 1955 by Errol Barrow and other BLP dissidents was responsible for splintering and fragmenting the working class and retarding its development as an independent political force in the society. This issue will be addressed against the background of the agro-commercial–dominated political economy, with attention to the roles that the political parties, the BWU, and dominant capitalist interests played to anchor and strengthen the "historic compromise"[1] around which political consensus was forged, with the effect of subordinating the majority working-class interests to those of the dominant minority. The "historic compromise" was the main strut that supported the consensus the political parties reached for governing Barbados, beginning before independence. The working class was not necessarily an innocent bystander in its own subordination, bearing in mind that it did develop into a "class in itself" that lacked the means to become a "class for itself". Its relatively large numbers did not translate into independent political strength: everything was done by the political parties, the leadership of organized labour and the capitalist interests to control the space within which it developed and reproduced itself.

MERCHANT'S CAPITAL, AGRO-COMMERCIAL CAPITAL
AND CAPITALISM IN LATE COLONIAL BARBADOS

Commodity production in Barbados was organized mainly around the use of basic tools and techniques for participation in the international division of labour. The economic specialization did not result from the social needs of the society, but rather from business decisions that agro-commercial interests made in relation to what was permitted under the imperialist division of labour that the British ruling class imposed on the British Empire. The form of capitalist organization of production in Barbados reflected the pervasive influence of merchant capital in the economic organization of political power and governance in Barbados, bearing in mind that politics is the concentrated expression of economics. The point here is that those who dominate economic life are never indifferent to politics and the distribution of power in society.

In its historical context merchant's capital is expressed in and through the dominance of money-dealing capital in economic and commercial activities. The dominance of merchant capital in the agro-commercial economic process in Barbados set the parameters within which labour had to reproduce capital and therefore its capacity to reproduce itself. Uneven and combined development is characteristic of the international spatial organization of capitalist production. By extension, the discourse of development versus underdevelopment as two distinct spheres that characterize advanced capitalist countries (development) and economically retarded countries (underdevelopment) is ideologically weighted and theoretically and empirically difficult to defend. Objectively, so-called underdevelopment is a sign that the capitalist process in the colonies was not organized to transform the productive forces and exploit labour at highly intense levels because of imperialist priorities that were seen in the fact that modern science and technology and innovation were far more expensive to produce and apply to the production process than was unskilled and semi-skilled labour power (Kay 1975; Warren 1980; Watson 2015a). The antisocial private accumulation imperatives of capitalists inform the logic and process of uneven and combined development (Pradella 2015, 152).

Karl Marx argues that the "real science of modern economy only begins when theoretical analysis passes from the process of circulation to the process of production". Marx emphasizes that "merchant's capital is older than the capitalist mode of production, is . . . historically the oldest free state of existence of capital" ([1894] 1971, 323).[2] In distinguishing between merchant's capital and industrial capital, Marx points out that "nothing could be more absurd than to regard merchant's capital, whether in the shape of commercial or of money-dealing capital, as a variety of industrial capital, such as . . . mining, agriculture, cattle-raising, manufacturing, transport, etc., which are sidelines of industrial capital occasioned by the division of social labour, and hence different spheres of investment". Marx's point is that when "manufacture gains sufficient strength, and particularly large-scale industry", then "commerce becomes the servant of industrial production, for which expansion of the market becomes a vital necessity". The "industrial capitalist always has the world-market before him . . . and must constantly compare his own cost-price with the market-prices at home, and throughout the world" ([1894] 1971, 336, 337). The home market is therefore one part of the real market of the industrial capitalist.

Marx notes that the "capitalist mode of production presupposes production for trade, selling on a large scale . . . hence also a merchant who does not buy to satisfy his personal wants but concentrates the purchases of many buyers in his one purchase". Historically, when merchant capital "holds a position of dominance, [it] stands everywhere for a system of robbery, so that its development among the trading nations of old and modern times is always directly connected with plundering, piracy, kidnapping slaves, and colonial conquest; as in Carthage, Rome, and later among the Venetians, Portuguese, Dutch, etc." ([1894] 1971, 327, 331). The "law that the independent development of merchant's capital is inversely proportional to the degree of development of capitalist production is particularly evident in the history of the carrying trade . . . where the principal gains were not . . . made by exporting domestic products, but by promoting the exchange of products of commercially and otherwise economically undeveloped societies, and by exploiting . . . producing countries". For Marx this "monopoly of the carrying trade disintegrates, and with it this trade itself, proportionately to the economic development of the peoples whom it exploits at both ends of its course, and whose lack of development was the basis of its existence" ([1894] 1971, 328–29; see also Pradella 2015).

In attempting to make sense of the development of the capitalist (agro-commercial) production processes that dominated the political economy in Barbados, it is necessary to appreciate what Marx says about the place of merchant capital in the development of capitalism. The capitalist forces in colonial Barbados were compelled to specialize in activities that complemented the industrial transformation of Britain over time, such that the development of a productive industrial base was never the driving force in the economic and social development of Barbados and other West Indian colonies. The colonies and their economic specializations were controlled by the political decisions that were set by sterling, in keeping with the interests of Britain's ruling class, with its far-flung interests, confirming that the political economy is organized to function as part of the larger political process. The separation of economics from politics is socially determined rather than the result of natural evolution. The social class structure of accumulation in Barbados reflected the deformities of economic retardation with reference to the relative backwardness of the productive forces (Lewis 1949, 1978).

The situation in which the circulation of commodities dominated economic activity and social life forced the state under the BLP and DLP to follow a trajectory they did not control. With independence the DLP became what Michael Howard labelled a "limited entrepreneur" via "limited direct participation in . . . agro-industry, agricultural marketing, and the hotel industry . . . in areas normally considered the preserve of the private sector" (Howard 2006, 30). Assertions by any government, its technocrats and organic intellectuals notwithstanding, at no time was it the concern of international (foreign) capital to enter Barbados to transform the economy and raise the quality of life of the population. Capitalists invest productive capital to expand the cycle of capital accumulation, which is substantively a global process.

Governments see things in national terms; however, capitalists, for whom the world economy is their real market, aim to banish national obstacles to the free movement of capital in the interest of private accumulation. Governments and their technocrats will emphasize that they are pursuing economic development to achieve national economic autonomy, which is far from the motive or vocation of international capital. This is where it is possible to discern the tension in the relationship between national states, with reference to the determination of national development priorities, and those of private capital accumulation.

SUBJECTIVE AND OBJECTIVE FACTORS IN THE MAKING OF THE WORKING CLASS IN BARBADOS

At the end of World War II, the Colonial Office declared, "The colonies . . . are primarily agricultural and they must continue to rely on agricultural production . . . for their main source of national wealth. This does not . . . mean that the total income of particular colonies cannot be enhanced by the improvement of existing industries or by the introduction of new ones" (Colonial Office 1947, 90; see also Howard 2006, 25). Keith Hunte (1988) argues that the DL organized and mobilized on behalf of a working class that was fragmented and forced to reproduce itself in largely isolated urban and rural villages, consistent with the low level of the development of the productive powers of labour and industry. As sites of captive labour supplies, those village communities were reproduced as integral part of racialized capitalist social relations in which merchant's capital dominated agro-commercial production and conditioned the exercise of state power.

The Colonial Office made it clear that British imperialism in the Caribbean did not need modern economic and industrial techniques for producing commodities to transform the material conditions of production and integrate the labouring population into a modern society in a rapidly changing world. Dialectically, village life also provided space for working-class people and their communities to resist attempts by the agro-commercial capitalists to deepen the commoditization of their existence, by creating friendly societies and other social entities to anchor social life and thereby hold at bay some of the most egregious features of the dehumanizing order. It would take decades for Barbados to be transformed from a large number of villages that were tied to sugar-dependent agriculture into a modern society in which primary production would play a less pronounced role relative to its contribution to output, employment, income, exports, and gross domestic product (Worrell 1994–95).

The decline of plantation agriculture in Barbados was occasioned by transformations that were occurring in the international political economy to which the Barbadian state and business interests were compelled to respond. The systematic decline of the sugar industry and of export-dependent agriculture coincided with the transition from colony to independence, and profoundly affected village life and the fortunes of the working class. The productive landscape and village life[3] in Barbados were transformed, giving way to a modern society in which tourism, light manufacturing, assembly activities (such as garments and electronics) and banking and non-bank financial activities and the expansion of the public sector as a leading employer of labour, as well as other services, would play important roles.

The DL and the BPL were effective in mobilizing, politicizing and educating the public with a view to framing the narrative about how the working class should respond to the difficulties and challenges they were forced to endure. Robert Morris notes that the pervasiveness of seasonal employment in agriculture compounded the uncertainty and insecurity that stalked the rural working class (1988, 40–46, 47, 50, 51). The DL and the BPL, and later on the WINCP, the BLP and the BWU, became the most active and effective organizations that mobilized and politicized the working class within fairly narrow limits. For a class in itself to become a class for itself that is capable of self-consciously fighting for its interests, it must come to understand its history, its role and mission, and the associated contradictions and possibilities that exist; even then its members have a responsibility to learn how to navigate the rapids of individualism, disorganization, fragmentation, insecurity and alienation that capitalism and liberalism impose on society under particular conditions of market anarchy.

Workers must also come to understand why their social reproduction is heavily bound up with being compelled to produce their opposite, which is capital. The starting point, therefore, is to understand the political basis of their separation as workers from the means of production, which left them with only their labour power to exchange for wages. In order for the working class to "stop making capital" (Holloway 2005) and work toward achieving real human dignity, it must understand fragmentation and splintering as normal in the uneven spatial division of labour and social reproduction under capitalism, and how such conditions work to reinforce class power and rule.

When the Great Depression erupted with the Wall Street crash of 1929, the sugar industry throughout the Caribbean was severely affected by the precipitous decline in the world price of sugar from 2.18 cents per pound in 1928 to 0.57 cents per pound by 1932, which compounded "economic disaster throughout the region" and became one of the main causes of "the social and political changes that followed. All Caribbean territories, whether . . . British, French, or US-dominated, were seriously affected . . . in similar ways" (Bolland 2012, 5; see Mordecai 1968, 21; Marshall 1988, 2, 12; Worrell 1994–95, 75–76; Hart 2002, 6–7). Capitalist crisis also creates opportunities for counter-hegemonic political struggles such as occurred in the working-class rebellion in the Caribbean during the 1930s, from which labour unions and political parties emerged and helped to bolster greater resistance to colonial oppression and racialized economic exploitation that resulted in reforms under the bourgeois democratic revolution.

Richard Hart associates "low wages; high unemployment and underemployment; arrogant racist attitudes of the colonial administrators and employers in their relations with black workers; lack of adequate . . . representation; and no established structure for the resolution of industrial disputes by collective bargaining" with the "common causes of working class unrest" throughout the Caribbean. For Hart the "fact that the grievances caused by these factors existed in all these colonies explains why, despite the lack of inter-colony contacts, the labour rebellions of the 1930s were an inter-colony phenomenon, sweeping like a wave across the region" (2002, 3–4).

Bolland argues that there were certain continuities that the post-emancipation societies in the British, Dutch, French and Spanish colonies experienced, including the "persistence of the plantation system and the concentration of land ownership associated with the production of sugar, the extreme social inequalities that resulted from this economic system, and the ideological and political systems that helped to perpetuate the hegemony of the planter class". Bolland notes that various "forms of resistance to these systems of domination were widespread and persistent, including the withdrawal of labour through strikes and emigration, the sabotage of planters' property, and a growing racial and class consciousness among working people that challenged their inferior social status" (2012, 1; see Hart 2002, 5–7; Will 1992, 10).[4]

Physical and political persecution and abuse of Jamaican, Haitian and other immigrant workers in Cuba and the Dominican Republic were directly linked to the unemployment situation, which capitalist crisis creates, and the same capitalists and the state routinely exploit as part of waging class struggle against the working class, dividing workers along ethnic, national and gender lines, often resorting to xenophobia to whip up nationalist and racist ideology, hostility and violence. Unemployment reinforces insecurity among workers, often producing psychological problems and alienating groups of workers from one another at the expense of contributing to building solidarity among them. Capitalists adopt tactics to separate their need for the labour power of workers from the workers' sense of their humanity, such as Haitians experienced in the Dominican Republic, where between twelve thousand and twenty thousand who toiled as sugar plantation workers were massacred in 1937 under the brutal regime of Rafael Trujillo (Bolland 2012, 5).

The aftermath of the Great Depression and the outbreak of World War II compounded problems for the entire Caribbean, which was an import-dependent zone, in bolstering export trade with the colonial powers. The prices of most imports increased, as did the cost of living in general, and the war led to an acute shortage of imports. The great "majority of the population experienced a decline in the standard of living between 1929 and 1945" (Bolland 2012, 6). C.L.R. James (1962) argues that the process leading from 1937 to independence in the West Indies inflicted terrible damage upon the population. He says, "In reality our people were miseducated, our political consciousness was twisted and broken. Far from being guided to Independence by the 1960s . . . the Imperial government poisoned and corrupted that sense of self-confidence and political dynamic needed for any people about to embark on the uncharted sea of independence and nationhood" (quoted in Belle 1988, 87).

According to Richard Hart, "In the 1930s, apart from the regional organisations established by the sugar manufacturers and the governing bodies of the sport of cricket, there was little or no inter-colony contact." There was also "migration to Trinidad of workers from the smaller eastern Caribbean islands, particularly Grenada, for employment in the oil industry. There had also been migration from these islands and Barbados to Guiana. But apart from these migrations, the workers in each colony had remained isolated from their counterparts in the other colonies" (Hart 2002, 3). The British colonial order discouraged the development of a clear sense of social and political consciousness among the colonized of their contributions to world history and culture; they also made it difficult for the people to acquire a clear appreciation of a British West Indian identity, much less a Caribbean identity. Colonial education extolled the virtues of imperialism, war, conquest and other racialized, antisocial values about the "white man's burden".

The experience Charles Duncan O'Neal gained from building the DL led him to conclude in retrospect, in a fit of frustration, that an important part of any effort to build self-confidence and political consciousness among the working class in Barbados had to be a systematic programme of political education.[5] O'Neal understood that human agency develops and expresses itself within the constraints that result from particular historical conditions; he would have agreed with Marx that "with destitution the struggle for necessities and all the old filthy business would necessarily be reproduced" (quoted in Valdes 2016).

The economic crisis and attendant political struggles that beset Barbados during the 1930s did not develop into an objective revolutionary situation. The makers of the working-class rebellion fought to reform the harsh conditions they endured under the colonial political economy, never failing to describe themselves as loyal colonial subjects of the Crown, and insisting on singing "God Save the King" in their moments of rebellious assertiveness and resistance. In the minds of many of them, the "Mother Country" was hardly the source of their predicament. George Lamming observed that to colonial subjects, the king and the empire became "bigger than the garden . . . and nothing else mattered but the empire. . . . The empire and the garden . . . both belong to God." Their wild misconception that God had "saved the king" led them to project the myth that they could also expect to "see the garden again" to realize "a sort of salvation . . . through grace" (1953, 67, 68).[6]

Mordecai argues that during the interwar years and after in the West Indies, the rising leaders supported adult suffrage, with many of them showing an interest in "only a limited suffrage". He notes that during that time, "West Indian politics was dominated by middle-class leaders, who sought the support of the urban working classes, but were not primarily interested in working-class problems. Their chief objective was greater middle-class participation in government" (Mordecai 1968, 18; see also James 1962). The middle-strata leaders used the working class to advance their narrow interests and they were quite comfortable with the gradualism that informed the Bushe Experiment, which set the context for the bourgeois democratic revolution (Belle 1988).

It is necessary to consider the oppressive dimensions of gender within the context of racialized class contradictions. In 1921, as Mary Chamberlain points out, the proportion of females to males in the population of Barbados was 59.7 per cent to 40.3 per cent, with 148 females per 100 males (2010, table 2). There are broad implications that stemmed from this demographic profile. Chamberlain says it

> contributed significantly to the low pay of the rural workers. Women . . . were paid less than men for the same work. . . . Poverty was . . . gendered and generational. . . . Moreover, mother-headed households, in which the woman was the main or sole wage earner, were a predominant feature of Barbadian (and Caribbean) family structures. . . . Barbados was one of the poorest of the British West Indies colonies. Public health was "peculiarly deplorable". Infant mortality was at devastating levels. (2010, 53–54)

Marvin Will describes the precarious condition of working-class black women in Barbados during the 1930s as follows:

> Despite their frequent head-of-household responsibilities, women seemed to encounter the worst treatment. Many worked as common "manual" labourers, frequently carrying very heavy loads (more than seventy

pounds) on their heads. As domestic servants, they generally received no board or sick leave and earned but 6–12s. per week for six to nine daily hours of hard labour – an amount that declined to as little as 1s. 6d. per week when food was included! Female employees in the smaller shops laboured long hours for 16s. per month. (1992, 14–15)

Most women did not meet the property qualification for the franchise, as most did not own property or derive the requisite income from property or education, so they could not vote.[7] Women gave birth, headed households, worked in a variety of capacities in households, the state and capitalist sector, served as caregivers, political activists and canvassers for candidates, joined political parties and labour unions, raised their and other people's children and paid their dues in other ways without which labour power could not be reproduced (Bolles 1996). Many women continue to endure patriarchal oppression at the hands of men and state and non-state institutions.

THE FRAGMENTATION AND DISORGANIZATION OF THE WORKING CLASS IN BARBADOS

The working class in Barbados did not simply become a victim of splintering as a result of the creation of the DLP in 1955. There is no compelling evidence that either the BLP or DLP has been a working-class political party, according to any realistic criteria. The split within the BPL that resulted in the creation of the WINCP and the BLP reflected great dissatisfaction by Crawford and company with Adams's political management style, which subordinated working-class interests and needs to colonial imperatives. Adams also worked deliberately to expel progressive and revolutionary cadres from the BPL, the BLP and the BWU.

Barbados Superior Court judge John Connell argues that the formation of the DLP in 1955 played a decisive role in fragmenting the working class.[8] Connell made the plausible claim that the security, strength and power of the working class, when understood in relation to the development of its ideological and political consciousness, were hampered by the increase in the number of political parties, which divided workers along party lines under parliamentary government. It is worth paying closer attention to Connell's contention, considering that the fragmentation of the working class in historical perspective did not originate with the rise and development of competitive party politics.

Modern party politics, which has been a distinctive feature of the development of liberal democracy, forms an important component of capitalist "social control formation". At the level of civil society, party politics plays an important role via formal political participation by helping to channel the political energies of the working class into predictable paths of regulation and control. The working class arises under capitalism first as a labouring mass that becomes a class in itself. Separated from the means of production, the working class is compelled to reproduce capital as the necessary precondition for reproducing itself. Patrick Emmanuel identifies and describes the "principal landmarks" for contextualizing the relationship between the trade unions and political parties in Barbados. He provides important dates and events, paying attention to certain changes that occurred in the island's "constitutional rules", the forms and process of "political mobilization and institutional formation" that occurred in the "non-official political system", the "concrete policy issues" around the struggles between officialdom and the mass struggle, and the "ideological dispositions" of the political figures who sought to manage and control the working class as a mass (1988, 94, 95).

The BLP and BWU emerged from the BPL, which was an umbrella organization that became differentiated only in 1941, when the BWU was registered. Marvin Will stresses that Wynter Crawford's "significant role . . . in the development of Barbadian labour party politics has been frequently ignored by contemporary historians" (1992, 9, 10, 73). Will says, "Despite the lack of mass political and labour organizations in Barbados, the officialdom of the Barbados Progressive League was not an association of amateurs", considering the names of the associates:

> C. Brathwaite, C.E. Talma, Martineau, H. Seale, G. Adams, W. Crawford, and others. Hon. C.E. Talma said it was "during 1938 . . . that the Barbados Progressive League was born, and Sir Grantley Adams was the first Vice-President. He then became President and I had the privilege of serving as the first General Secretary both of the Barbados Progressive League and the Barbados Labour Party. The Progressive League was the parent

body which founded the Barbados Labour Party and the Barbados Workers Union, [of] both of which organizations Sir Grantley was the founder and leader for many . . . years since 1940." (Will 1992, 66)

Harold Hoyte quotes Torrey Pilgrim, who did "considerable research on Crawford", as saying,

> Contemporary historians dealing with the builders of Barbados have highlighted the role played by Sir Grantley and Tom Adams as well as Errol Barrow in the post-1937 restructuring of its social, economic and political life. However . . . in-depth research into the activities of the period reveals that, in terms of his Congress Party platform projections and the resolutions he tabled in the House of Assembly as far back as the 1940s, Crawford must be credited with the blueprint of modern Barbados. (Hoyte 2015, 428)

It is indisputable that Wynter Crawford and the WINCP represented a "radical political force" in the immediate postwar Barbadian political environment, significantly ahead of the BLP and the DLP (Drayton 2014, 121–22).

Marvin Will notes that the "membership of the Progressive League soared to 20,000–30,000 adherents within approximately one year", and despite the extremely difficult economic circumstances for urban and rural working-class folks "and the reality of economic depression which made regular payment of the six cents (rural) and twelve cents (urban) monthly dues impossible for many, a bankroll of some $10,000 was raised by November 1939 to facilitate the purchase of a much-needed building for permanent headquarters on Roebuck Street". Will stresses that "conflicts among the BPL leaders soon emerged and made cooperation difficult if not impossible around strategy and tactics, ideology, and significant personality differences" (1992, 66).

The differences and tensions were remarkable between Adams, with his gradualist, Asquithian liberal stance (Phillips 1998), and Herbert Seale and Wynter Crawford, men who exhibited an explicitly progressive and pro-working-class outlook. Sir Hilary Beckles captures a critical dimension of Crawford's progressive and socialist-oriented worldview, saying, "The Congress Party was most incisive in its evaluation of those events (1937) and made no compromises in its self-assertion as the radical wing of the labour movement; and Crawford in particular suggested that both Adams and the Electors Association were involved in plots to undermine the workers' search for power and to deflect the movement from socialism" (quoted in Hoyte 2015, 426–27).

Edwy Talma, who recorded the original notes of the founding meetings of the BPL (March–April 1938), insisted that the organization was officially named the Barbados Progressive League; Talma acknowledges, however, that the "party concept was promoted in the early sessions". Marvin Will notes that Grantley Adams, who was in St Lucia "on professional (legal) business at the time of the inaugural meeting, was elected Vice-President of the League" (1992, 18, 74n 2). Will emphasizes that Crawford's name[9] does not appear in F. A. Hoyos's account of the founding of the BPL in 1938, "even though the initial meeting would not have been held without his input and that of Hope Stevens, a Tortolan then residing in the United States, whom Crawford invited" to the meeting (Will 1992, 74; see also Crawford 1991, 15).[10]

Hoyos claims that Grantley Adams was regarded as a dangerous agitator and caused much discomfort and consternation among the oligarchs, as he reminded them of the great distress in the country and warned them of the lessons to be learned from the French Revolution. A major price Adams paid, according to Hoyos, was that the predominantly white Bridgetown solicitors, who had close contacts with the regime, "began to withdraw their briefs from Grantley", reducing his "lucrative practice . . . to a trickle and he had to rely mainly on such modest fees as the poor could afford to pay for his services" (Hoyos 1988, 3–4). L.E. Smith remarked from the House of Assembly floor that Sir Grantley made significant sacrifices to advance the interests of the "barefooted people" and he "went forward and made history". During the days of "blood and fire" he was "fighting money without a cent. . . . But he was fighting for the people of Barbados. . . . He has done a . . . job that none of us will ever be able to do the way he did it because he did it without material . . . he fought a battle without ammunition and won."[11]

Some of the initiatives that O'Neal and the DL fought for and put on the political agenda were incorporated into the BPL's political programme.

Adams's strategy was to harness the workers' movement to the liberal political goals that reflected his personal outlook and career objectives, which were consistent with the gradualism that Whitehall preferred for managing decolonization. Adams was caught in the cauldron of rapidly and unpredictably changing political circumstances he could not effectively control; he therefore conveniently employed progressive-sounding, populist rhetoric to reach and control the working class. Hoyos made the candid observation that he was personally charged with the task of seeing to it that Adams did not go over to the side of the socialists (Hoyos 1988).

With Clennell Wickham's removal from high political visibility, with the politically orchestrated closure of the *Weekly Herald* newspaper, and following O'Neal's death in 1936, "Adams was well positioned at the Parliamentary level to subordinate what was . . . a socialist workers' movement under the umbrella of a radical civil rights movement. . . . While Adams was consolidating his position within the House of Assembly, radical workers, some of whom remained sceptical and hostile to his liberal political style and ideas, saw the need for autonomous organizations to further the process of agitation" (Beckles 2004a, 192). Beckles emphasizes that Adams emerged on the Barbadian political scene as a critic of O'Neal and his socialist vision, when he suggested that the realistic path was for the workers' movement to acknowledge the power of the merchant and planter ruling forces and "recognize that only gradualist non-confrontational policies could gain important concessions from employers". Beckles adds that Adams's "criticisms of the Democratic League did much to undermine its potential as a Parliamentary force". By 1936, however, Adams was forced to support some of the changes the DL proposed or introduced in the House of Assembly that were popular with workers, including the extension of the franchise, compulsory education for black children, abolition of child labour laws, and workers' rights to combine in trade unions (Beckles 2004a, 191).[12]

Marvin Will accurately portrays Adams as a late convert to "progressivism" and a reluctant supporter of a quickly changing reality and momentum that neither Whitehall nor the local capitalist forces that dominated local politics could readily control.[13] The claim that the "masses" saw Adams as "Moses . . . who led us from the wilderness to the promised land"

(Will 1992, 79) should not be dismissed, given the very high expectations of the working class of a messiah in the person of an educated, middle-strata leader they felt they could trust to deliver them from the dreadful conditions of racialized capitalist domination and oppression. The broad mass of working-class people believed that the educated "middle-class" leadership (see James 1962) possessed the skills, knowledge, training and competence to join forces in a common cause and direct the charge to overcome the obstacles that the ruling forces in Barbados put up to maintain their racialized class power and rule.

Hugh Springer was treasurer of the League of Coloured Peoples in London in 1937. After completing university studies in London, he returned to Barbados in 1938 and "teamed up with Grantley, who had then taken the leadership of the Barbados Progressive League" – "a partnership that ended when Springer left Barbados to become the first Registrar of the University College of the West Indies in Jamaica" (Sealy 1991, 15; see Hoyos 1988, 34; Mark 1966, 131–32).[14] Springer observed in 1959 that he did not agree with "several of Adams' early positions, but when he returned to Barbados in 1938", and Adams pleaded with him to assist him, he agreed to join forces with him because he was convinced that Adams had the driving ambition and "the greatest potential for leadership"; he was therefore "happy working with Adams in both the party and the Barbados Workers Union".[15]

Clennell Wickham, one of Adams's most uncompromising critics from the 1920s, also decided to support Adams's leadership of the working-class and labour movement (Will 1992, 79n33). Marvin Will points out that Wickham wrote to H.A. Vaughan, urging him: "support Adams, Saul has become Paul" (Will 1992, 79–80n2).[16] Beckles says, "Wickham . . . also noted that Adams had become increasingly concerned with defending and extending workers' rights by constitutional reform, and welcomed him as a critic of and opposer of planter chauvinism and oligarchy", and as one who seemed capable of arranging a marriage of convenience between the "representation of workers, and the general pursuit of civil rights" (2004a, 192).

The political terrain on which working-class struggles are waged under capitalism does not constitute a non-negotiable ground floor of freedom

(Žižek 2012) that workers can assume to be protected from being under-mined or abolished. Capitalists are always searching for ways to reduce production costs and raise the rate of profit, and they try to ensure that laws and administrative procedures, guidelines and programmes are framed to subsume freedom, rights, justice, equality and democracy under their right to exploit labour and force workers to bear the brunt of economic crisis. In fact, capitalists are never comfortable with any given regime of accumulation, given that crisis inheres in the capital relation, and they never commit to the pursuit of democracy with social content.

In 1941 the BWU registered as a labour organization, the same year the Conservative Electors' Association was formed to represent the interests of capitalists and certain others in the society. In 1942 the BPL contested the general election and won four seats to the twenty seats the Conservative Electors' Association won. Legislation was enacted in 1943 to reform the franchise, extend the franchise to women who met the requirements to vote, and amend the newly enacted trade union law. The extension of the franchise in the 1940s under the Representation of the People Act of 1943 lowered the income qualification to vote to £25, which extended the franchise to a limited number of women.

In 1944 Wynter Crawford and certain BPL defectors "supported by Chrissie Brathwaite, Talma and J.E.T. Brancker, among others, left the Progressive League under Adams to form Crawford's WINCP. The party proclaimed having a 'vigorously socialistic programme' and . . . won as many seats (8) as the League in the 1944 elections" (Emmanuel 1988, 100). The creation of the WINCP and the seats it won in 1944 signalled that the work O'Neal and the DL had done was yielding respectable results among the electorate. Chamberlain notes that largely, "the goals and membership of the WINCP were interchangeable with other West Indian organizations, reflecting the chameleon nature of political activism as it formed and reformed in response to particular situations and crises in the West Indies. Thus in 1947, Richard B. Moore, as Secretary of the American Committee for West Indian Federation, was addressing the Caribbean Labour Congress in September 1947" (2010, 158). Clearly, the small size of the WINCP did not prevent it from punching above its weight.

Crawford had been sceptical about Adams's tactics dating back to the 1930s, especially his claim that he was a champion of working-class interests. The BLP under Adams drew a line between "the island's law-abiding inhabitants, as distinct from the so-called lawless poor among whom [Clement] Payne was alleged to have extensive support" (Beckles 1990, 170). Adams made clear his class commitments and strivings, which transcended his objective class position.

THE BUSHE EXPERIMENT AND THE RESTRUCTURING OF WHITE SUPREMACY IN BARBADOS

The Bushe Experiment, which was implemented in Barbados in 1946, was a British initiative on which the "historic compromise" would be built to supervise the gradual deconstruction of colonialism in the West Indies, based on capitalist hegemony and the protection of white supremacy in a somewhat modified form. The process that unfolded in the House of Assembly was not entirely under the control of any group of white or black politicians: the two groups shared a general interest in preventing the fledgling working class from shaping the trajectory of the postwar politics and political economy of the territory. The white-dominated colonial administration shared power with Whitehall through the Office of the Governor, the colonial secretary and others, in an arrangement that satisfied Grantley Adams's Asquithian, liberal perspective, according to which the colonized had to be carefully supervised to determine their readiness for self-government (Lewis 1999, 198–202 and passim).

With the response of the recalcitrant elements among the ruling class forces in mind, George Belle (1988, 78–79) argues that there were "some 'hard headed' people" in Barbados who were "resisting even the gradualist approach":

> They are told that they have to learn, and some of their own class then start to teach them, like Attorney General E.K. Walcott. You see him lecturing them in the House of Assembly: they have to let trade unions come in; they have to allow reforms; they have to let the vote be given to the people. Do it gradually, but do it, that is the way you will save yourselves.

Belle makes a statement that resonates with Gary Lewis's observation, according to which the colonial state was ahead of Adams in its readiness to accelerate the pace of decolonization. Belle says, "In 1946, in Barbados, the Governor is ahead of even the leader of the labour movement. The Governor is ready to give adult suffrage, and the leader of the labour movement is saying: 'We not ready yet.'" The hardheadedness and resentment that the capitalists were displaying revealed much about how the ruling class felt as it was losing direct control of the colonial state under British guidance. The point to bear in mind here is that the white segment of the population was not enthusiastic about the "historic compromise": they did not set out to showcase it, although it was designed to protect their general interest.

White supremacy anchored the racialization of social life in Barbados, and white economic and political hegemony produced a "unifying effect on Barbadian whites", bearing in mind that a serious appreciation of objective class differences within the small white population should temper any attempt to portray white Barbadians as an irreducibly monolithic racial group. Karl Watson (1998, 18, 25) argues that the persistence of the "myth of a white monolithic social structure" in Barbados stems from the habit of objectifying biological differences and misrepresenting the situation in linear terms of black and white. Watson's concept of the "myth of a white monolithic social structure" reminds us that race is itself an ideology (see Reed Jr 2013). The white segment of the Barbadian population is best seen in class terms, with attention to the dominant capitalist strata, the middling business and professional strata (petit-bourgeois elements) and working-class elements. Most whites in Barbados have had to reproduce themselves by selling labour power to the dominant local capitalists and foreign investors in exchange for wages and salaries. They comprise an extremely small portion of the population and also of the working class. Their embrace of white supremacy reflects their ideological prejudices and preferences; however, it does not negate their objective class position and the fact that they share much more in common with their non-white counterparts than with their exploiters, a fact that is not objectively negated even if they choose the "unobtainable" thing, race, over class.

With respect to the ongoing deterioration of Britain's international position after World War II, Ed Conway notes that George Bolton, who served as Britain's representative at the International Monetary Fund, spoke unflatteringly about the systemic decline of the country as a world power and of the marginalization of the British Empire that began even before the war. Bolton said,

> England and the Empire are, of course, entirely disregarded in any argument or summing up of the situation, and I have to accept the fact that we are perhaps of roughly the same importance in the world, either individually or as a group, as one of the Latin American countries. The recent decisions about India and Egypt are instances of indisputable proof of the approaching complete dissolution of the Commonwealth and the relegation of England to the level comparable with that of say Sweden or France. (Quoted in Conway 2015, 354; see Chamberlain 2010, 157)

Bolton's observations about Britain's systematic decline as a world power carried implications for that country's white supremacist masculinity that were reflected in opposition to the Universal Declaration of Human Rights and in the brutal response to the Mau Mau rebellion in Kenya (Elkins 2005).

The fact that Britain's growing powerlessness hardly registered with the West Indian decolonizing elites did not mean that the working class was supine in its behaviour. On the Barbados scene, the engineers went on strike in 1946, a move that gave the BWU the first major victory in an industrial dispute. The BLP won nine seats to the WINCP's seven seats in the 1946 election. The powers of the Legislative Council were reduced in 1949, in line with the curtailment of the powers of the House of Lords under the British Parliament Act of 1949. In the 1948 election the BLP won twelve seats to three seats for the WINCP. In 1951, when universal adult suffrage came into effect under the Representation of the People Act (1950), the BLP won fifteen seats to the Conservative Electors' Association's four, the Congress Party's two, and independents got three.

The electoral and political fortunes of the Conservative Electors' Association and Congress Party declined dramatically between 1946 and 1956 (see Chamberlain 2010, 156–57), a sign that the introduction of universal adult suffrage was having a significant impact on how the working-class majority was responding to political change. In 1952 J. Cameron Tudor resigned from the BLP, citing irreconcilable differences with Adams and the government. Ministerial government was introduced in 1954 with the creation of the office of premier. Disputes continued inside the BLP in the House of Assembly and on the political trail, to the point where Errol Barrow and other dissident parliamentarians left the BLP and formed the DLP in 1955.

The DLP fared poorly in the 1956 elections, winning only four of twenty-four seats to fifteen for the BLP; the Conservative Electors' Association won three seats; independents got the remaining two; the WINCP failed to win any parliamentary seats and was absorbed into the newly formed DLP shortly after (Emmanuel 1988, 96, 97). The political demise of the WINCP did not mean that the principles for which Crawford and the party fought and stalwartly defended, on the foundation the DL laid, had come to naught. In fact, Crawford's political footprint could be seen in the progressive programmes the DLP would adopt in due course (Chamberlain 2010, 158).

Ministerial government advanced in 1958 with the introduction of cabinet government, consistent with provisions of the Bushe Experiment. Adams resigned as premier in 1958 to become the prime minister of the Federation of the West Indies, after Norman Manley and Eric Williams had declined the offer from Whitehall to lead the federation (Chamberlain 2010, 162). The Conservative Electors' Association reorganized itself as the Progressive Conservative Party, which soon morphed into the Barbados National Party under the leadership of Ernest D. Mottley. The work of the DLP paid major dividends in 1961, when it won the general election with fourteen seats of twenty-four, against five for the BLP, four for the Barbados National Party, and one to an independent. The process of reorganization that was initiated by the capitalists occurred partly in the creation or strengthening of key business organizations such as the "Chamber of Commerce . . . the Manufacturers' Association . . . the Sugar Producers Association and the Barbados Employers' Confederation" (Cheltenham 1970, 252, 254–55).

The business organizations the capitalist forces created represented a strategic move to ensure that the black majority governments would not implement public policies that were injurious to their particular business imperatives and their general class interests. The inability of black majority governments to put the economy at the disposal of the state reflected the fact that private capital remained in control of the economy and strengthened its power in public policymaking, a move that made it more difficult to discern exactly how the ruling class would rule under changing conditions. Whatever improvements accrued to the black majority, the dominant white business forces gave up little or nothing of substance in exchange, which bolstered their ability to influence the pace and content of economic and social change.

Karl Watson notes that the conservative view had persisted among the Barbadian agro-commercial and associated "white minority" interests that the "exercise of political power should be linked to high social status and economic well-being. Lack of economic power should thus disqualify individuals from representing the community" (1998, 24).[17] Conservatives strongly believe that high social rank and status are natural, as opposed to stemming from economic, financial and other practices, some of which were bound up with expropriation, enslavement, genocide and other forms of primitive accumulation and crimes that are committed against the weak.

The hegemony of white supremacy rests on unsupportable claims for the existence of distinct biological human races, a tenet of scientific racism that features in the coding of liberalism and Western modernity (Goldberg 2002). Paul Broca referred to race as an "abstract conception . . . a conception of continuity in discontinuity, of unity in diversity . . . the rehabilitation of a . . . directly unobtainable thing" (quoted in Malik 1996, 120). Kenan Malik notes that Harvard University anthropologist Richard Dixon argued that when raciologists discovered that it would be impossible to derive any reliable criteria for measuring race, they settled for arbitrary, capricious and unreliable ways of representing race. It hardly mattered that race is a social construction and an ideology. Proponents of raciology began with "something that did not exist" as the "starting point for proving that it did". Raciologists created race as a modern category and container into which they could deposit whatever they fancied, to construct white supremacy to represent structures of local and global domination based on racial hierarchy (see Malik 1996, 121). This is what informs white supremacy as the "norm of world order". For Nancy Stepan, "the history of racial science is a history of a series of accommodations of the sciences to deeply held convictions about the naturalness of the inequalities between human races" (1982, xx–xxi; see also Goldberg 2002).

SOCIAL CLASS FORMATION AND THE "SPLINTERING" OF THE WORKING CLASS IN BARBADOS

Patrick Emmanuel notes that at the time of the 1946 census in Barbados "the population was 192,800 persons with blacks comprising 77.2 per cent . . . mixed race 17.5 per cent, whites 5.1 per cent and Asiatics 0.1 per cent". Blacks accounted for 49.0 per cent of employers compared with 28.0 white employers, while blacks accounted for 81.0 per cent of wage and salaried workers and whites 5.0 per cent. Blacks accounted for 78.0 per cent of the "self-employed (farmers, skilled trades, artisans, etc.) . . . 20.0 per cent were mixed and 2.0 per cent white" (1988, 102). DeLisle Worrell argues that the changes wrought in Barbados in the decade after World War II contributed to Adams's growing popular appeal among the working class. Worrell stresses that inequality remained entrenched even as output and national income improved, "permitting higher levels of consumption expenditure and attracting new investment" (1994–95, 76; see also Chamberlain 2010, 51–75). Real property in the means of production was concentrated in a number of predominantly white (capitalist) hands, which explain why blacks formed the vast majority of wage and salaried workers in a highly racialized class society.

The outlook of the black petite bourgeoisie made up of small business-people, who accounted for 49 per cent of employers, was conditioned broadly by the economic, financial and commercial rhythm and dictates of the dominant (white) capitalist sector, which was itself subject to the rhythm of international market forces and policies. The majority of black employers consisted predominantly of small merchants and shopkeepers who operated on the lower rungs of money-dealing (merchant's) capital and lacked the means and institutional support to transform themselves into big capitalists.

Conditions appeared to be changing for the mass of workers, partly on account of developments in the international economy. The export price of sugar more than doubled from the 1938 price to $87.8 per tonne in 1946 and "GDP at factor cost in 1946 of $40 million was two and one-half times as great as in 1938". There was expansion in agriculture, government, investment, building construction and domestic services, and private consumption rose in 1946, somewhat more slowly than gross domestic product, and the "balance of payments deficit on current account was made up by net capital inflows which contributed 42 per cent of domestic capital formation between 1946 and 1950". Wages rose in 1946 over the pre-World War II and World War II levels; however; the cost of living increased more quickly. The "public service rose from 2,600 persons to 3,600 persons between the fiscal years 1938–39 and 1946–47", with the "new jobs and the rising demand for the services of small traders, artisans, and domestic workers . . . [as] the main avenues by which the working class gained from the postwar expansion, but unemployment and underemployment remained chronic" (Worrell 1994–95, 76, 77).

Worrell alludes to another aspect of the class formation process and change in postwar Barbados that was reflected in a modest expansion of the middle strata and the blue-collar segments of the working class. He argues that in "social areas like education primary and secondary school enrolments improved between 1938–39 and 1945–46", though only "9 per cent of the primary school population made it to secondary school" (1994–95, 76, 77). The capitalist economy, which was organized predominantly around primary agricultural specialization and services, lacked a capital goods sector and a modern manufacturing base that was linked to research and development and technological innovation, and therefore had no need for large numbers of highly educated and technically trained and proficient cadres of workers.

The death rate declined "from 20 per thousand in the late 1930s to 16 per thousand in 1946 . . . though still high infant mortality fell into the range of 125–160 per thousand in 1946–50 considerably below the 1937 and 1938 figures of 217 and 22 respectively". Housing for the working class did not show any qualitative improvement (Worrell 1994–95, 77). The persistence of rigid class inequality in the period after 1951 would become an important issue inside the BLP that was reflected in the demand by Errol Barrow and certain other backbenchers for Adams to adopt a much more expansionary, neo-Keynesian approach, and a forward-looking strategy to attack the problem and improve the general situation.

The dominant capitalist interests were strategically situated and eager to service the expanding requirements of the state bureaucracy and meet the pent-up demand of the blue-collar and white-collar middle-strata workers and professionals for loans for housing and home furnishings, vehicles for personal transport, and other requirements. The Barbados Mutual and J.N. Goddard and Sons were among the companies that expanded and strengthened their positions, while maintaining close ties with the state as beneficiaries of incentives (Karch 1997, 2008). They also outgrew the spatial extent of the political economy of Barbados and expanded on a regional and international scale to overcome the constraints that were imposed by the limited economic scale and productive base of the territory.

The postwar working-class struggles in Barbados revolved largely around competing forces that battled for control of the decolonizing state to acquire the power to set agendas and determine priorities. The central issue revolves therefore around the location of political and economic power and who controls those levers in the state and civil society. By 1947, political and policy differences with Adams had intensified to the point where Crawford withdrew from the executive committee, on which he had served from 1946. Emmanuel argues that the political "hegemony" of the BLP was "bolstered by the patient and fruitful work of the Barbados Workers' Union from ten years previously" (1988, 100). Adams championed a juridical (deontological) conception of equal political rights for all. Crawford and the WINCP championed a progressive rights agenda that called for the nationalization of the essential means of production. Not to be completely upstaged by Crawford and the WINCP, Adams publicly announced his support for state acquisition of the sugar cane plantations and breaking them up into smallholdings for distribution among the small cane farmers.

This suggestion was a totally idealistic, petit-bourgeois, populist idea, the implementation of which would have triggered a far more profound crisis in the industry and society for the mass of small cane farmers and for foreign-exchange earnings for Barbados. As already noted, the international sugar industry was undergoing major techno-industrial restructuring that was accompanied by the ongoing concentration and centralization of capital and production in the industry worldwide (Deerr 1949). Barbados was an extremely marginal sugar producer, with backward productive forces, in an increasingly competitive international industry. It would have been impossible for a proliferation of smallholdings based exclusively on labour-intensive techniques of production and low productivity to contribute to any qualitative improvement in the performance of the sugar industry and the condition of the mass of new smallholders.

No doubt a viable alternative to sugar in Barbados was definitely worth considering; however, the plausible ideas that Adams and Crawford expressed for providing black agricultural labourers with ready access to land had gained the attention of the landless and otherwise property-less workers and seasonal small farmers much earlier. Would the land be distributed on the basis of freehold or leasehold? How would the owners be compensated, and at what cost to the state and society? Would productivity and competitiveness increase? Would the new tillers produce for export or subsistence? What might be the foreign-exchange implications, among other important considerations? Distribution of land to small tillers does not necessarily mean that the tillers own the land or have the resources, skills and technical proficiency to make things better for themselves and the society at large.

In 1935 William Macmillan made what sounded like a plausible case in *Warning from the West Indies* for a wholesome "mixed community of Europeans and Africans" to develop in the colonies, where "black people" would be left "economically and industrially free" with "command of their food supply by possessing their own land, and not . . . be deprived of it" (1936, 436–37). What Macmillan proposed was by no means the norm in the leading capitalist countries. Macmillan seemed to have overlooked the fact that capitalism must have a mass of dispossessed, propertyless people who are compelled to sell their labour power for wages if and when they can find work; it is also a fact that the abiding wish of every peasant and small farmer is to become a big capitalist.

The history of the sugar industry in Barbados from 1860 to 1976 was marked by the relentless concentration and centralization of capital in plantation holdings, even as the total acreage committed to plantation production systematically declined. In 1860 the average size of plantations was 194 acres, with some five hundred plantations which accounted for "a total acreage . . . of 89,264". A century later, in 1961, "the average size of plantations was 286 acres on a total acreage under plantation control of 71,910", which reflected a withdrawal of 17,354 acres from plantation production. Five years later (1966), "the total number of plantations had declined to 207 on a total acreage . . . of 68,712 with the average size of plantations of 347 acres". In 1976 there were two hundred plantations with an average size of 290 acres, and the total acreage under plantation control was 58,000 (Innis 1999, 9). There was a net decline in the number of plantations by 40 per cent and of total acreage under plantation control of 31, 264 acres over 116 years from 1860 to 1976.

The decline of plantation acreage under cultivation between 1966 and 1976 was 10,712 acres, or 35 per cent (Innis 1999, 9, table 1), which was significant by Barbadian standards. Much of the acreage withdrawn from plantation-based production in Barbados between 1961 and 1976 was used especially for housing development that was associated with the creation of new middle-strata residential suburbs; however, there was limited improvement in the scientific and technological modernization of the plantation production process. Patrick Emmanuel noted in 1988 that "the plantation system in Barbados is on its death-bed not because of any internal socio-political assault on it, but because of the same international forces of prices and competition with which it had so long battled" (1988, 111). The decline of large-scale plantation production in Barbados contributed to an ongoing shift of plantation workers into non-agricultural employment. The "politics of stable gradualism prevailed over the movement for rapid democratization" (1988, 103). The transfer of formal executive power from the governor to the elected House of Assembly and the abolition of veto power over House bills in the Legislative Council were not designed to give substantive power to the working-class majority within the scope of the bourgeois democratic revolution.

In a 2008 interview with the author, Woodville Marshall questions the claim that the rise of two-party politics in Barbados under the BLP and DLP is the main cause of the splintering of the working class under parliamentary democracy, where political fragmentation and alienation are legendary. Social and political fragmentation is a fact of life under capitalism, where the production process becomes more fragmented, in line with the concentration of capital and wealth. The alignment between the BWU with the BLP and DLP contributed to the fragmentation of the working class (Emmanuel 1988, 103; Horne 2007), considering that both parties became co-sponsors of Cold War–inspired, anti-working-class labour and trade union politics. At the West Indian level it was "Bustamante, Bird, Bramble, Bradshaw, Butler – the five great Bs – [who] emerged as trade union leaders later to develop political apparatuses as arms of their unions" (Emmanuel 1988, 104). Robert Bradshaw argued that Grantley Adams created an unnecessary problem for himself when he ceded control of the BWU to Frank Walcott, with politically costly consequences for the BLP in 1961 and after (Sealy 1991, 44, 107). In 1971 Adams echoed Bradshaw when he reminisced that "the best way to preserve the unity of the labour movement in Barbados was to have one organization, as the parent political party, and a trade union working together in close harmonious relations" (*Advocate News*, 14 February 1971, quoted in Emmanuel 1988, 104).

The unity of the labour movement Adams had in mind rested on keeping the working class disorganized. Bradshaw's perspective reflects the entrenched colonial and postcolonial political authoritarianism and centralism that continue to define the trajectory of party politics and trade union democracy in the British Caribbean (Bolland 2001, 2012). The rise of political movements, labour unions and political parties in Barbados in the twentieth century followed a path on which the parties and unions brought the working class under their control in ways that redounded to the benefit of the hegemonic project of capitalism and liberal democracy. The splintering of the working class is a function of bourgeois party politics, liberalism and capitalist organization of production.

LABOUR PARTY POLITICS, LABOUR AND WORKING-CLASS POLITICAL DEVELOPMENT IN BARBADOS

Grantley Adams, Frank Walcott and Frederick "Sleepy" Smith agreed that their participation in the labour movement and party politics was important in their own political development. Frederick Smith combined formal academic studies in classics at Codrington College with the study of law at Gray's Inn in London; he also studied Labour Party politics and British trade unionism in London. Smith notes that in the United Kingdom he "attended several Labour Party summer schools as well as a course with the Trade Union Congress . . . with Grantley Adams' consent". He said in an interview with Sharon Sealy, "Adams . . . trained me and sent me on a course to take over the union when he went to the Federal Government" (Sealy 2001, 19; see Smith and Smith 2015).

Smith joined the BLP in 1952 after he returned from the United Kingdom, confident about bringing his UK training and experience to bear on the development of the BWU, with the building of a mass base of political support for the BLP in mind. When he returned to Barbados he initially taught English to BWU secretaries to improve their oral and written language skills (Sealy 2001, 19). He forged a close relationship with Frank Walcott and with Adams, who was still head of the union. Adams appreciated the importance of attracting qualified individuals into the BLP, and he leveraged his middle-strata background, his Oxford University education and legal training to attract a critical mass of other British-educated individuals to the party, among them Hugh Springer, J. Cameron Tudor, Errol Barrow and Frederick Smith.

According to Sharon Sealy, Frederick Smith said: "Sir Grantley had been grooming him and Mr. Barrow to take up active positions in government. He was selected for union president and Mr. Barrow was to become leader of the BLP upon Sir Grantley's departure to lead the Federal Government" (2001, 24–25).[18] Smith enthusiastically entered the competition for the presidency of the BWU in 1954; however, Adams threw his support behind Walcott and McDonald Blunt (Sealy 2001, 1–19, 25; Bradshaw 1989, 14), to Smith's utter disappointment. Adams's commitment to Asquithian liberalism (Phillips 1998) contrasted with the eagerness of BLP junior members to experiment with social democratic approaches with a neo-Keynesian policy emphasis to address economic and social problems. Smith broke with Adams and the BLP in 1955, about two weeks before the DLP constitution was adopted and a week before the DLP was formally launched.[19]

Errol Barrow emphasized that it was never his intention to separate from the BLP to create a second labour party; however, he insisted that it became impossible to remain in the BLP and follow the very slow and accommodationist pace of change on which Adams had embarked, in the face of the harrowing conditions that plagued the great majority of the population.[20] Mainstream labour unions in capitalist societies are largely organized to address and respond to working conditions and bread-and-butter issues and other concerns of dues-paying members; they also set out to control their members, typically under top-down centralized leadership. It was this particular tendency that the CLC had the potential to overcome. Mainstream labour organizations tend to be heavily invested in free-market capitalism and liberal individualism. It is therefore predictable that they will try to keep their rank-and-file members politically fragmented, compromised and subordinated to capitalist economic interests and liberal politics and political party hegemony, consistent with tendencies in the bourgeois democratic revolution.

Typically, when political parties and labour unions began to develop in the West Indies, British political parties and trade union leaders worked systematically and intentionally to influence the political direction of the colonial political parties and unions, by promoting competing, pluralistic organizations, on the ground that such forms foster Western democratic values. The real intention, however, has been to steer them away from building ties with international socialist and communist organizations. The British entities encouraged them to adopt the liberal line of least resistance that leaves labour matters to trade union leaders, politics and government to political parties and politicians, government to those who exercise state power, and economics and the markets to capitalists – a division of labour that deprives the working class of an independent voice and role. Gordon Lewis notes that British trade unionist Sir Walter Citrine, a member of the Moyne Commission, recommended for

Barbados a "united Owen-like type of a general union . . . thus avoiding the fratricidal rivalry of different warring factions so characteristic of the Trinidad labour scene" (Lewis 1968, 235; see Howard 2006, 5–8). In the case of Jamaica, Theodore Sealy mentions that Norman Manley tried to get Bustamante to go along with one parent union connecting the JLP and PNP; Bustamante balked at the idea (1991). It did not mean, however, that Sir Walter Citrine favoured a labour union with an independent working-class, socialist outlook.

Emmanuel argues that the BWU, when compared with the Bustamante Industrial Trade Union in Jamaica and Eric Gairy's trade unions in Grenada, as well as those led by the "Big Bs", appeared to have developed a distinct form of internal structuring around a clearly defined division of labour, a distinctively non-charismatic "bureaucracy and leadership", worker education and other features that could enhance the professional character of the organization. At the outset the BWU was led by educated individuals like Adams and Hugh Springer, men who appreciated the importance of professionalism, discipline and unity for the advancement of the labour movement (Emmanuel 1988, 96, 97; see Mark 1966). Given Adams's pro-Cold War, anti-working-class and anti-communist disposition, the manner in which he expelled the left from the BPL, the BLP and the BWU and the relentless way he went about destroying the CLC, there was little doubt that he intended to keep the BWU beyond capture by progressive working-class leaders. Employers in Barbados[21] and throughout the West Indies welcomed the destruction of the CLC, enthusiastically embraced CADORIT and became eager "fellow travellers" of the Cold War.

Between 1954 and 1961, with Frank Walcott leading the BWU, the union moved from having close ties with the BLP to parting ways with the ruling party, reducing any temptation for Barrow and the DLP to promote a competing labour organization to bolster their mass political and electoral base. Barbadian society was still predominantly agricultural, and it suited the DLP to work with the existing mass union in keeping with the consensus the parties and the BWU reached for governing the territory. The BWU has been strongly committed to capitalist hegemony and therefore to the capital accumulation strategy the DLP adopted, which stressed nominal indicative planning with emphasis on an active neo-Keynesian economic role for the state, attracting international capital and deepening the integration of the country into the international economy (Howard 2006, 29–32). Barrow and the DLP also preferred a BWU that emphasized negotiation with employers over working-class militancy in dealing with foreign investors. The DLP convinced the public that economic and political stability was necessary to promote job creation, rising living standards and the achievement of what was viewed as a "middle-class" society.

The three consecutive electoral victories the DLP won between 1961 and 1971 were not marked by a dramatic swing in the popular vote away from the BLP. The BLP lost the 1961 elections to the DLP on the basis of the number of parliamentary seats each party won; however, the BLP won slightly more of the popular vote than the DLP, which won fourteen of the twenty-four seats, with 36.3 per cent of the poll; the BLP won five seats with 36.8 per cent of the vote; the Barbados National Party won four seats with 22 per cent of the votes cast; and Frank Walcott was elected as the sole Independent. The BLP and Barbados National Party won a total of nine seats, with 58.8 per cent of the poll, compared with the DLP's fourteen seats and 36.3 per cent of the total votes cast, an outcome which shows that the majoritarian "first past the post" electoral system can yield results that do not necessarily reflect the actual voting preferences of the electorate (Emmanuel 1988, 108).

Sir John Mordecai says, "Mr. Barrow's assumption of office was nevertheless immensely popular, even to those who had not voted with him but were fed up with the 'old guard' and with the slow pace at which things habitually moved" (1968, 436). In the 1966 elections the DLP again won fourteen seats, and the BLP won more seats than it did in 1961; however, it fared rather poorly in 1971, when the DLP won 18 of the twenty-four seats in the House of Assembly (Emmanuel 1988, 96, 97).

The DLP intensified its efforts to attract international investment, which created business opportunities for local capital and expanded tourism and light export manufacturing (Howard 2006; Worrell 1994–95). The DLP government continued to subsidize the crisis-ridden sugar industry, which was being propped up by the protectionist provisions of the British Commonwealth Sugar Agreement to the satisfaction of the sugar producers and the state, as the agreement's provisions also helped to stabilize employment, income and consumption for the vulnerable sugar workers and their dependents. The BWU never stretched its imagination beyond the zone of pragmatic trade union democracy that connected neo-Keynesian income redistribution to electoral politics and representative government. This form of democracy "without social content" is rooted in the alienation of political power (Wood 1995) from any popular accountability. The DLP acted as a pragmatic political party that understood the scope and depth of the economic power and control by the dominant capitalists of the life of the society. Barrow made a priority of modernizing the economy and promoting class peace: he acted on the idea that for the programmes the DLP adopted to benefit the working class, the capitalists would have to reap the lion's share in conditions where they held an economic stranglehold on virtually every aspect of the economy, and where the aspirations of the rising blue-collar and middle-strata population were still relatively modest.

Decolonization in Barbados and the West Indies was based largely on the deepening of the "Westminster model"[22] of government. Two-party politics and the "orderly transfer of power" in Barbados have revolved around nominal competition between the BLP and DLP. The BWU political realignment has tended to favour the DLP; however, it has not resulted in any systemic political or electoral disasters that threatened to destroy the BLP. The reality is that both political parties have uncompromisingly united around the political consensus for governing Barbados that stemmed from the "historic compromise" discussed at length in this study. The strong voter support that the two political parties share is reflected in the fact that the swing vote tends to be a small percentage of the electorate. The point here is that the differences between the two parties are more technical than substantive.

The BWU claims to support those who support the workers. In fact, the position of the BWU oscillates between the centre-right social democracy of the BLP and the centre-left social democracy of the DLP. The political parties and the labour unions adopt centrist policies that are indicative of the risks that come with basing a country's development (capital accumulation) strategy on ready access to international capital to fuel economic growth (Worrell 1994–95). Such a strategy always imposes severe constraints on the options that are open to the working class, considering that for the political leaders and their labour-union allies, investment, jobs, foreign exchange and stability are too important to allow working-class political autonomy to shape the development trajectory and political priorities. The fact that capitalism is an international form of production limits the options that are open to any state that is strapped for investment capital to find national solutions to economic problems, where the balance of payments is routinely in negative territory, and international competitiveness is elusive.

The DLP, BLP and the labour unions nominally embrace an ideological notion of socialism that reflexively protects capitalists and capitalism from necessary working-class critique and resistance, which means also that the business strata in Barbados have had nothing to fear from socialism. In fact, they are hardly repulsed by social democracy, which has benefited them consistently. Richard Cheltenham noted that the BLP and the DLP have been united in embracing the political consensus on which "mercantile/planter interest within a mixed economy" was built (1970, 252). The fact, however, is that capitalists are always nervous about any given capital accumulation strategy, a predisposition that makes them mercurial.[23]

The changing class structure of Barbadian society is reflected partly in the presence of groups of black professionals in middle-management positions in the major business enterprises and in branches of foreign firms; however, senior executive decision-making authority remains largely under the control of white families (Howard 2006, 45; Beckles 1989). The working class, including the middle-strata workers, accepts the populist claim that entitlement to social democratic provisions is socialism in practice, as defined by the political consensus that is shared by the state, the political parties, organized labour, private capital and society at large. The social democratic entitlements that the state began to dispense on an expanded scale in the early 1960s strengthened its ability to control people's access to employment and social goods, thereby effectively shaping the contours of working-class social and political consciousness and behaviour. The insecurity that accompanies separation from the means of production, the extent of the uncertainty that is associated with overproduction and the alienation of power that characterize the marketization of politics make it easier to control the behaviour of the working class, regardless of political party affiliation. The situation is rendered more problematic for the working class where organized labour is technically pro-labour but substantively anti-working-class in values and political commitments.

Under Barrow the modernization process between 1961 and 1966 gathered momentum on a foundation the BLP gradually built from the early 1950s (Worrell 1994–95). Capital cooperated broadly with social democratic initiatives "such . . . as enforceable wage agreements, workmen's compensation, holidays with pay, factory supervision, shorter shop-opening hours, higher pensions; free and compulsory education, free books, free school meals . . . slum clearance and housing development; state ownership of public utilities, oil and natural gas resources" (Emmanuel 1988, 107). Richard Cheltenham addresses an aspect of the contradiction between politics (black majority control of state power) and economics (concentration of economic and financial power) in the hands of a small, white capitalist class. He argues that the BLP

> had demonstrated, while in office, that it was prepared to accommodate the mercantile/planter interest within a mixed economy. The D.L.P. contrary to protestations had done nothing thus far to suggest it differed from the B.L.P. on this issue. This class, which was the inspirational and financial backbone of the B.N.P., operating through "front men" like E.D. Mottley, L.A. Lynch and others, was thus content to make political representation through their professional associations. (1970, 252; see Karch 1982)

Cheltenham's argument is corroborated by Howard Johnson and Karl Watson's account of how the white minority in the Caribbean has intentionally and systematically acted to "shape and dominate the social and economic environment in a region which is predominantly non-white". Johnson and Watson (1998, back cover) stress that "in spite of changing relationships with other races in the Caribbean, the white minority has maintained its elite position by uniting its constituent ethnic and social groups whenever its dominance has been challenged. Other strategies included cementing links to political power and maintaining access to domestic and foreign capital." The particular class-protection project and survival strategy of the white minority also rests on predictable political support from the global white-supremacist norm of the world order, which operates via the dominant institutions that anchor liberal internationalism.

In Barbados the postwar capital accumulation strategy favours the white minority primarily because the capitalist class is drawn almost exclusively from its ranks and both political parties are beholden to it. Capitalists will compete with one another in the most vigorous ways for market share, which also coincides with defending their class interests; however, they will not hesitate to lock arms to defend the right to exploit labour, accumulate capital and help to shape the political and policy agendas of the state. The fact that class trumps race is disguised by the emphasis that is placed on the identity politics of race, which is an ideology rather than a concrete social category.

The racialized class-protection strategy pursued by the capitalist minority in Barbados under the "historic compromise" has been upheld by the political parties, the state managers and organized labour and by civil society largely to manage and regulate the process of social reproduction and mobility among the black majority. It simply did not contribute to the development of a visible stratum of black capitalists with the wherewithal to organize production or compete with the handful of white capitalists who own the bulk of the means of production. Blacks won the political kingdom in Barbados in ways that reinforced the formal separation of economics from politics and deepened the subsuming of black labour under white capital.

The introduction under Barrow of free secondary and tertiary education helped to quench the thirst for higher education and professional advancement among the working class, a development that made it possible for blacks to achieve what ostensibly resembles a virtual "monopoly of this vast system" (Emmanuel 1988, 110; see Stafford 2005, ii), with modest qualitative change in the relations between the classes. The fact that politics is the concentrated expression of economics suggests that the systemic monopoly to which Emmanuel refers necessarily rests on a material base. Free secondary and tertiary education brought into existence a large pool of educated labour in need of employment and in pursuit of social mobility. The Barbados Independence Constitution – which J. Cameron Tudor referred to as an agreed document between both sides[24] – updated the "historic compromise" and strengthened the political consensus on which the racialized class peace was based, in ways that continue to favour white-supremacist hegemony as the dominant norm of societal order. It is this phenomenon that forms part of the ruling-class strategy, which remains covered over in the tracks of social democratic politics within the bourgeois democratic revolution.

LABOUR POLITICS, CLASS EXPLOITATION AND THE WORKING CLASS IN BARBADOS

Capitalist (economic) control and state (political) repression of the working class operate in the sphere of the market through which contradictory social relations between humans are treated as technical relations between things (commodities). Contextually, capitalists do not have to define themselves as a ruling class, given that everyday life under liberal capitalism appears chaotic, fragmented, individualized and anarchic (Rosenberg 1994). It is in the capital-wage labour relation that the law of value asserts itself, which is also where members of the ruling class represent themselves largely as self-interested individual businesspeople who are naturally driven to maximize their self-interest in neo-Smithian ways that miraculously redound to the general good. This form of ideological dissembling by the ruling class and its organic intellectuals is part of how myth-making becomes normalized (Agnew 2009).

As the decolonization moment came to an end, the stage was being set in Barbados for the state to become the largest single employer of labour. When this happens in any society, much of the antagonism between capital and labour becomes absorbed and displaced via the state (but not resolved), considering that displacement is a form of preservation. The investment by organized labour in the political consensus project of nation-building and national unity, and the eagerness of its leadership to defend the right to exploit, translate into a defence of private interests over the public good. It has therefore been easy for the state, the political parties and the leadership of organized labour to cast the class struggle as a non-contradictory, transactional and residual bread-and-butter issue and a moral issue that can be resolved through income redistribution, while leaving the concentration of wealth largely undisturbed. This way of treating class exploitation as a secondary and technical matter satisfies the nationalists, who reduce the structural contradictions of capitalism to technical problems.

Nationalists view the market, which is a site of intense class struggle, as little more than an arena where citizens negotiate the working day as juridically equal individuals, with the market assumed to operate independently of politics and the class struggle. Anwar Shaikh argues that the central problem with neoclassical economic analysis is that it assumes an "idealized framework" that bears no connection to actual social reality. Shaikh says, "Neoclassical economics skirts the din of real markets by pretending that individual production plans mesh perfectly with social needs. This pretense is called general equilibrium. In point of fact, the turbulent order arising from real markets is achieved on in-and-through disorder, and money is its general agent" (2016, 10; see Marx [1894] 1967, 820).

Slavoj Žižek argues compellingly that substantive freedom is impossible to protect without constructing "a ground floor" that counts as its "zero". Žižek's point is that "before . . . decisions or choices are made – there has to be a ground of tradition . . . that . . . cannot be counted". Žižek warns against starting "directly with self-legislated freedom" because it erases the history of struggles through which the zero floor of freedom must be constructed (2012, 1, 2). The liberal strategy is to define us as simultaneously juridically equal, while misrepresenting the socially produced economic dependence and inequality as natural (Teschke and Heine 2002; Losurdo 2011; Holloway 2005), an outcome that is inevitable where the means of production are organized for the ends of private capital accumulation, as is the case in Barbados.

The fact that state power is a form of organized ruling-class despotism (Agnew 2009) means that labour cannot hope to liberate itself by embracing as substantive democracy power relations that are based on domination, which is enshrined in law (Gullí 2010; Drayton 2016). It is necessary to fight for the disalienation of power in the pursuit of rights, freedom, justice and substantive democracy (Wood 1995; Holloway 2002; Gullí 2010). The commonsense assertion that Barbadians are a conservative lot seems uncharacteristic of a society that supports two political parties that openly assert their democratic-socialist credentials.

Errol Barrow insisted that he was born a socialist, and Grantley Adams claimed he became a convert to Fabian socialism around 1938. Barrow could appeal to the legacy of Dr O'Neal to assert his socialist bona fides. Tom Adams, on the other hand, could hardly afford to draw too much attention to his father's "right-wing" socialist legacy (Holder 2015, 61; Sealy 1991) on his own behalf. The BLP and DLP, studied with reference to how they have consistently protected the bargain around the "historic compromise", are very much like two wings of the same bird. Beginning in the late colonial period, both political parties helped to reinforce white supremacy as the norm of the domestic political order by nominally mobilizing the black working class while intentionally depoliticizing it to prevent it from organizing and practising politics with its own interests in mind.

CONCLUSION

In Barbados and in other West Indian territories during the late colonial period, there arose a dominant nationalist, ideologically informed, anti-imperialist (but not necessarily anti-capitalist) sentimentalism that adds nothing to an informed critique of capitalism or the bourgeois democratic revolution that Richard Drayton appropriately labels "Westminster undemocracy" (2016, 9). West Indian leaders seemed unmindful that British imperialism had already entered a state of terminal crisis. The United Kingdom was forced to implement decolonization in the territories on account of its growing powerlessness in the international arena; however, it effectively managed decolonization from a position that was aided and abetted by US hegemony.

A careful study of decolonization in Barbados reveals that the implementation of the Bushe Experiment drew lessons from the 1937 working-class rebellion and the recommendations of the Moyne Commission. The package of reforms ranged from the introduction of party politics, the labour and trade union movement, universal adult suffrage, ministerial government and parliamentary democracy, a set of reforms that were part of the bourgeois democratic revolution, which was inspired also by the important work that was undertaken by the DL. Black majority rule became part of a class compromise under the bourgeois democratic revolution, the framework for which was set out under the Bushe Experiment, which anticipated postwar working-class militancy and attempted to short-circuit it in the "historic compromise".

The bourgeois democratic revolution was designed to reinforce the right of private capital to exploit labour; it therefore inevitably deepened the subsumption of labour under capital and subordinated workers' interests and rights to the hegemony of the political parties and the leadership of organized labour. This strategic move fuelled the populist (nationalist) notion that it was possible for the black majority to win the political kingdom and govern democratically without bringing the commanding heights of the economy under substantive state-mediated political control.

The plausible assertion that the Barbadian working class became splintered and fragmented as a result of the rise of political party pluralism, when the DLP emerged from a split in the BLP, remains an inadequate response that ignores the centrality of the social relations of production and discounts the primacy of the control of state power in explanations of social change. Neither the BLP nor the DLP is a socialist or working-class party; however, they necessarily rely on working-class mass support for their political survival under the bourgeois democratic revolution. Both parties have worked very closely with the dominant capitalist strata and with organized labour to maintain the capitalist "social control formation" (Perry 2010, 1) to manage the society.

Grantley Adams and the BLP acted strategically with Anglo-American Cold War approval to kill two birds with one stone. First, they played a major role in the destruction of the CLC before the DLP arose, and thereby rendered the labour movement at the territorial and regional level less capable of responding to domestic and regional challenges to working-class advancement. Second, the leading capitalist forces throughout the West Indies celebrated the anti-working-class, anti-CLC coup, and Adams was knighted for the job he did in that context and for his unstinting loyalty to the decaying British Empire. The dramatic expansion of the state bureaucracy in Barbados created a buffer to protect the capitalists from the resentment of the exploited, who were fed a consumerist logic based on the pursuit of elusive "middle-class" aspirations and lifestyles. The political leaders and the head of the BWU revealed their plausible pro-labour but substantively anti-working-class commitments when they declared that the "constituted leaders" created the only acceptable framework for addressing the enduring problem of racialized, economic (class) inequality and domination in Barbados.

It was not an accident that the BWU was unambiguous in its defence of the right of private capital to exploit labour, which also made it that much easier for foreign capital to operate in Barbados. The BWU and the two political parties became self-monitoring and self-regulating agents for the political consensus, attesting thereby to the effectiveness of hegemony in mediating contradictory class relations in the society through the "passive revolution". The reforms that were introduced under Barrow and the DLP benefited racialized capitalism at every stage, a development that also compounded problems for the emergence of any semblance of productive and competitive black capitalist strata in Barbados. The discourse of socialism in party politics and society in Barbados has been politically opportunistic, intellectually vacuous and informed by nationalist ideology that dominates existential consciousness and political discourse in the society, in ways that are consistent with the aims of the bourgeois democratic revolution.

CONCLUSION

THE INDEPENDENCE CONSTITUTION THAT announced the formal end to colonialism in Barbados was a landmark in the institutionalization of the bourgeois democratic revolution in the country's political culture. It was a statement in continuity more than discontinuity, in the sense that it was intentionally crafted with the "historic compromise" and the political consensus in mind that stemmed from the Bushe Experiment. The UK government and the "authorized leaders" in Barbados were confident that Barbados was about to embark on a course that would not pose any threats to the paramountcy of US or British security interests in the Caribbean. The dominant agro-commercial interests and the decolonizing elites were satisfied that it would not be difficult to control the working-class majority.

The study shows that everything was done to recast the contributions and legacies of Dr O'Neal and the DL, the WA, the UNIA, and countless working-class stalwarts and other progressive male and female leaders of the 1937 rebellion by making them palatable to the bourgeois democratic dispensation. The political modernization of Barbados, with reference to the rise of party politics, trade union democracy and working-class assertiveness, was no small achievement when considered in terms of the battle for the rights of workers at the workplace, in the political arena and in their villages and beyond. The problem posed for the working class, however, was that its interests were submerged in the bureaucratic trade union movement under the leadership of anti-working-class, anti-communist agents who acted in consonance with the Anglo-American Cold War project to rid the leadership of the labour movement of progressives and revolutionaries, destroy the CLC and deprive the working class of an organized, independent voice in the process.

The form of social democracy the DLP and BLP portray as socialism was well designed to lend agro-commercial capitalism a "human face" during the transition to black majority government. The study did not contend or conclude that socialism could be easily instituted in societies like Barbados; however, it questioned the populist manner in which both political parties went out of their way to conflate social democracy with socialism, thereby protecting capitalism and the bourgeois democratic revolution from appropriate exposure and critique. The political parties successfully set the boundaries of appropriate discourse by demobilizing the working class and depoliticizing politics and class conflict between the exploiters and exploited. Organized labour in Barbados has actively participated in treating contradictions between capital and labour largely as workplace and bread-and-butter and related problems.

The real motive behind the Cold War project in its geopolitical, military, economic, financial and ideological manifestations has been to prevent socialism from developing and surviving as a viable alternative to capitalism on a world scale, confirming that freedom begins where necessity is vanquished. The real opposition to socialism has come foremost from liberal capitalist states led by the United States, which works relentlessly to impose a closure on history by insisting that capitalism and liberal democracy represent the end of history and the highest possible form of human civilization. Errol Barrow's declaration that he was "born a socialist" contributed to the impression that his worldview and the policies of the DLP reflected the limits of scientific "socialist" values and commitments, in contrast with Grantley Adams's self-described "right-wing" socialism; the two differed by degree more than kind.

Most of the West Indian decolonizing elite did not seem to appreciate that the British Empire at the end of World War II was rapidly becoming a "superseded empire". Fully aware of the strength of the pro-British values and commitments of the West Indian elite, their failure to acknowledge the implications for the colonies of Britain's growing powerlessness, and their eagerness to gain control of the levers of state power on terms that were acceptable to London (and Washington), the British understood that it would not be difficult to order and supervise the transition to independence.

This study questions and contradicts assertions by nationalist intellectuals that Barbados and other West Indian territories demanded independence from the United Kingdom and won it on their own terms. The evidence shows that the leaders of Barbados embraced the juridical architecture and institutional norms of the Westminster system by accepting the savings clauses that were written into the West Indian independence constitutions at the insistence of the UK government. The very act of changing Barbados's colonial status at independence to a monarchy, with the Queen as head of state, represented a conscious and conservative embrace of continuity over change, in defining the priorities of the newly sovereign state for meeting the needs of the society.

The black majority in Barbados has never made the case for the deconstruction of white supremacy, which it reduced to racism, in its fight for economic and political justice. The nationalist rhetoric about the primacy of race over class and of the need to make the fight a struggle against racism kept attention away from the fact that the right to exploit anchors all manner of rights, freedom, justice and equality in capitalist society. As the key philosophical doctrine of modernity, liberalism makes the individual in history the unit of analysis and the central actor in the struggle for societal change, a tactic that weakens and disarms the social, gives advantage to the powerful in society who exercise disproportionate power, and normalizes exploitation. Understanding these basic facts makes it all the more urgent to put class analysis rather than individualism and anti-racism at the centre of analysis in the struggle against white supremacy as somatic norm and as the norm of world order. The nationalist project in Barbados is best understood as an extension of the bourgeois democratic revolution.

The study confirms also that Errol Barrow and the DLP embraced Fabian social democracy under conditions that differed from O'Neal's time. Barrow's approach to social democracy assumed form under nominally more propitious circumstances of international neo-Keynesianism. The Fabian socialists in Britain from whom Barrow and others learned their craft were a paternalistic lot who never imagined the possibility of the British working-class majority (or their counterparts in the colonies) determining their own destinies. The idea of a workers' state invested with the power to consolidate socialist power in the political economy is anathema to social democrats of all persuasions.

Neil Davidson reminds us that "constructing an argument for why a particular group should determine their own future has to be done on the basis of a political argument, and not by circumventing it through reliance on the notion of a right". The concept of right under the bourgeois democratic revolution begins foremost with the right of capital to exploit labour, which provided the material basis for independence in the West Indies in a "subordinate position . . . within the capitalist system of nation-states" (Davidson 2015, 9, 13). The fact that the two labour parties in Barbados put socialism on the agenda makes it appropriate to interrogate their claims, bearing in mind that the problem of building socialism in Barbados was compounded by structural constraints posed by capitalism and liberalism in the domestic and international environment.

Barbados simply lacked a modern bourgeoisie and a modern proletariat, as there did not exist modern science, technology, industry or manufacturing with an advanced material and intellectual culture to support the development of a modern, organized, industrial working class. Widespread landlessness in Barbados has been the product of high population density on a limited territorial land mass, coincidental with the extreme concentration of available arable land in few hands. The discourse of social democracy as socialism in Barbados emerged in conditions of backward productive forces with largely parasitic capitalists who reproduced themselves within the British (imperialist) division of labour. Their economic specializations emphasized merchant-capital-mediated, comprador activities that depended heavily on access to the British market on protectionist terms. They simply did not develop into a modern, productive capitalist class. Under capitalism the working class, having been separated from its means of production, is forced to reproduce itself with the tools that capital puts at its disposal, which means that the working class in Barbados was put at a tremendous disadvantage to produce capital and reproduce itself socially. It did not come as a surprise that the political parties, labour movement and the society then and now failed to produce a critical mass of organic intellectuals of the working class that made it a priority to think about the possibility of governing itself.

The US strategy for dominating the Caribbean remains an integral part of its pursuit of absolute global supremacy, an unattainable and costly project that puts the struggle for our universal humanity on a collision course with its hegemonic project. Barrow and the DLP core leadership remained largely silent in the face of the Cold War assault on Cheddi Jagan and the PPP, on the ground that Jagan posed a mortal threat to US security interests and freedom and democracy in the Western Hemisphere. The reality, however, is that at no time did the United States need any communist-inspired revolutionary movements in the Caribbean or Latin America as the pretext for promoting counter-revolution anywhere in the hemisphere. The Cold War project was constructed on the idea that the survival of international capitalism necessitates waging global anti-socialist, anti-communist and therefore anti-working-class warfare; hence the US pursuit of unconditional global supremacy. It is difficult to sustain any claim that the United States is the natural ally of the working class in any society anywhere in the world.

This study shows that the BLP and the DLP were assertively anti-communist, which is consistent with the social democratic tradition. The political party programmes and policies that brought material benefits to the working class and the society under Barrow were self-consciously defined within the parameters of the bourgeois democratic revolution which foremost benefited those whose vocation is the private accumulation of capital. The study confirms that British imperialism was not an alien force that denied freedom to the West Indian colonies; rather, imperialism and the colonial experience were mutually constitutive, with contradictory expressions and reverberations in Britain and the colonies.

The research suggests that it is time to part with the ideologically inspired, false inside-outside dichotomies that are inspired by anti-colonial nationalism, through which imperialism is viewed as an alien political form and the world as comprising an assemblage of independent national states, each with its autonomous economy. This state-centrist, geographically determined outlook on the formation of nations, national states and the modern international system makes history the servant of geography, and adds nothing to critical thinking about universal history. National states and the international system form a heterogeneous, open-ended, mutually constitutive order in which contentious struggles persist over the organization, control and exercise of state power.

The state, which is not coterminous with the territorial (spatial) extent of any country and its population, is a site of organized class power which makes it a site of control, domination and intense struggle, bearing in mind that social classes and their factions in society are constituted by their contradictory interests and relationships. The experience in late colonial societies like Barbados confirms that nationalists speak in the name of the "people" while simultaneously submerging the interests of the working class in populist "people" discourse. There is no compelling evidence, however, that nationalists are the natural allies of the working class, regardless of the objective class position of any nationalist. They simultaneously invoke social democracy while defending capitalism, national (sovereign) state rights and nation-building, with working-class rights subsumed thereunder, to protect the right to exploit from critical exposure. Nationalists do not see a problem with local capitalists exploiting their workers; however, they seldom recoil from decrying exploitation by foreign capitalists, in effect making the nationality of capital, rather than the exploitation of man by man, the real problem. The fact that capital accumulation is a global process makes the nationality of capital secondary. From the liberal and the social democratic perspective, the real subsumption of labour under capital and class exploitation are inevitable, given that labour is seen as naturally self-alienating under commodity production. This neo-Hegelian logic is indicative of "an extraordinary form of collective false consciousness" (Davidson 2015, 13) and self-delusion.

The study points to the conclusion that the state and its sovereign power are foregrounded in domination, which is hidden in the political and economic crevices of the bourgeois democratic revolution. It is therefore not in the interest of the exploited and oppressed to rely on the system of domination to secure their liberation. Under capitalism and liberal democracy, reality assumes the fantastic form of mythmaking, with social reality appearing to the naked eye as naturally fragmented and chaotic. Everything therefore is portrayed as separated: politics from economics, the state from civil society, the individual from the state and society, and the domestic realm from the international arena, with laws of nature assumed to be in control. This form of dissembling benefits exploiters and oppressors.

Sir Frederick Smith's observation that the white capitalist strata in Barbados significantly strengthened their economic power throughout the period of black majority political rule in Barbados confirms that the bourgeois democratic revolution facilitated the realization of the anti-working-class objective of consolidating private capitalist power over social needs and ends, with the direct supervision and participation of black majority governments. The study shows also that when political parties, labour unions and capitalists are compelled by circumstances beyond their control to pursue policies and programmes that improve the material, social and political welfare of the working class, they try to make sure that the working class is denied access to the levers and instruments of state power. The study also shows that capitalists are never indifferent to the organization and exercise of state power and the production of culture and ideology in society.

The study did not claim, however, that the working-class majority should disparage or become cynical about participating in the political process. Rather, the argument has been that the bourgeois democratic revolution and its processes operate in the tracks of the class struggle and it is therefore imperative for the working class to exploit the process to fight for higher ends to build a solid, non-negotiable ground floor of freedom that can offer the possibility of withstanding anti-working-class predations from any quarter. The embrace by the Barbadian working class of the bourgeois democratic revolution was partly informed by the belief that social democracy is a settled issue, according to the way the argument was framed and communicated by the "constituted leaders" and their organic intellectuals. In contrast, the political parties, labour organizations and capitalist forces view social democracy and workers' rights in transactional terms, which means that they treat them as subject to renegotiation and even reversal.

When Errol Barrow railed against the insular prejudices and insecurities of what he described as "pettifogging" Eastern Caribbean political leaders in the aftermath of the dissolution of the federation, he seemed to discount the fact that the United Kingdom, with US support, had determined that a federal system with a strong central government with residual powers reserved for the unit territories was not acceptable. Everything Whitehall had done to augment the powers of the governor general as the federation was preparing to embark on independence confirmed that Britain had fully endorsed the official US position, which was against a strong federal state. The most unambiguous expression came in Downing Street's promise to Norman Manley that Jamaica would not suffer any penalty for withdrawing from the federation. The United Kingdom also embraced the US demand that the West Indian working class had to be excluded from playing any important role in shaping the trajectory of self-government, federation and independence.

The savings clauses Barrow agreed to keep in the Independence Constitution, which his government negotiated at Lancaster House in 1966, signalled that independence was negotiated from a position of weakness vis-à-vis the UK state and therefore that the sovereign monarchy that Barbados became at independence was not negotiated on terms that the decolonizing elites set according to their preferences. The UK strategy for managing the transition to independence in Barbados and throughout the West Indies included neocolonial provisions in the form of the savings clauses, which were built in as safeguards to ensure that the postcolonial state managers would be subject to administrative oversight and review by unelected bodies – a signature of what Drayton calls "Westminster undemocracy".

The savings clauses might therefore be seen as an extension of the "historic compromise" that worked so well in Barbados and in other West Indian territories. They ensured the continuity of British hegemony over the exercise of sovereign authority at the domestic level in ways that limited the scope for the exercise of sovereign autonomy by the newly independent state on the world stage. The UK position confirmed that the UN model of sovereignty was not designed to give newly independent states the right to define and exercise sovereignty according to their preferences. The British insistence on tucking the savings clauses away in the Independence Constitution reinforced the substantively anti-working-class character of social democracy in late colonial and postcolonial Barbados.

NOTES

CHAPTER 1

1. Cmnd. 7958; Cmnd. 6713, Despatch from the Secretary of State for the Colonies to the Colonial Governments, 12 November 1945, HMSO, 1945, in Phillips (1977, 12).
2. Cheddi Jagan (British Guiana) began publishing about British Guiana and the Caribbean in the wider international context in the 1950s; he produced a body of broadly quoted and cited political material and scholarship that covered the Cold War period. Michael Manley published material on Jamaica and embraced an explicitly Third World internationalist stance in defence of "democratic socialism" in Jamaica and on nonalignment. Eric Williams, an Oxford University–trained historian and Trinidad and Tobago's first prime minister, published *Capitalism and Slavery* (1944). In his autobiography, *Inward Hunger* ([1969] 1971), Williams expressed strong nationalist political views and commitments, without imagining any possibilities beyond the limits of British and Western economic, political and geopolitical hegemony. Colin Palmer published a biography of Eric Williams (Palmer 2006) that pays limited attention to Williams's tense relationship with Grantley Adams during the time of the Federation of the West Indies and his scepticism toward Barrow's interest in promoting post-federation regional initiatives like the Little Eight. Palmer also published a biography of Cheddi Jagan (Palmer 2010) in which he locates British Guiana's struggle for independence within the broader Caribbean and international context and addresses issues that are relevant for this study. Selwyn Ryan's biography of Eric Williams is extensive in its scope and reach (Ryan 2009). More recently, Maurice St Pierre published a biography of Eric Williams (St Pierre 2015). Biographical work on Norman Manley and Alexander Bustamante of Jamaica exists, along with a limited number of biographies of other former West Indian and Commonwealth

Caribbean leaders, for example, Paget Henry's biography of Antigua's Vere Bird (Henry 2010).

3. House of Assembly Debates (Official Report), Third Session, 1966–71, 19 May 1970, 1691; the Juries Act 1970.

4. There were ten original members of the Federation of the West Indies. When Jamaica and Trinidad withdrew from the federation, eight members remained, and they were referred to as the Little Eight. When Barbados withdrew to pursue independence alone, seven remained, hence the Little Seven.

CHAPTER 2

1. For additional information about the early development of both sides of Errol Barrow's family see also transcript: Graham Barrow, interviewed by Robert Morris, 1976 (Oral History Project, Barbados Nation Builders Series, University of the West Indies, Cave Hill, Barbados).

2. Christopher "Chrissie" Augustus Brathwaite was a black merchant who operated on Roebuck Street, Bridgetown; he was a political activist and was elected to the Barbados House of Assembly on the DL ticket. See Marshall 2003, 56n7.

3. Bishop Reginald Grant Barrow was born in St Vincent on 24 September 1889. His father, Robert Barrow, was director of prisons in St Vincent and "had been an Anglican Clergyman, presiding Elder of the Episcopal Methodist Church, Bishop of the African/Orthodox Church, a Roman Catholic, Bahai Lecturer, an ardent Garveyite, Headmaster of a secondary school, Dean of a private college, university professor, journalist, magazine publisher and newspaper editor, a trade union organizer, a political activist, as well as a farmer, chiropractor, herbalist and an amateur chef and winemaker" (Pilgrim 1988a, 28).

4. See Pilgrim (1988a, 1988b) for relevant information on the racism that the Reverend Barrow endured at the hands of the white supremacist Anglican Church and its senior officers in Barbados.

5. Alleyne was awarded a baronetcy by King George III in 1769. He owned plantations in the parish of St Andrew, including Greenland, River, and Sedge Pond (Pilgrim 1988b, 31).

6. In addition to providing vital medical service to impoverished people in the mining community of Newcastle, O'Neal also worked with the Miners' Union, which backed him to contest the seat on the Sunderland County

Council that he won. His political relationship with the Miners' Union also brought him into close contact with Scottish miner Keir Hardie, a founder of the Independent Labour Party, which was allied with the trade unions. Hardie's declared aim was to help to establish a new social order with "an economic and social system based on socialist principles" (Simpson 1973, 35, 36; Hoyos 1972, 109).

7. Charles Duncan O'Neal, Christopher "Chrissie" Brathwaite and Clennell Wickham were founding members of the DL. Brathwaite was the first member of the DL to win a seat in a by-election to the House of Assembly, giving the working class a "symbolic" taste of possibilities that could be realized under the banner of the DL. O'Neal first contested a seat in the city in 1925 but withdrew before the election. Successful DL candidates during the 1930s included Erskine Ward, Lee Sargeant, Henry Reece, Charlie Elder and Charles Duncan O'Neal, who was elected to the House of Assembly in 1932 with 346 votes against Bridgetown businessman Harold G. Austin, who received 345 votes. O'Neal held the seat for four years until his death in 1936 at fifty-six. His campaign emphasized ways to reduce high unemployment, lower the franchise qualification to increase the number of eligible voters and bring the franchise to the working class, compulsory free education, workmen's compensation, and higher wages for workers (Farley 1987, 44–50 passim).

8. O'Neal's involvement in political and working-class issues in Trinidad influenced his decision to form the WA in Barbados. Sir John Mordecai reports that Captain Andrew Cipriani revived the "moribund" WA in 1919 and "immediately attracted a tremendous following. The growth of the Association was such that by the early nineteen thirties a membership of 120,000 was claimed for it out of a population of 450,000. It never functioned as a trade union, but concentrated attention on legislative reforms, although consistently agitating for proper trade union and factory legislation, land settlement, slum clearance, education reforms, and above all popular representation by election to the legislature" (Mordecai 1968, 18; see also Beckles 2004a, 186–88).

9. *Supplement to Official Gazette*, no. 52, 30 June 1952, 35; see Hunte 1988, 32.

10. *Supplement to the Official Gazette*, no. 101, 17 December 1936, 788.

11. In the "Third Thesis on Feuerbach", Marx ([1888] 1976, 61) says, "The materialist doctrine that men are products of circumstances and upbringing and that . . . changed men are products of other circumstances and

changed upbringing, forgets that men themselves change circumstances and that the educator . . . must be educated. Hence, this doctrine necessarily arrives at dividing society into two parts, of which one is superior to society. . . . The coincidence of the changing of circumstances and of human activity can be conceived and rationally understood only as revolutionizing practice."

12. Barrow graduated from Harrison College (sixth form) in 1939. He won a scholarship to Codrington College in 1940 to study classics (see Morgan 1994, 15–16; Sealy 1991, 25; *Nation Keepsake*, 10 June 1987, 4A).

13. House of Assembly Debates (Official Report), Second Session, 1961–66, 26 April 1966, 23.

14. Frank Walcott took over as general secretary of the BWU.

15. I address these issues in a chapter on harmonious progress and the Public Order Bill in volume 2. Additional details about the "historic compromise" will be provided in the second volume of this study.

16. Jean Holder mentions that Grantley Adams, in contrast with Errol Barrow, who described himself as socialist from birth, described himself as a "Right-Wing Socialist" (2015, 61), a notion that raises serious questions about Adams's knowledge and understanding of socialism. Hoyos (1988) acknowledged that he was assigned the task of seeing that Adams did not join the political left in Barbados.

17. House of Assembly Debates (Official Report), Third Session, 1966–71, 1691.

CHAPTER 3

1. On the occasion of the presentation of his credentials to President Lyndon Johnson in Washington on 15 January 1968, Ambassador Hilton Vaughan observed in his address that "the virtual declaration of independence with the Governors, Lords in Council and Members of the Assembly of Barbados, declared from the Commonwealth of Cromwell's England in 1651, was echoed in the American Declaration of Independence in 1776". *Barbados High Commission to the United Kingdom Newsletter* 2, no. 1 (January 1968): 2–3.

2. See Anievas and Nişancioğlu (2015) for a relevant discussion of the concept of an "internationalist theory of history".

3. There is a tendency to Hegel that Jonathan Israel (2006) and Jack Goody (2007) discuss (see also Watson 2008a).

4. Anthony De V. Phillips's account of the role Governor Pope Hennessy played in the events and riots of 1876 includes the involvement of a sizeable number of black Barbadians in events that occurred over a period of eight days. The black population was largely and deliberately excluded from ownership of property and did not have the right to vote. The dominant idea was that only Englishmen had the rational capacity for political participation. The vast majority of people of African descent was also politically marginalized (1987, 81–84, 72; see also Belle 1988).

5. See Phillips 1977, 12.

6. House of Assembly Debates (Official Report), Third Session, 1966–71, 20 October 1970, 1991.

7. Ibid.

8. West Indies, West Indian Conference, Terms of Reference, CO 1042/45.

9. Philip Hewitt-Myring to Sir John McPherson, "A Report on Public Relations at the Second Session of the West Indian Conference (St Thomas, VI, March–April, 1946)", West Indian Conference, Terms of Reference, Reference: S 0009, CO 1042/45.

10. Gerald Horne (2007) argues that West Indians in the United States, particularly in Harlem, New York, played an instrumental role in influencing the discourse on decolonization in the West Indies. According to the *West India Committee Circular* 60, no. 1173 of September 1945, 163, there were in 1945 approximately 32,000 West Indian permanent residents in the United States, of whom some 28,000 were from Jamaica (see Ayearst 1960, 135).

11. West Indies, West Indian Conference, Terms of Reference, CO 1042/45.

12. Ibid.

13. Ibid.

14. CO 1042/45. See also Marshall (2003, 92–114 passim).

15. Memorandum by P. Rogers, File 71295 (1946), CO 318/466/2.

16. For details on the BGWILC see Bolland 2001, 475–78 and passim.

17. Cmnd. 6174 (1940). Also Cmnd. 6607 (1945), quoted by Mordecai 1968, 28.

18. Anthony De V. Phillips refers to the Old Representative System as "a system which had been found in all the several colonies of the First British Empire, including the North American colonies such as Virginia, New York, and Massachusetts". Phillips notes that among the problems the British authorities found with the Old Representative System was that "the elected assemblies had encroached upon the prerogatives of the executive government, notably by not voting money for projects but also by insisting

on carrying them through by means of boards and Committees. Secondly, there was no control of financial affairs since each member as an individual member of the assembly was free to propose expenditure at any time during a session so that there could be no estimates and obviously no annual budget" (1987, 70, 71).

19. John Connell, interview with the author, Sanford, St Philip, Barbados, 6 July 2006; Woodville Marshall, interview with the author, Paradise Heights, St Michael, 19 November 2008; Mitchell Codrington, interview with the author, Husbands, St James, Barbados, 6 July 2006.

20. *Political Report of the Governor*, December 1953, February 1955 and May 1955, CO 1031/1810.

21. *Supplement to the Official Gazette* 88, no. 47, 12 June 1952, 166.

22. See *Political Report of the Governor*, December 1953, February 1955 and May 1955, CO 1031/1810.

23. Phillips (1998, 19n12) quotes the lyrics of "The Red Flag":
The people's flag is deepest red
It shrouded oft our martyred dead
And ere their limbs grew stiff and cold
Their heart's blood dyed its every fold.
Chorus:
Then raise the scarlet standard high!
Beneath its shade we'll live and die.
Though cowards flinch and traitors sneer,
We'll keep the red flag flying here!

24. Barrow's "No Loitering on Colonial Premises" speech appears also in Holder (2007, 65–67, appendix).

25. "Barbados was settled under Letters Patent granted by King Charles I to the Earl of Carlisle. In 1628 sixty-four persons came out with the intention of taking up 100 acres of land each and by 1638 practically the whole available cultivable acreage had been granted to nearly 800 persons." The Property and Conveyancing Act of 1891 "enforced the registration of title deeds" and facilitated a "system of absolute freehold ownership"; by 1946 there were "some 378 plantations covering 52,000 arable acres" (Barbados 1945, 2).

26. House of Assembly Debates (Official Record), Second Session, 1961–66, 26 April 1966, 6.

27. See also Report of the Barbados Constitutional Conference 1966, Cmnd. 3058.

28. House of Assembly Debates (Official Record), Second Session, 1961–66, 26 April 1966, 6.
29. Note to Mr Wallace from D. Williams (Colonial Office), 6 January 1966, CO 1031/5060.
30. House of Assembly Debates (Official Report), Second Session, 1961–66, 26 April 1966, 3.
31. House of Assembly Debates (Official Report), Third Session, 1966–71, 1691.
32. *Supplement to the Official Gazette* 87, no. 10, 4 February 1952, 14, CO 32/126.
33. Ibid.
34. Gerald Horne (2007, 200) notes that Adams, when soon to be knighted for his unstinting service to the British Empire, was compelled to endure "racial discrimination . . . whilst in Canada". He was en route from London (on official business) to Barbados and was booked at the Windsor Hotel, which "refused him admission on racial grounds"; he was forced to find other accommodation.
35. Report, 29 October 1954, CO 1031/1464.
36. Grantley Adams became an important West Indian agent for the ICFTU (see Bolland 2001, 498; Watson 2004).
37. Secretary of State's Annual Report to Parliament for the West Indies, CO 1031/4205.
38. Ibid. See also Defence of the West Indies Coordination with the United States, CO 1031/4238.
39. West Indies, West Indian Conference, Terms of Reference, CO 1042/45.
40. George Price of Belize commented in 1976 that the People's United Party, which was formed on 29 September 1950, suffered defections in 1956 on the issue of the Federation of the West Indies. Price and some party members opposed the federation on the following grounds: (1) representation: Belize had a very small population but was the largest territory among the British colonies after British Guiana and was concerned about under-representation in a federation; (2) geographical name of the organization – Federation of the West Indies – Belizeans did not see themselves as part of the West Indies; (3) constitutional status of the organization – the Federation was to comprise colonies and "we did not see any political advancement in that"; (4) immigration and ethnic identity – Belizeans feared large-scale immigration by blacks from the West Indies; (5) unethical

conduct by one party member who used to attend meetings of the CC and "some Caribbean or West Indian regional meetings" without informing the party of the nature of their involvement in those regional activities – a factor that led to their expulsion from the party (Sealy 1991, 185, 186). Price appeared to have been flexible on the prospect of the federation becoming a much more inclusive project than a West Indian project. He said, "Belize is a Central American country geographically and . . . it has a Central American destiny. . . . The Caribbean Sea is so wide that it . . . washes Mexico, it washes Central America, and it washes South America and the island countries. So there came about an evolution of thinking . . . of regional development. There was this Caribbean Community, a new concept of the old West Indian Federation. Belize is Caribbean . . . Belize cannot live alone in this world; we have to join with someone. So we joined CARIFTA [the Caribbean Free Trade Association], first, then CARICOM. . . . And I think CARICOM has helped very well. But for the . . . Caribbean Development Bank, we would not have been able to finance many of our projects today – electrification, agriculture, industry, tourism, housing" (quoted in Sealy 1991, 176–77).

41. The Barbados Democratic Labour Party Memorandum to Her Majesty's Principal Secretary of State for the Colonies, Rt Hon Mr Ian McLeod, CO/1381/4272.

42. CA/1403/62. Short report by J.D. Hennings, British Embassy, Washington, DC, "on how Barrow's visit to Washington has gone", CO 1031/3760.

43. Eric Williams also viewed Adams as lazy and incompetent (Sealy 1991, 192).

44. Short report by J.D. Hennings, British Embassy, Washington, DC.

45. Proceedings of Conference on the Closer Association of the British West Indian Colonies, 1947, col. no. 218, part 1: Report, 7, quoted in Sir Fred Phillips 1977, 22.

46. This was Williams's way of referencing his contempt for Grantley Adams by alluding to Adams's alleged laziness and his drinking problem.

47. Inward telegram to the secretary of state for the colonies from chairman, Regional Council of Ministers, Barbados, 23 July 1963, CO 1031/4454.

48. Barbados Legislative Council (Official Report), 3 September 1963, 7.

49. See also inward telegram to the secretary of state for the colonies, from chairman, Regional Council of Ministers, Barbados, 23 July 1963, CO 1031/4454.

50. See also "Greaves: We Have a Mandate for Independence", *Barbados Advocate*, 26 January 1966, 2; inward telegram to the secretary of state for the colonies from Barbados (governor's deputy), 7 January 1966, CO 1031/5060.

51. Sir Shridath Ramphal, interview with the author, St Michael, Barbados, 4 December 2008.

52. The reference is to a light Cessna aircraft Barrow usually flew to other Caribbean islands for meetings with their leaders.

53. "The Future Constitutional Development of the Leeward and Windward Islands in the Event of a Failure to Attain Federation", Government House, St Kitts, Nevis, Anguilla, 20 November 1964, CO 1031/4454. R.S.: S 11.A/9.

54. Summary of Replies to Circular Letter at 20–26 from Dominica's Chief Minister Le Blanc, Secret and Personal, Government House, St Vincent, 22 October 1964 to Douglas Williams, Esq., Colonial Office, London, CO 1031/4480.

55. CO 1031/445.

56. House of Assembly Debates (Official Report), 12 February 1963, 17, 18; see also Marshall (2003, 115–22 passim).

57. Antigua, No. 267, Colonial Office, London, CO 1031/4480.

58. Ibid.

59. Personal and confidential reference from John Stow, 7 November 1964, CO 1031/4480.

60. S&P.4/61 G.J. Bryan, Government House, St Lucia, 23 October 1964, CO 1031/4480.

61. Letter from N.E. Costar, British High Commission, Trinidad and Tobago, 10 October 1964, to D.M. Cleary, Esq., Atlantic Department, Commonwealth Relations Office, London, POS 20/37/1.

62. Dispatch no. 2, POL 314/13/2, CO 1031/4454.

63. Ibid.

64. Ref. No. A.8/P. & S.4, Administrator's Office, Roseau, Dominica, 8 October 1964, CO 1031/4480; inward telegram to the secretary of state for the colonies from Barbados (governor's deputy), 7 January 1966, CO 1031/5060.

65. Governor John Stow, Personal Report for the Month of April 1964, CO 1031/4765.

66. Ref. No. A.8/P. & S.4, Administrator's Office, Roseau, Dominica, 8 October 1964, CO 1031/4480.

67. Western Samoa reportedly opted for "independence with assistance . . . from New Zealand", based on the Treaty of Friendship it signed with New

Zealand. The treaty allowed New Zealand to "afford assistance to Western Samoa in the conduct of its foreign relations. When requested, New Zealand acts as the channel of communication with other Governments and international organizations, represents Western Samoa at international conferences and supplies it with information on international affairs". New Zealand did not have legal power to intervene in Western Samoa's internal affairs under the treaty (United Nations Charter, article 73; CO 1031/4480; Douglas Williams, memo to R.M.K. Slater, Esq., CMG, Foreign Office. 29 September 1964, CO 1031/4480).

68. CO Ref: WIS 64/629/023, 28 October 1964, Colonial Office.

69. See also House of Assembly Debates (Official Record), 31 July 1962, 663; House of Assembly Debates (Official Report), 25 January 1963, 1,057.

70. Grenada, St Lucia, Dominica, Antigua and St Kitts made up the West Indies Associated States.

71. UN General Assembly Resolution XV, 14 December 1960.

72. See also the introduction, *Annual Report of the Secretary-General for Period 16 June 1966 to 15 June 1976*, published in *UN Monthly Chronicle*, no. 4, 9 October 1967, 135.

73. Appendix, extract from Colonial Office Secret and Personal Letter to Administrators, 28 September 1964, CO 1031/4480.

74. Ibid.

75. CO 1031/4454.

76. Letter from Government House, Plymouth, Montserrat, 24 November 1964, to D.R. Gibbs, CO 1031/4480.

77. Douglas Williams mentioned as much in a memo to R.M.K. Slater, Esq, CMG, Foreign Office, 29 September 1964, CO 1031/4480.

78. Ibid.

CHAPTER 4

1. Lamming was selected on the recommendation of his former high school (Combermere) teacher, Frank Collymore, to teach English at El Colegio de Venezuela, a boarding school in Port of Spain, Trinidad, for Venezuelan boys. He taught there between 1946 and 1950, the year he migrated to the United Kingdom.

2. Leah Rosenberg (2007, 157, 159) mentions that there was a Readers' and Writers' Club in Jamaica from at least the 1930s. Lamming's novels, especially *In the Castle of My Skin* (1953), *The Emigrants* (1954), *Of Age and*

Innocence (1958) and *Season of Adventure* (1960), provide a sophisticated interpretation of the complex historical, political, social and ideological challenges the nationalist, decolonizing elites in the West Indian territories faced.

3. West Indies, West Indian Conference, Terms of Reference, CO 1042/45.

4. Cmd. 6713, despatch from the secretary of state for the colonies to the colonial governments, 12 November 1945, HMSO, 1945 (quoted in Phillips 1977, 12).

5. CADORIT was replaced by the CIA-dominated American Institute for Free Labor Development at the time of the creation of the Alliance for Progress in the wake of the Cuban Revolution taking power in 1959 (Watson 2004, 107).

6. George Orwell (1945) used the term "Cold War" in relation to the "world-view, beliefs and social structure of . . . the Soviet Union and the United States, and also the undeclared state of war that would come to exist between them" (Westad 2005, 2). Orwell suggested that the "atomic bomb" seemed to be "robbing the exploited classes and peoples of all power to revolt, and at the same time putting the possessors of the bomb on a basis of equality. Unable to conquer one another they are likely to continue ruling the world between them" (quoted in Westad 2005, 2).

7. West Indian Conference, Terms of Reference, S 0009. Philip Hewitt-Myring to Sir John McPherson, "A Report on Public Relations at the Second Session of the West Indian Conference (St Thomas, VI, March–April, 1946)". West Indian Conference, Terms of Reference, Reference: S 0009, CO 1042/45. See also Palmer (2006, 26).

8. According to Hans Morgenthau, "Neither the Southeast Asia Treaty Organization (SEATO) nor the Baghdad Pact . . . adds anything material to the strength of the West. All the nations concerned, with the exception of Iran, Pakistan, and Thailand, were already members of one or another Western military alignment before the conclusion of those pacts. . . . Iran and Thailand would be liabilities rather than assets for whatever side they would join in case of actual war" (1962, 260).

9. West Indian Department, "Government Campaign Against Illegal Immigrants into Trinidad" (Richard Hart, Ken and Frank Hill, A. Henry), File WIS 22/12/08, CO1031/15.

10. Winston Churchill delivered his "Iron Curtain" speech at Fulton, Missouri, in 1946, in which he laid the conceptual and geopolitical foundation for the

Cold War. In 1947 the US Congress passed the National Security Act and the Taft-Hartley Act, the same year the Marshall Plan was announced for the reconstruction of Western Europe. The USSR announced the creation of the Cominform. The highly militaristic containment and counter-revolutionary components of the Cold War project were thereby set in place.

11. According to the governor's report for February 1954 (CO 1031/1080), Grantley Adams said "regretfully . . . he and the 12,000 white residents of Barbados do not talk the same language. They are the old plantocracy and are unwilling to surrender any of their privileges". See also Personal Report for the Month of January 1966 to W.I.J. Wallace, Esq, CMG, OBE, Secret and Personal, Ref: 173/S.11, File Number WIS 64/2/01, CO 1031/5060.

12. University of the West Indies historian Dr Karl Watson notes that Grantley Adams resisted "racial prejudice and bias during his courtship of Grace Thorne, daughter of Herbert and Millicent Thorne, a member of one of the elite planter families of the island". Mr Thorne pleaded with Adams to "stay away from his daughter", saying, "It will bring disgrace to the family if she marries you. Do not tempt her, please" (1998, 23, 24; see also Hoyos 1988, 2; Sealy 1991, 13).

13. Gerald Horne (2007, 116) quotes Paul Blanshard as saying about Bustamante, "I have met [men] . . . who have borrowed money from him at the rate of 250 percent a year."

14. West Indians of the stature of Hubert Harrison, Cyril Briggs, Marcus Garvey, Otto Huiswoud, Claude McKay, W.A. Domingo, Richard B. Moore, Robert Pierpoint, and Ramón Emeterio Betances and Eugenio María de Hostos from Puerto Rico brought with them from the Caribbean to the United States an established tradition of "resistance with few parallels in the New World" (Horne 2007, 85–86; see also James 1998).

15. Bolland (2001, 510) gives the original source of Adams's call for a socialist Commonwealth as the official report of the CLC Conference held in Barbados, 17–27 September 1945. Barbados Department of Archives Box 395, University of the West Indies, Cave Hill, Barbados.

16. Colonel Vivian to "My Dear Harrington", CO968/121/4.

17. The reference is to Walter White, at the time the head of the NAACP.

18. Incoming telegram from secretary of state to governor general, dispatched 14 March 1962, University of the West Indies Federal Archives Box 395, Cave Hill, Barbados. See also West Indies Gazette 5, no. 6 (14 March 1962), Legal Supplement appendix.

19. Cary Fraser (2007, 114–16) argues that Cheddi Jagan and Janet Jagan "were able to recruit the majority of Hindus in the Indo-Guyanese community to follow their banner". Fraser draws attention to the "anti-intellectualism that . . . marked the PPP" and emphasizes that in the 1956 and 1961 election campaigns the PPP shaped its election strategy with appeals to "racial loyalty to keep the factions of the Indo-Guyanese community, including . . . capitalists and landlords, behind the PPP". Fraser also highlights the historical roots of the authoritarian culture of the PPP.

20. Bustamante sent a message to the secretary of state for the colonies registering his support for British action to remove the democratically elected Jagan government in British Guiana in 1953 (Sealy 1991, 112–13). CO 32/127.

21. Horne (2007, 164) notes that the name of the PPP, an outgrowth of the Political Affairs Committee, which the Jagans, Ashton Chase and Jocelyn Hubbard founded, was an "amalgam of the left-leaning Progressive Party of the United States (endorsed by W.E.B. Du Bois) and the People's National Party of Jamaica, to which Richard Hart belonged".

22. *Supplement to the Official Gazette* 88, no. 47 (12 June 1952), 155, CO 32/127.

23. *Supplement to the Official Gazette* 88, no. 47 (12 June 1952), 161.

24. Letter from Grantley Adams to Rt Hon Reginald Maudling, secretary of state for the colonies, 12 March 1962. University of the West Indies Federal Archives Box 395, Cave Hill, Barbados.

25. "Defence of the West Indies Co-ordination with the United States", CO 1031/4238 (WIS 1261/175/02)

26. See Horne (2007, 164) for details of Hart's role in assisting the PPP to become an affiliate of the CLC. Horne notes that Burnham was vice president of the CLC London Branch, which also spearheaded antiracist and anti-imperialist activities in the United Kingdom.

27. Originally in *Congressional Record*, 57th Congress, 1st session, 1902, 35: 7639–40.

28. *Supplement to the Official Gazette* 87, no. 3 (10 January 1952), 771.

29. "West Indies: Extent of Its Diplomatic Network", File Number WIS 1278/175/01, CO 1031/4254. See also *Official Gazette* 86, no. 4 (5 July 1951), 418, CO 32/126.

30. CO 1031/4225, File 1238/390/01.

31. "Defence of the West Indies Coordination with the United States", CO 1031/4238, File WIS 1261/175/2; "Defence of the West Indies after Independence", WIS 1261/175/01; Rabe 2005, 112–25.

32. Confidential Caribbean Committee of the Alliance for Progress Country Reviews, C.J. Hayes to the Hon. R.E.L. Johnstone, MVO, British Embassy, Washington, December 1967, DC FCO 23/200, File No. GR 2/1, CLA 254/04 7

33. "Emergency in Cuba", CO 1031/4225, WIS 1238/390/01.

34. Confidential outward telegram from Commonwealth Relations Office, W. no. 565, West Indies Department WID 126/142/1, CO 1031/4225.

35. Joint Chiefs of Staff, memorandum to the secretary of defense, Report by the Department of Defense and Joint Chiefs of Staff Representative on Caribbean Survey Group to the Joint Chiefs of Staff on Cuba, Project (TS). Unclassified.

36. "Emergency in Cuba", outward telegram from the secretary of state for the colonies, 26 October 1962, CO 1031/4225, File WIS 1238/390/01.

37. See CO 1031/5060.

38. Richard Cheltenham stresses that Adams wanted to retain control of the BWU while "simultaneously remaining political head of the country", and that the *Barbados Advocate* insisted that it was undemocratic for Adams to combine "political government with other tendentious activity", implying that such a combination of party and union headship "could set the stage for the unprincipled dictator should he arrive on the scene". The *Advocate* also objected to Walcott's being assigned a ministerial position in the government in addition to taking over the BWU (Cheltenham 1970, 103; *Barbados Advocate*, 7 August 1952; *Barbados Advocate*, 2 July 1953).

39. In 1956 the name of the monthly publication was changed from *Political Report of the Governor* to the *Barbados Intelligence Report*.

40. CO 1031/1534 File WIS 105/2/0, note by W.A. Ward 22/6 Colonial Office. The letter from the CPA gave the address of the Caribbean Socialist Party as c/o L.B. Brathwaite, 47 Swan Street, Bridgetown, St Michael, Barbados.

41. *Supplement to the Official Gazette* 87, no. 16 (25 February 1952), 58, 59.

42. CO 1031/1810. Wynter A. Crawford identified himself with the DLP in June 1956; *Monthly Intelligence Report (Barbados Intelligence Report)*, June 1956, CO 1031/1810.

43. Governor to Secretary of State for the Colonies, our reference: S 424/vol. 4, File WIS185/236/01, CO 1031/1810.

44. Ibid.

45. Beckles argues that the process of social justice in Barbados "reached maturity in 1994 when Owen Seymour Arthur, a young man from the

chattel house in the plantation tenantry became prime minister. This event brought closure to the culture of formal institutional denial and exclusion based on class" (2004b, xii).

It would be more accurate and realistic to suggest that the selection of Owen Arthur as prime minister of Barbados offered hope for strengthening and advancing the cause of social justice in the country, bearing in mind that any gains made by the working class in areas like justice and freedom are simply never guaranteed in any class society, of which Barbados is one. The working-class origins of a political leader do not and simply cannot guarantee the maturity of conditions for social justice, considering also that many working-class people do not necessarily act politically or otherwise in their own interest. Arthur's role as prime minister did not change power relations, the concentration of economic power and wealth in a few hands or the subsumption of labour under capital which compels labour to produce its opposite, which is capital.

46. *Political Report of the Governor for the Month of March 1954*, CO 1031/1810; see also Lewis 1999.

47. *Political Report of the Governor for the Month of June 1954*, CO 1031/1810.

48. *Political Report of the Governor for the Month of September 1954*, CO 1031/1810.

49. Marvin Will says based on an interview he conducted with Sir Ronald Mapp in Barbados on 25 October 1991 that Mapp accused Adams of running Parliament in a "manner that kept BLP parliamentarians uninformed of agenda items" which "contributed to a cleavage in labour and the formation in 1955 of the Democratic Labour Party" (Will 1992, 81n40).

50. The DLP was launched on 1 May 1955. *Political Report of the Governor for the Month of April 1955*, CO 1031/1810. The report for March 1955 cites an editorial from the *Barbados Advocate* which "squarely blamed the leaders of the Labour Party for the troubles which had occurred within its ranks and concluded that 'what finally drove these men from the ranks of the Labour Party was the persistent disregard of the views and opinions of the rank and file by the leaders of the Party'". The report for June 1955 mentioned that the DLP claimed it was opposed to Adams not on personal grounds "but because his policies are not in the best interests of the people of the Island".

51. On the official British view of opposition political parties in Barbados during the 1950s, see "The Strength of the Opposition Parties in Barbados", CO 1031/1290.

52. The report for December 1955 noted, "So far as is known the supply of Communist literature to Ulrick Grant dried up completely during the month, but it is understood that he proposes to resume requests for supplies during the New Year." CO 1031/1810.

53. *Political Report of the Governor for the Month of January 1955*, CO 1031/1810; see Elkins (2005) and Furedi (1998).

54. *Political Reports of the Governor for the Months of March and April 1955*, CO 1031/1810.

55. *Political Report of the Governor for the Month of January 1955*, CO 1031/1810.

56. *Political Report of the Governor for the Month of February 1955*, CO 1031/1810.

57. *Political Report of the Governor for the Month of May 1955* and *Political Report of the Governor for the Month of February 1955*, CO 1031/1810. The report for February 1956 mentioned that a local newspaper "received three copies of the publication 'For a Lasting Peace, for a People's democracy' dated 20th January and 3rd and 10th February. These were handed over to the Police." The report for April 1956 mentioned that during the month "about half a dozen copies of 'The Soviet Weekly' published during 1955 were handed over to the Police". These were said to have been received by a member of the public along with twelve copies of the *African Voice* – January/February issues. The handing over of the documents to the police highlights the strong authoritarianism that was in vogue and the anti-communist hysteria that prevailed.

58. *Monthly Intelligence Report (Barbados Intelligence Report)*, July 1956, Report of Barbados Intelligence Committee. See also *Monthly Intelligence Report (Barbados Intelligence Report)* for August, September and October 1956, CO 1031/1810.

59. *Supplement to the Official Gazette 87*, no. 31 (17 April 1952) [House], 92.

60. *Report of Barbados Intelligence Committee for July 1956*, CO 1031/1810.

61. *Report of Barbados Intelligence Committee for the months of July to October 1956*, CO 1031/1810.

CHAPTER 5

1. See Emmanuel (1988, 96–97) for details of the constitutional and political arrangements under the "old representative system" created under the 1751 Order in Council.

2. See Watson 2015a for a more extensive discussion of Marx's concept of merchant's capital in relation to industrial capitalism.

3. The study considers extensively the structural factors and the environment in which "the concrete day-to-day activities of the working masses" occurred. Those "working masses" were mainly the products of a system that was based on the dominance of agriculture and sugar in the division of labour within the political economy of Barbados at the time. They were far from passive actors, as they struggled against the odds they encountered in their everyday lives. Barbados's sugar industry had been declining over several decades; however, the Colonial Office declared just after World War II that the West Indian territories would have to continue to focus on sugar and agriculture. The United Kingdom enacted the Commonwealth Sugar Agreement Act in 1950, which I discuss, to shore up agriculture and extend the life of the declining sugar industry. The legislation was to guarantee Britain's access to cheap agricultural commodities from its colonies as it attempted to restructure its industrial and manufacturing base in the postwar years. The conditions associated with the "day-to-day activities of the working masses" were largely beyond their control. The report raises several interesting and intriguing questions and points that reflect the research orientation and priorities of anthropologists and others for whom ethnographic emphasis in research is paramount. I did not set out to conduct ethnographic research on Barbados in the late colonial period. The specific matters raised in the report about the quotidian situation pertain to symptoms rather than causal factors. My priority has been to contextualize and situate the political role Errol Barrow played in the larger societal context as part of the Caribbean and the wider world. The following sources should prove useful and helpful in filling some of the gaps for readers interested in finding out more about the issues raised in the report: Hunte (1988), Will (1992), Worrell (1994–95), Emmanuel (1988), Morgan (1994), Sutton (2005), Beckles (2004a), Clarke (2000), Bolland (2001), Chamberlain (2010), and Gmelch and Gmelch (2012).

4. Bolland (2012, 2–3) discusses specific characteristics of the social, economic and geopolitical situation in Cuba, Haiti and the Dominican Republic with attention to the forces and processes that shaped class struggles in those three societies. He argues that in the case of Cuba, "a powerful labour movement in the early 1930s became a revolution in 1933. The revolutionary government achieved some reforms but it was not recognized by the United States and was soon overthrown by Fulgencio Batista, with US support. This Cuban revolution was effectively postponed rather than

destroyed, and opposition to the status quo grew in the late 1940s. Fidel
Castro and his followers brought together powerful socialist and nationalist traditions, succeeded in overthrowing Batista in 1959, and restored the
revolutionary agenda."

5. Graham Barrow, interview by Robert Morris, 1976 (transcript).

6. See Harold Hoyte (2015, 381–82) for information about Sydney Burnett-
    Alleyne's romantic and exaggerated anti-historical fantasy. Alleyne said to
    Hoyte, "I was born in the British Empire and therefore will not subordinate
    the British Empire to any other country. I am British and proud of that. I
    am a citizen of the Holy Roman Empire and of the British Empire. That
    means that the Pope is Christ on Earth and the Queen is the princess of
    the Monarchy. I owe my duties and obligations to their dictates and if they
    do not want this, I am not going to do it." Alleyne's wild notion that the
    "Pope is Christ on Earth" is a sign of his personal delusion.

7. The Representation of the People Act 1901 provided for an income qualifi-
    cation of £50 per year on the franchise and a qualification of £5 on freehold
    land and properties. The sugar crisis, which hit Barbados quite hard from
    the early 1920s, degraded further the material conditions of those artisans
    and lower middle-strata blacks, threatening their ability to remain eligible
    to exercise the franchise (Beckles 2004a, 187).

8. John Connell, interview with the author, Sanford, St Philip, Barbados, 6
    July 2006; Mitchell Codrington, interview with the author, Husbands, St
    James, Barbados, 6 July 2006.

9. House of Assembly Debates (Official Report), Third Session, 1966–71,
    28 July 1970, 1991. The late Cecil Crawford, brother of the late Wynter
    Crawford, shared with the author certain documents including one with a
    photo of Adams appearing on the front, though he was first vice-president
    and Chrissie Brathwaite was president of the BPL.

10. See *Daily Nation*, 13 July 1991, 18, for Crawford's personal account that
    historians have slighted his role and contribution to the founding of the
    BLP. On Hope Stevens see *Barbados Advocate*, 9 February 1973, "Tortolan
    Looks Back on His Part in Formation of BLP". See also Gerald Horne
    (2007) for more about Hope Stevens. These and other important points
    were discussed in several conversations between the author and the late
    Cecil Crawford, brother of the late Wynter Crawford. Cecil Crawford also
    permitted the author to peruse some of his private papers which con-
    tained documents detailing the founding of the BPL and the "intrigue"

that informed how Wynter Crawford was marginalized in the archive of the BPL and BLP. Attempts by the author to schedule an interview with Wynter Crawford during the early 1990s proved unsuccessful, owing to Crawford's deteriorating eyesight and general health.

11. House of Assembly Debates (Official Report), Third Session, 1966–71, 20 October 1970, 1992.

12. Woodville Marshall, interview with the author, Paradise Heights, St Michael, Barbados, 19 November 2008.

13. Grantley Adams led the BPL from its founding in 1938 to its transition to the BLP, and remained leader of the BLP until he resigned from the House of Assembly in 1958 to become prime minister of the Federation of the West Indies. He also assumed the leadership of the BWU from its founding until 1954. Adams headed the Barbados government under the Bushe Experiment, which set the terms and conditions for the implementation of internal self-government (Will 1992, 67–68; House of Assembly Debates [Official Report], Third Session, 1966–71, 20 October 1970, 1991). The Trade Union Act was enacted in 1939 and took effect in 1940; under the new legislation the BWU became an independent organization in 1941. Before universal adult suffrage came into effect in 1951, the BWU was the largest, most effective and most important civil-society organization that represented the broad interests of the working class in Barbados until the BLP became ascendant.

14. Robert Bradshaw (St Kitts) asserted that it was unwise and politically risky for any political leader in the West Indies/CARICOM countries to separate their leadership of the labour and trade union movement from their leadership of their political parties. He also insisted that Grantley Adams "did not take the advice and as a result his party lost because he tried to separate the Trade Unions from politics which does not work out here because political representation has grown out of the labour movement. Maybe it is unfortunate but there it is, a fact of life. If I were to say to my people in St. Kitts today that I am going to withdraw from the Presidency of the Union to which they elected me and retain the Premiership of the State, the people's reaction would be violent and predictable. 'Oh, you get too big for us now, eh?' It is as simple as that'" (quoted in Theodore Sealy 1991, 44; see also Bolland (2001) and Horne (2007) on the authoritarian tendencies of West Indian leaders and politics). Bradshaw also claimed that Vere Bird lost the election in Antigua to Selwyn Walter because he made a

similar mistake. Sealy points out that when Alexander Bustamante's JLP won the Jamaican general election in 1944 with "22 seats out of 32 seats to the House of Representatives", polling 41.4 per cent of the votes cast, and he "became Chief Minister of Jamaica to sit on the Executive Council with the Governor", he "elected to take the portfolio of Communications and Works but he never surrendered his Union leadership. Indeed, well past 90 years of age, and partly invalid at his mountain home at Irish Town, Bustamante remained nominally and de facto Leader of the Bustamante Industrial Trade Union, having completed 23 years of service in Jamaica's legislature and Parliament" (Sealy 1991, 107).

15. Frank Walcott became general secretary of the BWU in November 1947, replacing Hugh Springer, who resigned to become registrar of the University College of the West Indies, Mona, Jamaica. Walcott served as Springer's assistant in the BWU. Walcott's working-class background made a difference to how the rank and file in the BWU came to relate to the leadership of the union (see Will 1992, 80; Marshall 1991, 11–13).

16. Hoyos (1972, 128) says in reference to Grantley Adams, "It is perhaps a curious irony that the man who now led the new movement was the same man who had played a major part in bringing the *Herald* newspaper to a standstill in 1930. But Wickham, with the magnanimity that was typical of him, had long forgiven Adams for that. Indeed, he joined forces with Adams from the time he entered the House of Assembly."

17. Sydney Burnett-Alleyne claims that he believes in "equal opportunity" but does not "believe in the equality of all people". He rejects social equality because nature (not history) designs each to "have a particular purpose" (Hoyte 2015, 381). In his thinking, social equality, which develops via the institutions humans create to reproduce themselves, violates the laws of nature – a sign of self-delusion and abysmal ignorance of history.

18. F.A. Hoyos (1972, 137) notes that Grantley Adams introduced Errol Barrow to the St George electors at a mass meeting at Ellerton during the 1951 general election campaign, and "presented him as a man who might well succeed him as leader of the Party and Barrow replied in a speech that was lustily cheered by the thousands present at the meeting".

19. The members of the first provisional council of the DLP were O.T. Allder, E.W. Barrow, J. Best, O. Blackman, J.M. Bonnett, C.L. Brathwaite, L.B. Brathwaite, L.D. Burrows, H. Coulson, L. Wood, C.A. Gill, D. Holder, E.S. Lewis, A.H. Lewis, F.G. Smith, J.B. Springer, Sr., J.B. Springer, Jr, D.

Straker, E. Tudor, J.C. Tudor (all males). See *DLP Manifesto 1961*, in Sealy (2001, 65, appendix I).

20. *Supplement to the Official Gazette 87*, no. 47 (12 June 1952): 154.

21. The Barbados Employers' Confederation looked forward to the work of CADORIT in the Caribbean to help channel the energies of organized labour in the appropriate direction. See *CADORIT Information Bulletin*, May–June 1959, 14; *Barbados Employers' Confederation Newsletter*, no. 22 (31 July 1959), 1.

22. Elements of the liberal democratic order include the primacy of private property and rightful property income, the right of private capital to exploit labour, universal adult suffrage, protection of individual rights under the law, trade union rights, a free press, freedom of association and allowance for gradual change and adjustment in the status quo over time.

23. The *Barbados Employers' Confederation Newsletter*, no. 27 (December 1959), advised its "member organizations to watch most carefully the workings of Wages Councils for these can be dangerous to private enterprise in the hands of a government using them for political reasons".

24. House of Assembly Debates (Official Report), Third Session, 1966–71, 1579.

REFERENCES

Agnew, John. 2005. *Hegemony: The New Shape of Global Power*. Philadelphia: Temple University Press.

———. 2009. *Globalization and Sovereignty*. Lanham, MD: Rowman and Littlefield.

Allahar, Anton, ed. 2001. *Caribbean Charisma: Reflections on Leadership, Legitimacy and Populist Politics*. Boulder: Lynne Rienner.

Anievas, Alexander and Kerem Nişancioğlu. 2015. *How the West Came to Rule: The Geopolitical Origins of Capitalism*. London: Pluto.

Arrighi, Giovanni. 1982. *The Geometry of Imperialism: The Limits of Hobson's Paradigm*. London: Verso.

Arrighi, Giovanni and John Saul. 1973. *Essays on the Political Economy of Africa*. New York: Monthly Review Press.

Ayearst, Morley. 1960. *The British West Indies: The Search for Self-Government*. New York: New York University Press.

Azzarà, Stefano G. 2007. "Domenico Losurdo: Classical German Philosophy, a Critique of Liberalism and 'Critical Marxism'". 14 May. http://domenicolosurdopresentazazing.blogspot.com/.

Balibar, Etienne. 1991. "The Nation Form: History and Ideology". In *Race, Nation, Class: Ambiguous Identities*, by Etienne Balibar and Immanuel Wallerstein, 86–106. London: Verso.

Barbados. 1945. *A Ten-Year Development Plan for Barbados: Sketch Plan of Development, 1946–56*. Bridgetown, Barbados: Advocate Company, for the Government of Barbados.

———. 1965. *Barbados Development Programme 1962–65*. Bridgetown: Government Printing Office.

Barkawi, Tarak and Mark Laffey. 1999. "The Imperial Peace: Democracy, Force and Globalization". *European Journal of International Relations* 5 (4): 403–34.

Beckles, Hilary. 1989. *Corporate Power in Barbados: The Mutual Affair – Economic Injustice in a Political Democracy*. Bridgetown, Barbados: Lighthouse Communications.

————. 1990. *A History of Barbados: From Amerindian Settlement to Nation-State.* New York: Cambridge University Press.

————. 2001. "Radicalism and Errol Barrow in the Political Tradition of Barbados". In *The Empowering Impulse: The Nationalist Tradition of Barbados,* edited by Glenford D. Howe and Don D. Marshall, 221–31. Kingston: Canoe Press.

————. 2004a. *Great House Rules: Landless Emancipation and Workers' Protest in Barbados 1838–1938.* Kingston: Ian Randle.

————. 2004b. *Chattel House Blues: Making of a Democratic Society in Barbados, from Clement Payne to Owen Arthur.* Kingston: Ian Randle.

Belle, George V. 1988. "The Struggle for Political Democracy: The 1937 Riots". In *Emancipation III: Aspects of the Post-Slavery Experience of Barbados. Lectures to commemorate the 150th Anniversary of Emancipation,* edited by Woodville Marshall, 56–91. Kingston: n.p.

Bilgin, Pinar, and Adam Morton. 2002. "Historicizing Representations of 'Failed States': Beyond the Cold-War Annexation of the Social Sciences". *Third World Quarterly* 23 (1): 55–80.

Blackman, Francis. 1995. *Dame Nita: Caribbean Woman, World Citizen.* Kingston: Ian Randle.

Blanshard, Paul. 1947. *Democracy and Empire in the Caribbean.* New York: Macmillan.

Blaut, James. 1976. "Where Was Capitalism Born?" *Antipode* 8 (2): 1–11.

Bolland, Nigel. 2001. *The Politics of Labour in the Caribbean: the Social Origins of Authoritarianism and Democracy in the Labour Movement.* Kingston: Ian Randle.

————. 2012. "The Barbados Labour Rebellion, 1937, in a Comparative, Caribbean Perspective". Elsa Goveia Memorial Lecture presented at the University of the West Indies, Cave Hill, Barbados, 25 April.

Bolles, A. Lynn. 1996. *We Paid Our Dues: Women Trade Union Leaders of the Caribbean.* Washington, DC: Howard University Press.

Bradshaw, William. 1989. "'Sleepy' Smith: The Champion of the Small Man". *New Bajan* Special Issue, May.

Brynjolfsson, Erik, and Andrew McAfee. 2014. *The Second Machine Age: Work, Progress, and Prosperity in A Time of Brilliant Technologies.* New York: Norton.

Buck-Morss, Susan. 2009. *Hegel, Haiti and Universal History.* Pittsburgh: University of Pittsburgh Press.

Burke, Willie. 1966. "Premier Raps Vested Class". *Barbados Advocate,* 5 January.

Chamberlain, Mary. 2010. *Empire and Nation-Building in the Caribbean: Barbados 1937–66*. Manchester: Manchester University Press.

Cheltenham, Richard. 1970. "Constitutional and Political Development in Barbados 1946–66". PhD dissertation, University of Manchester, UK.

Chomsky, Noam. 2000. *Rogue States: The Rule of Force in World Affairs*. Boston: South End Press.

CIA (Central Intelligence Agency). 1947. "Soviet Objectives in Latin America". ORE 16/1, 1 November. http://www.foia.cia.gov.

Clarke, Austin. 2000. *Pig Tails 'n' Breadfruit: Rituals of Slave Food*. Toronto: Vintage Canada.

Clymer, Jeffory A. 2003. *America's Culture of Terrorism: Violence, Capitalism, and the Written Word*. Chapel Hill: University of North Carolina Press.

Colonial Office. 1947. *The Colonial Empire, 1939–1947*. Cmd. 7167. London: HMSO.

Conway, Ed. 2015. *The Summit, Bretton Woods, 1944: J.M. Keynes and the Reshaping of the Global Economy*. New York: Pegasus.

Cowling, J.W. 1943. *Forced Labour in the Colonies*. London: Peace News.

Cozier, E.L. 1981. "The Man 'TT' Lewis". *Barbados Advocate*. 2 March.

Crawford, Wynter A. 1991. "How the BLP Was founded". *Daily Nation*. 3 July.

Davidson, Neil. 2015. "Is Social Revolution Still Possible in the Twenty-First Century?" *Journal of Contemporary Central and Eastern Europe* 23 (2–3): 105–50.

Dear, Jack. 1992. "The Birth of the Nation". *Journal of the Barbados Museum and Historical Society* 40:1–8.

Deerr, Nöel. 1949. *The History of Sugar*. Vol. 1. London: Chapman and Hall.

DeSmith, Stanley A. 1964. *The New Commonwealth and its Constitutions*. London: Stevens and Sons.

Dray, Philip. 2002. *At the Hands of Persons Unknown: the Lynching of Black America*. New York: Random House.

Drayton, Richard. 2014. "Secondary Decolonization: The Black Power Moment in Barbados, c. 1970". In *Black Power in the Caribbean*, edited by Kate Quinn, 117–35. Gainesville: University Press of Florida.

———. 2016. "Whose Constitution? Law, Justice and History in the Caribbean". 2016 Distinguished Jurist Lecture, Judicial Education Institute of Trinidad and Tobago, Port of Spain, Trinidad, 2 March.

Duncan, Neville. 1988. "Barbados and the Federation". In *Emancipation III: Aspects of the Post-Slavery Experience of Barbados – Lectures to Commemorate the 150th Anniversary of Emancipation*, edited by Woodville Marshall, 112–22. Kingston: n.p.

Edsall, Thomas. 2018. "Industrial Revolutions Are Political Wrecking Balls". *New York Times.* 3 May. www.nytimes.com/2018/05/03/opinion/trump -industrial-revolutions.html.

Elden, Stuart. 2009. *Terror and Territory: The Spatial Extent of Sovereignty.* Minneapolis: University of Minnesota Press.

Elkins, Caroline. 2005. *Britain's Gulag: The Brutal End of Empire in Kenya.* London: Jonathan Cape.

Emmanuel, Patrick. 1988. "Shifts in the Balance of Political Power: Unions and Parties". In *Emancipation III: Aspects of the Post-Slavery Experience of Barbados. Lectures to Commemorate the 150th Anniversary of Emancipation,* edited by Woodville Marshall, 92–111. Kingston: n.p.

Farber, Samuel. 2006. *The Origins of the Cuban Revolution Reconsidered.* Chapel Hill, NC: University of North Carolina Press.

Farley, Martel A. 1987. "Charles Duncan O'Neal: A Study of His Life and Times". BA dissertation, University of the West Indies, Cave Hill, Barbados.

Finamore, C. 2014. "Radical Ideas for Radical Times". *CounterPunch,* 24 September. https://www.counterpunch.org/2014/09/24/radical-ideas-for -radical-times/.

Foner, Eric. 2002. *Who Owns History? Rethinking the Past in a Changing World.* New York: Hill and Wang.

Fraser, Cary. 2007. Review of *Sacred Duty: Hinduism and Violence in Guyana* by Kean Gibson.

Furedi, Frank. 1998. *The Silent War: Imperialism and the Changing Perception of Race.* New Brunswick, NJ: Rutgers University Press.

Gill, Stephen. 2003. *Power and Resistance in the New World Order.* Basingstoke, UK: Palgrave Macmillan.

Gmelch, Sharon B., and George Gmelch. 2012. *The Parish Behind God's Back.* 2nd ed. Long Grove, IL: Waveland.

Goldberg, David Theo. 2002. *The Racial State.* Malden, MA: Blackwell.

Gomes, Albert. 1974. *Through a Maze of Colour.* Port of Spain, Trinidad: Key Caribbean.

Goody, Jack. 2007. *The Theft of History.* Cambridge: Cambridge University Press.

Gullí, Bruno. 2010. *Earthly Plenitudes: A Study on Sovereignty and Labor.* Philadelphia: Temple University Press.

Hammond, Thomas. T., ed. 1982. *Witnesses to the Origins of the Cold War.* Seattle: University of Washington Press.

Haniff, Yusuf, ed. 1987. *Speeches by Errol Barrow.* London: Hansib.

Hardt, Michael, and Antonio Negri. 2008. *Commonwealth*. Cambridge, MA: Harvard University Press.

Hart, Richard. 1998. *From Occupation to Independence: A Short History of the Peoples of the English-Speaking Caribbean Region*. London: Pluto.

————. 2002. *Labour Rebellions of the 1930s in the British Caribbean Region Colonies*. London: Caribbean Labour Solidarity and Socialist History Society.

————. 2004. *Time for a Change: Constitutional, Political and Labour Developments in Jamaica and other Colonies in the Caribbean Region, 1944–1955*. Kingston: Arawak.

Harvey, David. 1989. *The Condition of Postmodernity: An Inquiry into the Origins of Social Change*. Oxford: Blackwell.

Henry, Paget. 2010. *Shouldering Antigua and Barbuda: The Life of V.C. Bird*. Hertford, Hertfordshire, UK: Hansib.

Hobson, J.A. 1902. *Imperialism: A Study*. New York: James Pott.

Hofstadter, Richard. 1973. *The American Political Tradition and the Men Who Made It*. New York: Vintage.

Holder, Jean. S. 2007. *The Right Excellent Errol Walton Barrow: National Hero and Father of Independence – A Souvenir*. Barbados: Jean S. Holder.

————. 2015. *The Right Excellent Errol Walton Barrow: An Intimate Portrait, the Little Eight Experiment and the March to Independence*. Rev. ed. Barbados: Jean S. Holder.

Holloway, John. 1995. "Global Capital and the National State". In *Global Capital, National State and the Politics of Money*, edited by Werner Bonefeld and John Holloway, 116–40. Basingstoke, UK: Palgrave Macmillan.

————. 2002. *Change the World without Taking Power: The Meaning of Revolution Today*. London: Pluto.

————. 2005. "Stop Making Capitalism". In *Human Dignity*, edited by Werner Bonefeld and Kosmas Psychopedis, 173–80. London: Ashgate.

Holt, Thomas. 2000. *The Problem of Racism in the 21st Century*. The Nathan I. Huggins Lectures. Cambridge, MA: Harvard University Press.

Horne, Gerald. 2007. *Cold War in a Hot Zone: The United States Confronts Labor and Independence Struggles in the British West Indies*. Philadelphia: Temple University Press.

Horsman, Reginald. 1981. *Race and Manifest Destiny: The Origins of American Racial Anglo-Saxonism*. Cambridge, MA: Harvard University Press.

Howard, Michael. 2006. *The Economic Development of Barbados*. Kingston: University of the West Indies Press.

Howe, Glenford D., and Don D. Marshall, eds. 2001. *The Empowering Impulse: The Nationalist Tradition of Barbados*. Kingston: Canoe Press.

Hoyos, F.A. 1963. *The Rise of West Indian Democracy: The Life and Times of Sir Grantley Adams*. Bridgetown, Barbados: Advocate Press.

———. 1972. *Builders of Barbados*. London: Macmillan Education.

———. 1974. *Grantley Adams and the Social Revolution: The Story of the Movement that Changed the Pattern of West Indian Society*. London: Macmillan.

———. 1984. *The Quiet Revolutionary: The Autobiography of F.A. Hoyos*. London: Macmillan.

———. 1988. *Tom Adams: A Biography*. London: Macmillan.

Hoyte, Harold. 2012. *Eyewitness to Order and Disorder*. Ayshford, Barbados: HH Investments.

———. 2015. *Political Warriors of Barbados: Generals, Lieutenants and Foot Soldiers*. Ayshford, Barbados: HH Investments.

Hunte, Keith. 1988. "The Struggle for Political Democracy: Charles Duncan O'Neal and the Democratic League". In *Emancipation III: Aspects of the Post-Slavery Experience of Barbados. Lectures to Commemorate the 150th Anniversary of Emancipation*, edited by Woodville Marshall, 20–38. Kingston: n.p.

Innis, Trevor. 1999. "The Shifting Patterns of Land Use in Barbados since Independence 1966–1995". BA thesis, University of West Indies, Cave Hill, Barbados.

Israel, Jonathan. 2006. *Enlightenment Contested: Philosophy, Modernity, and the Emancipation of Man 1670–1752*. New York: Oxford University Press.

Jagan, Cheddi. 1972. *The West on Trial: The Fight for Guiana's Freedom*. New York: International Publishers.

Jahn, Beate. 1998. "One Step Forward, Two Steps Backward: Critical Theory as Latest Edition of Liberal Idealism". *Millennium Journal of International Studies* 27 (3): 613–41.

———. 2000. *The Cultural Construction of International Relations*. New York: Palgrave Macmillan.

James, C.L.R. 1962. *Party Politics in the West Indies*. Trinidad: Vedic Enterprises .

James, Winston. 1998. *Holding Aloft the Banner of Ethiopia*. London: Verso.

———. 2007. "Dissent, Coercion, Containment and Marronage: The Agony and Trajectory of Radical Intellectuals in Barbadian History". In *The Locations of George Lamming*, edited by Bill Schwarz, 26–48. Oxford: Macmillan Caribbean.

Jemmott, Ralph, and Dan Carter. 1994–95. "Barbadian Educational Development

1933–1993, an Interpretative Analysis II". *Journal of the Barbados Museum and Historical Society* 42:91–150.

Johnson, Chalmers. 2004. *The Sorrows of Empire: Militarism, Secrecy and the End of the Republic.* New York: Metropolitan Books.

Johnson, Howard, and Karl Watson, eds. 1998. *The White Minority in the Caribbean.* Kingston: Ian Randle.

Karch, Cecilia A. 1982. "*The Growth of the Corporate Economy in Barbados, Class or Race Factors: 1890–1977*". In *The Contemporary Caribbean: A Sociological Reader, edited by Susan Craig,* 213–41. Port of Spain, Trinidad: College Press.

———. (with Henderson Carter). 1997. *The Rise of the Phoenix: The Barbados Mutual Life Assurance Society in Caribbean Economy and Society 1840–1990.* Kingston: Ian Randle.

———. 2008. *Corporate Culture in the Caribbean: A History of Goddard Enterprises Limited.* Bridgetown, Barbados: Goddard Enterprises.

Kay, Geoffrey. 1975. *Development and Underdevelopment.* New York: St Martin's.

Kellman, Ricardo. 2010. "A History of Barbados' Foreign Policy 1966–1998". PhD dissertation, University of the West Indies, Cave Hill Campus, Barbados.

Kennan, George. 1947. "X: The Sources of Soviet Conduct". *Foreign Affairs* 25 (4): 566–82.

Kiernan, Victor. 1969. *The Lords of Human Kind: European Attitudes to Other Cultures in the Imperial Age.* Chicago: University of Chicago Press.

Koenigsberg, Richard. 2016. "Ideology as Fantasy". Elmhurst, NY: Library of Social Science.

———. 2017. "Diseased Attachment to the Nation-State". https://www.library ofsocialscience.com/newsletter/posts/2017/2017-05-09-h.html.

Lamming, George. 1953. *In the Castle of My Skin.* New York: McGraw-Hill.

———. 1958. *Of Age and Innocence.* London: Michael Joseph.

———. 1960. *The Pleasures of Exile.* London: Michael Joseph.

———. [1954] 1980. *The Emigrants.* London: Allison and Busby.

———. [1960] 1999. *Season of Adventure.* London: Allison and Busby.

Landau, Saul. 1987. *The Dangerous Doctrine.* Boulder: Westview.

Layne, Christopher. 2006. *The Peace of Illusions: American Grand Strategy from 1940 to the Present.* Ithaca: Cornell University Press.

Lenin, V.I. [1917] 1972. *Imperialism: the Highest Stage of Capitalism.* Moscow: Progress Publishers.

Levins, Richard and Richard Lewontin. 1985. *The Dialectical Biologist.* Cambridge, MA: Harvard University Press.

Lewis, Gary. 1999. *White Rebel: The Life and Times of T.T. Lewis*. Kingston: University of the West Indies Press.

Lewis, Gordon K. 1968. *The Growth of the Modern West Indies*. New York: Monthly Review Press.

Lewis, W. Arthur. 1938. *Labour in the West Indies: The Birth of a Workers' Movement*. London: Fabian Society.

————. 1949. "Colonial Development". *Colonial Review* 4 (2 June): 37–41.

————. 1954. "Economic Development with Unlimited Supplies of Labour". *Manchester School of Economic and Social Studies* 22 (2): 139–91.

————. 1961. *Eastern Caribbean Report to the Prime Minister*. Port of Spain, Trinidad: Federal Government Printery.

————. 1965. *The Agony of the Eight*. Bridgetown, Barbados: Advocate Company.

————. 1968. Epilogue in Sir John Mordecai, *Federation of the West Indies*. Evanston, Illinois: Northwestern University Press.

————. [1939] 1977. *Labour in the West Indies: The Birth of a Workers' Movement*. London: New Beacon Books.

————. 1978. *Evolution of the International Economic Order*. Princeton, N.J.: Princeton University Press.

Losurdo, Domenico. 2011. *Liberalism: A Counter-History*. London: Verso.

Louis, William Roger. 1977. *Imperialism at Bay 1941–1945: The United States and the Decolonization of the British Empire*. Oxford: Oxford University Press.

Macmillan, W.M. 1936. *Warning from the West Indies*. London: Faber and Faber.

Malik, Kenan. 1996. *The Meaning of Race: Race, History and Culture in Western Society*. New York: New York University Press.

Manifesto of the Democratic Labour Party, Barbados General Election 1961. 1961. Bridgetown: Democratic Labour Party.

Mark, Francis. 1966. *The History of the Barbados Workers' Union*. Bridgetown, Barbados: Barbados Workers' Union.

Marqusee, Mike. 2003. *Crimes of Freedom*. New York: New Press.

————. 2007. "The Iron Click: American Exceptionalism and US Empire". In *Selling US Wars*, edited by Achin Vanaik, 89–118. Northampton, MA: Olive Branch Press.

Mars, Perry, and Alma Young, eds. 2004. *Caribbean Labour and Politics: Legacies of Cheddi Jagan and Michael Manley*. Detroit: Wayne State University Press.

Marshall, Woodville, ed. 1988. *Emancipation IV: A Series of Lectures to Commemorate the 150th Anniversary of Emancipation*. Kingston: Canoe Press.

————. 1991. *The Post-Slavery Labour Problem Revisited*. Elsa Goveia Lecture. Kingston: Department of History, the Univeristy of the West Indies.

————, ed. 2003. *I Speak for the People: The Memoirs of Wynter Crawford*. Kingston: Ian Randle.

Marx, Karl. [1894] 1967. *Capital: A Critique of Political Economy*. Vol. 3. New York: International Publishers.

————. [1894] 1971. *Capital: A Critique of Political Economy*. Vol. 3. Moscow: Progress Publishers.

————. [1939] 1973. *The Grundrisse*. London: Lawrence and Wishart.

————. [1888] 1976. "Theses on Feuerbach". In *Ludwig Feuerbach and the End of Classical German Philosophy*, by Frederich Engels. Peking: Foreign Languages Press. (Prepared for the Internet by David Romagnolo, January 1998.)

Marx, Karl, and Fredrich Engels. 1972. *The Communist Manifesto*. New York: Bantam Classics.

Mawby, Spencer. 2012. *Ordering Independence: The End of Empire in the Anglophone Caribbean, 1947–1969*. Basingstoke, UK: Palgrave Macmillan.

McIntosh, Simeon. 2002. *Caribbean Constitutional Reform: Rethinking the West Indian Polity*. Kingston: Ian Randle.

Mészáros, István. 2008. *The Challenge and Burden of Historical Time: Socialism in the Twenty-First Century*. New York: Monthly Review Press.

Mills, Charles. 2010. *Radical Theory, Caribbean Reality: Race, Class and Social Domination*. Kingston: University of the West Indies Press.

————. 2016. "Liberalizing Illiberal Liberalism: Liberalism and Racial Justice". Lecture delivered at Bucknell University, Lewisburg, Pennsylvania, 29 September.

Montagu, Ashley. [1942] 1997. *Man's Most Dangerous Myth: The Fallacy of Race*. Walnut Creek, CA: AltaMira.

Mordecai, Sir John. 1968. *Federation of the West Indies*. Evanston, IL: Northwestern University Press.

Morgan, Peter. 1994. *The Life and Times of Errol Barrow*. Bridgetown, Barbados: Caribbean Communications.

Morgenthau, Hans. 1962. *The Impasse of American Foreign Policy*. Chicago: University of Chicago Press.

Morris, Robert L. 1988. "The Effects of the Great Depression". In *Emancipation III: Aspects of the Post-Slavery Experience of Barbados. Lectures to Commemorate the 150th Anniversary of Emancipation*, edited by Woodville Marshall, 39–55. Kingston: n.p.

Munroe, Trevor. 1978. "The Marxist Left in Jamaica, 1940–1950". Working Paper no. 15. Kingston: Institute of Social and Economic Research, University of the West Indies.

Nasser, Alan. 2014. "Apolitical Economy: Democracy and Dynasty". *CounterPunch*, 2–4 May. https://www.counterpunch.org/2014/05/02/apolitical-economy -democracy-and-dynasty/.

Neocleous, Mark. 2008. *Critique of Security*. Montreal, PQ, and Kingston, ON: McGill-Queens University Press.

Newton, Velma. 1984. *The Silver Men: West Indian Migration to Panama 1850– 1914*. Kingston: Institute of Social and Economic Research, University of the West Indies.

Ninkovich, Frank. 1994. *Modernity and Power: A History of the Domino Theory in the Twentieth Century*. Chicago: University of Chicago Press.

Noble, David. 1998. "The Anglo-Protestant Monopolization of 'America'". In *José Martí's "Our America": From National to Hemispheric Cultural Studies*, edited by Jeffrey Belnap and Raúl Fernández, 253–74. Durham, NC: Duke University Press.

Orwell, George. 1945. "You and the Atomic Bomb". *Tribune*. 19 October.

Palmer, Colin. 2006. *Eric Williams and the Making of the Modern Caribbean*. Chapel Hill: University of North Carolina Press.

———. 2010. *Cheddi Jagan and the Politics of Power: British Guiana's Struggle for Independence*. Chapel Hill: University of North Carolina Press.

Panitch, Leo, and Sam Gindin. 2012. *The Making of Global Capitalism: The Political Economy of American Empire*. London: Verso.

Parker, Jason. 2002. "Remapping the Cold War in the Tropics: Race, Communism and Security in the British West Indies". *International History Review* 24 (2): 318–47.

Patterson, Orlando. 1991. *Freedom in the Making of Western Culture*. New York: Basic Books.

Pelling, Henry. [1953] 1965. *The Origins of the Labour Party 1880–1900*. London: Oxford University Press.

Perelman, Michael. 2011. *The Invisible Handcuffs of Capitalism: How Market Tyranny Stifles the Economy by Stunting Workers*. New York: Monthly Review Press.

Pérez, Louis A. Jr. 1998. *The War of 1898: The United States and Cuba in History and Historiography*. Chapel, Hill, NC: University of North Carolina Press.

Perry, Jeffrey. 2010. "The Developing Conjuncture and Some Insights from Hubert Harrison and Theodore W. Allen on the Centrality of the Fight against White Supremacy". *Cultural Logic: Marxist Theory and Practice* (July): 2–117.

Phillips, Anthony De V. 1987. "The Confederation Question". In *Emancipation*

II: Aspects of the Post-Slavery Experience in Barbados, edited by Woodville K. Marshall, 70–84. Bridgetown, Barbados: University of the West Indies and the National Cultural Foundation.

————. 1998. "Grantley Herbert Adams: Asquithian Liberalism and Socialism". Journal of the Barbados Museum and Historical Society 44 (November–December): 1–20.

Phillips, Sir Fred. 1977. Freedom in the Caribbean: A Study in Constitutional Change. Dobbs Ferry, NY: Oceana.

Pilgrim, Torrey. 1988a. Bajan, May.

————. 1988b. Bajan, June.

Poole, Bernard. 1951. The Caribbean Commission: Background of Cooperation in the West Indies. Columbia, SC: University of South Carolina Press.

Pradella, Lucia. 2015. Globalization and the Critique of Political Economy: New Insights from Marx's Writings. London: Routledge.

Rabe, Stephen. 2005. U.S. Intervention in British Guiana: A Cold War Story. Chapel Hill: University of North Carolina Press.

Radosh, Ronald. 1969. American Labor and United States Foreign Policy: The Cold War in the Unions from Gompers to Lovestone. New York: Random House.

Reed, Adolph Jr. 2013. "Marx, Race and Neoliberalism". New Labor Forum 22 (1): 49–57.

Reid, Ira. [1939] 1970. The Negro Immigrant: His Background, Characteristics and Social Adjustment 1899–1937. New York: AMS Press.

Richardson, Bonham. 1985. Panama Money in Barbados, 1900–1920. Knoxville: University of Tennessee Press.

Robinson, William I. 2004. A Theory of Global Capitalism. Baltimore: Johns Hopkins University Press.

————. 2014. Global Capitalism and the Crisis of Humanity. Cambridge: Cambridge University Press.

Rodney, Walter. 1981. A History of the Guyanese Working People, 1881–1905. Foreword by George Lamming. Baltimore: Johns Hopkins University Press.

Roberts, Michael. 2016. The Long Depression: How It Happened, Why It Happened, and What Happens Next. Chicago: Haymarket.

Rosenberg, Leah R. 2007. Nationalism and the Formation of Caribbean Literature. New York: Palgrave Macmillan.

Rosenberg, Justin. 1994. The Empire of Civil Society: A Critique of the Realist Theory of International Relations. London: Verso.

Ruppert, Michael C. 2003. Crossing the Rubicon: The Decline of the American Empire and the End of the Age of Oil. Gabriola Island, BC: New Society.

Ryan, Selwyn. 2009. *Eric Williams: The Myth and the Man*. Kingston: University of the West Indies Press.

Scott, David. 2002. "The Sovereignty of the Imagination: An Interview with George Lamming". *Small Axe* 12 (September): 72–200.

Sealy, Sharon. 2001. "A Biography of Sir Frederick Smith". BA thesis, University of the West Indies, Cave Hill, Barbados.

Sealy, Theodore. 1991. *Sealy's Caribbean Leaders: A Personal Perspective on Major Political Caribbean Leaders Pre and Post Independence*. Kingston: Eagle Merchant Bank of Jamaica in association with Kingston Publishers.

Seekings, Jeremy. 2006. "'Pa's Pension': The Origins of Non-contributory Old Age Pensions in Late Colonial Barbados". Centre for Social Science Research, Social Policy Series. Social Survey Unit, CSSR Working Paper no. 164, University of Cape Town, South Africa.

Selwyn, Benjamin. 2016. "The Struggle for Development". Lecture delivered at SOAS, University of London. 1 November.

Senior, Olive. 2014. *Dying to Better Themselves: West Indians and the Building of the Panama Canal*. Kingston: University of the West Indies Press.

Shaikh, Anwar. 2016. *Capitalism: Competition, Conflict, Crises*. New York: Oxford University Press.

Simpson, Bill. 1973. *Labour: The Unions and the Party*. London: Allen and Unwin.

Smith, Neil. 2003. *American Empire: Roosevelt's Geographer and the Prelude to Globalization*. Berkeley: University of California Press.

Smith, Sir Frederick, and Alan Smith. 2015. *Dreaming a Nation: Sir Frederick and the Barbados Journey in His Own Voice*. London: LifeBook.

St Pierre, Maurice. 2015. *Eric Williams and the Anticolonial Tradition: The Making of a Diasporan Intellectual*. Charlottesville: University of Virginia Press.

Stafford, Patricia. 2005. "The Growth and Development of the Brown and Black Middle Class, 1838–1988, and Its Role in the Shaping of Modern Barbados". PhD dissertation, University of the West Indies, Cave Hill, Barbados.

Stannard, David E. 1992. *American Holocaust: Columbus and the Conquest of the New World*. New York: Oxford University Press.

Stepan, Nancy. 1982. *The Idea of Race in Science: Great Britain 1800–1960*. London: Macmillan.

Sutton, Constance R. 2005. "Continuing the Fight for Economic Justice: The Barbadian Sugar Workers' 1958 Wildcat Strike". In *Revisiting Caribbean Labour: Essays in Honour of Nigel Bolland*, edited by Constance R. Sutton, 41–64. Kingston: Ian Randle.

Teschke, Benno. 2003. *The Myth of 1648*. London: Verso Books.

Teschke, Benno, and Christian Heine. 2002. "The Dialectic of Globalisation: A Critique of Social Constructivism". In *Historical Materialism and Globalization: Essays on Continuity and Change*, edited by Mark Rupert and Hazel Smith, 165–88. London: Routledge.

Therborn, Goran. 1976. *Science, Class and Society: On the Formation of Sociology and Historical Materialism*. London: New Left Books.

Thompson, Kenneth W. 1981. *Cold War Theories*. Volume 1: *World Polarization, 1943–1953*. Baton Rouge: Louisiana State University Press.

Tilly, Charles. 1985. "War Making and State Making as Organized Crime". In *Bringing the State Back In*, edited by Peter B. Evans, Dietrich Rueschemeyer and Theda Skocpol, 169–91. New York: Cambridge University Press.

Valdes, Nelson. 2016. "Cuba and the Future: A Great Debate Has Just Begun". *CounterPunch*, 25 April. https://www.counterpunch.org/.../cuba-and-the -future-a-great-debate-has-just-begun/.

Vitalis, Robert. 2000. "The Graceful and Generous Liberal Gesture: Making Racism Invisible in American International Relations". *Millennium: Journal of International Studies* 29 (2): 331–56.

Warren, Bill. 1980. *Imperialism: Pioneer of Capitalism*, edited by John Sender. London: New Left and Verso.

Wallace, E. 1977. *The British Caribbean: From the Decline of Colonialism to the End of Federation*. Toronto: University of Toronto Press.

Watson, Karl. 1998. "Sir Grantley Adams as Seen by Others: Oral Histories of the Private Man". *Journal of the Barbados Museum and Historical Society* 44 (November–December): 21–37.

Watson, Hilbourne A. 2001. "Errol Barrow (1920–1987): The Social Construction of Colonial and Post-colonial Charismatic Leadership in Barbados". In *Caribbean Charisma: Reflections on Leadership, Legitimacy and Populist Politics*, edited by Anton Allahar. Boulder: Lynne Rienner.

———. 2004. "Guyana, Jamaica and the Cold War Project: the Transformation of the British West Indian and CARICOM Labor Movements into Agents of Cold War Globalization". In *Caribbean Labor and Politics: Legacies of Cheddi Jagan and Michael Manley*, edited by Perry Mars and Alma H. Young, 89–125. Detroit: Wayne State University Press.

———. 2007. Review of *U.S. Intervention in British Guiana: A Cold War Story* by Stephen Rabe. *Americas: A Quarterly Review of Inter-American Cultural Life* 63 (4): 130–31.

————. 2008a. "Global Capitalist Crisis and the Caribbean: Theorizing the New Geography of Global Power, Transnational Hegemony and State Sovereignty". Paper delivered at the Thirty-Third Annual Caribbean Studies Association Conference, San Andrés Island, Colombia. 26–30 May.

————. 2008b. "W. Arthur Lewis and the New World Group: Variations within the Analytic Framework of Neoclassical Economics". *Nordic Journal of Latin American and Caribbean Studies* 38 (1–2): 49–79.

————. 2008c. "Alienation and Fetishization: A Critical Analysis of 'Radicalism and Innovation' in the New World Group's Approach to and Rejection of Metropolitan Intellectual and Political Hegemony". *Nordic Journal of Latin American and Caribbean Studies* 38 (1–2): 15–48

————. 2015a. "Oliver Cromwell Cox's Understanding of Capitalism and the Problem of His Materialist Perspective". *Canadian Journal of Latin American and Caribbean Studies* 39 (3): 382–402. http://dx.doi.org/10.1080/082636 63.2014.1013287.

————. 2015b. "State Sovereignty, Body Politic, NeoPatriarchy, and Citizenship in the Caribbean: Beyond Epistemological Territorialism and Sovereignty Myths". In *Globalization, Sovereignty, and Citizenship in the Caribbean*, edited by Hilbourne A. Watson, 31–67. Kingston: University of the West Indies Press.

Welch, Pedro L.V. 1992. "In Search of a Barbadian Identity: Historical Factors in the Evolution of a Barbadian Literary Tradition". *Journal of the Barbados Museum and Historical Society* 40: 37–47.

West Indian Royal Commission (WIRC). 1940. *West Indian Royal Commission Report 1938–39 (Recommendations)*. Cmnd. 6174. London: HMSO.

Westad, Odd Arne. 2005. *The Global Cold War: Third World Interventions and the Making of Our Times*. Cambridge: Cambridge University Press.

Wheare, Kenneth C. 1960. *Constitutional Structure of the Commonwealth*. Oxford: Oxford University Press.

Wickham, John. 1979. "The Environment as an Ingredient of the Cultural Expression". In *Perceptions of the Environment*, edited by Yves Renard. St Michael, Barbados: Caribbean Conservation Commission.

Wilder, Gary. 2015. *Freedom Time: Negritude, Decolonization, and the Future of the World*. Durham, NC: Duke University Press.

Will, Marvin W. 1992. "Insurrection and the Development of Political Institutions: The 1937 Rebellion and the Birth of Labour Parties and Labour Unions in Barbados". *Journal of the Barbados Museum and Historical Society* 40:9–18, 66–84.

Williams, Douglas. 1966. "The Case for Barbados Independence". *Daily Telegraph*, 10 January.

Williams, Eric. 1944. *Capitalism and Slavery*. Chapel Hill: University of North Carolina Press

———. 1961. *The Economics of Nationhood*. Port of Spain: PNM Publishing.

———. [1969] 1971. *Inward Hunger: The Education of a Prime Minister*. Chicago: University of Chicago Press.

Wolin, Sheldon. 2008. *Democracy Incorporated: Managed Democracy and the Specter of Inverted Totalitarianism*. Princeton, NJ: Princeton University Press.

Wood, Ellen Meiksins. 1991. *The Pristine Culture of Capitalism: A Historical Essay on Old Regimes and Modern States*. London: Verso.

———. 1995. *Capitalism against Democracy*. Cambridge: Cambridge University Press.

———. 1998. *The Retreat from Class: A New 'True' Socialism*. London: Verso.

———. 2003. *Empire of Capital*. London: Verso.

Worrell, DeLisle. 1994–95. "The Barbados Economy since the 1930s". *Journal of the Barbados Museum and Historical Society* 42:75–90.

Žižek, Slavoj. 2012. "Why Obama Is More Than Bush with a Human Face". *Guardian* (UK), 14 November.

INDEX

Achebe, Chinua, 9
Adams, Grantley Herbert, 27, 34,
43, 259n2; 266n42, 266n46,
270n11, 270n12, 270n15, 278n16;
and African diaspora, 177, 179–80;
anti-communism of, 66–67, 119,
150, 166, 185, 195–96, 198, 201–2;
attacks by Barrow, 123; awarded
knighthood, 35, 81, 115, 170; belief
in Barbadian exceptionalism,
35, 81, 86, 114–18, 143; and BLP,
16–18, 19, 28–29, 68–69, 95,
100, 103–4, 185, 220, 227, 238–39,
273n49, 273n50, 277n14; and
BPL, 221, 223–25, 277n13; Bushe
Experiment, 13, 89; and BWU,
102, 150, 221–22, 237, 240, 272n38;
defended British imperialism, ix,
3–5, 85, 112, 118, 169–72, 186–87;
embraced Cold War, 118–19, 173,
184, 249–50; Fabian socialism,
248, 252; and federation, 163; and
land tenure, 148, 235; invested
government funds in South Africa,
186; as a political conservative,
85–86, 96–98, 104, 110, 117, 158,
193–95, 199, 220, 222; as PM of
the Federation, 230; popular appeal
of, 232; position on nationalization
of sugar industry, 104–5, 148, 234;

racial discrimination experienced
by, 265n34; and relationship with
Walcott, 199, 204–6; as a "Right-
Wing Socialist", 262n16; support
for Manley, 167
Adams, Jon Michael Geoffrey
Manningham "Tom", 19, 27–28, 30,
69, 76, 112, 222, 248; criticism of
Barrow, 71–72
African Americans, 177
African Methodist Episcopal (AME)
Church, 15–16, 46–47, 71
Afro-Asian Solidarity Conference
(1965), 164
Agnew, John, 82
The Agony of the Eight (Lewis), 138
agro-commercial interests, 2, 49,
205, 210, 231, 251–52; in Barbados,
42–44, 95–96, 98, 102–3; and
exploitation of working-class, 11, 50,
55; and merchant capital, 211–14.
See also Conservative Electors'
Association
ALCOA, 154
Allahar, Anton, 8
Allder, Owen, 18, 199
Alleyne School, 34, 44–45, 59, 260,
276, 278
Alleyne, Sir John Gay, 44–45
Alliance for Progress, 190, 269, 272

297

CPSIA information can be obtained
at www.ICGtesting.com
Printed in the USA
FSHW020134100819
60910FS